Tooth
Decay
and
Cavities

Dr. Alvin Silverstein,

Virginia Silverstein, and

Laura Silverstein Nunn

My Health
Franklin Watts

A Division of Grolier Publishing
New York • London • Hong Kong • Sydney
Danbury, Connecticut

Special thanks to Dr. Jeffrey Rabinowitz, a partner in Park 56 Dental Group, New York, NY, for allowing photographs to be taken at his office.

Photographs ©: Custom Medical Stock Photo: 17 (Hossler, Ph. D.), 35 right; Peter Arnold Inc.: 19 (Dr. R. Gottsegen), 14 (Alex Grey); Photo Researchers: 16, 21, 23, 30 (Biophoto Associates/SS), 26 (Dr. Jeremy Burgess/SPL), 10 (Doug Martin), 33 (Lawrence Migdale), 31 (Science Pictures Limited/SPL), 35 left (Peter Skinner), 38 (Vision SRI); Randy Matusow: 24, 25, 27, 28; Rigoberto Quinteros: 4, 22; Tony Stone Images: 9 (Gus Butera), 8 (Robert E. Daemmrich); Visuals Unlimited: 11 (Charlie Heidecker), 7 (Joe McDonald), 6 (Science VU).

Medical illustrations by Leonard Morgan
Cartoons by Rick Stromoski

Visit Franklin Watts on the Internet at:
http://publishing.grolier.com

Library of Congress Cataloging-in-Publication Data

Silverstein, Alvin.
    Tooth decay and cavities / by Alvin Silverstein, Virginia Silverstein, and Laura Silverstein Nunn.
        p.   cm.—(My Health)
    Includes bibliographical references and index.
    Summary: Describes the structure and function of teeth and discusses how cavities form and how to prevent them.
    ISBN 0-531-11580-1 (lib. bdg.)   0-531-16412-8 (pbk.)
    1. Dental caries—Juvenile literature. 2. Dental caries in children—Juvenile literature. [1. Teeth—Care and hygiene.] I. Silverstein, Virginia B. II. Nunn, Laura Silverstein. III. Title. IV. Series.
RK331.S55   1999
617.6'7—dc21
                                      98-22024
                                          CIP
                                          AC

GROLIER
PUBLISHING

Contents

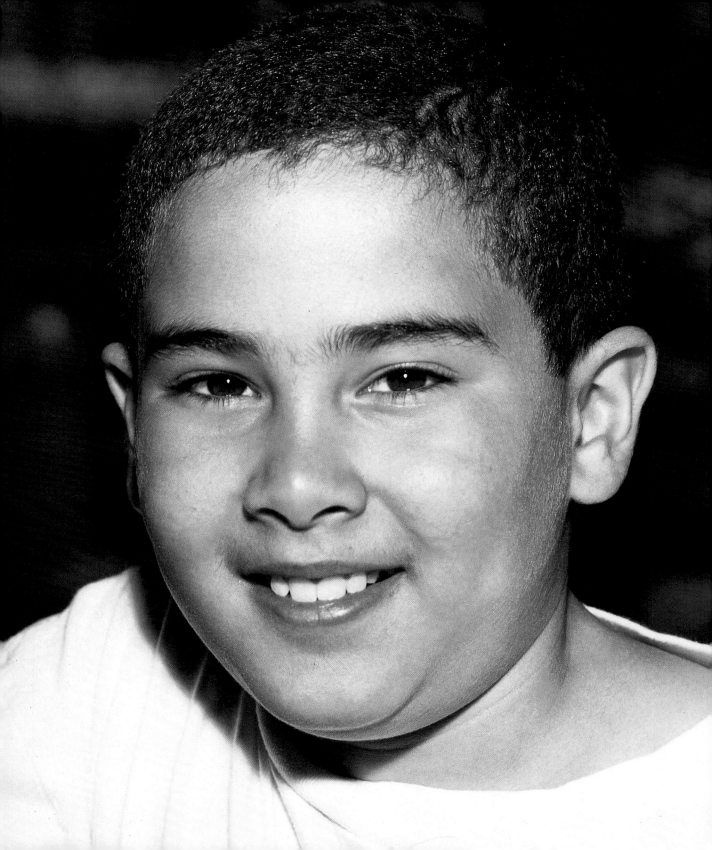

Teeth for a Lifetime

"Say cheese!" That's what people say when they want to take your picture. You give a big, wide smile for the camera to show that you're happy. And when you smile, you show off a nice set of pearly white teeth.

Your teeth aren't there just to make your smile look good. Teeth have a very important job to do—they chew up the food you eat into little pieces so you can swallow it more easily. Actually, you start to digest the food right in your mouth, while you are chewing it.

To help your teeth do their job, you need to take good care of them. If you do, your teeth can last a lifetime.

◀ **If you take care of your teeth, you can have a pearly white smile your whole life.**

Did You Know...

Some animals, such as birds, lizards, and frogs, do not have teeth. Birds use their strong beaks to tear up food before they swallow it. Lizards and frogs use their long, powerful tongues to snap up food.

Teeth Tell Tales

You can tell a lot about an animal by looking at its teeth. For example, some animals eat only plant foods—leaves, roots, fruits, or seeds. Many plant eaters have very good cutting teeth. Their front teeth are large and sharp so they can snip off leaves and stems or bite off roots with ease. The beaver's front teeth are so big and strong that it can even gnaw through tree trunks. Grazing animals such as horses

Plant eaters, such as this beaver, use their large front teeth to gnaw on branches, stems, and roots.

and cows are plant eaters, too. Their large back teeth are good for grinding up leaves or grains.

Some animals eat mainly meat. They hunt other animals for food. Their teeth are very different from those of plant eaters. Dogs, cats, and other meat eaters have long, pointed fangs. They use them to bite into their prey and tear the meat into pieces small enough to swallow. They have cutting and grinding teeth too, but those teeth are not very big or strong. (If you watch a pet cat or dog eating, you may notice that it does not chew its food very well. It just swallows it down in chunks.)

Meat eaters, such as this gray wolf, use their fangs to tear flesh into pieces small enough to swallow.

Think of all the different types of food on a piece of pizza—cheese, hamburger, pepperoni, mushrooms, onions, peppers, tomatoes. Your teeth can chew them all.

Now look inside your own mouth. Your front teeth are not as strong as a beaver's cutting teeth, but they are good enough to take a bite out of an apple or carrot. Your back teeth are not as big or wide as those of a horse, but you can still crunch vegetables and mash them into a soft pulp. And you don't have long fangs like a cat or a dog, but your teeth can handle meat—even a tough piece of steak—pretty well. People eat both plant foods and meat, so you have teeth that are good for chewing many different types of foods.

Two Sets of Teeth

Babies are born without any teeth at all. At first they can only drink liquids like milk, water, or juice. After a few months, they may eat some soft foods like apple-sauce, ground-up bananas, or mashed peas.

The first teeth, called **milk teeth,** appear when an infant is about 6 months old. One by one they pop

Babies have no teeth.

This 7-year-old girl is missing a front tooth.

out of the **gums**—first the cutting teeth in front, then some grinding teeth and tearing teeth. It takes about 2 years for all 20 milk teeth to come out.

When a child is about 5 or 6 years old, the milk teeth start to fall out. These "baby" teeth are replaced, one at a time, by larger ones called **permanent teeth**. There are 32 teeth in a complete set of permanent teeth. These are the teeth that we keep for the rest of our lives.

Did the Tooth Fairy ever visit your home? In the United States, when you lose a baby tooth, you put it under your pillow. That night, while you are sleeping, the Tooth Fairy takes the tooth, leaving money in its place. In some other countries, children put their baby teeth where a "Tooth Mouse" can find them. They hope their new teeth will be as strong and sharp as a mouse's teeth.

Why do people grow two sets of teeth? A complete set of permanent teeth can't fit into a baby's tiny mouth. That's why they come later, when a child is a little bigger.

Teeth and More Teeth

Animals such as cats and dogs have two sets of teeth, just like people do. Snakes and crocodiles, however, may have several sets of teeth during their lives. And sharks keep on replacing their teeth as long as they live.

A crocodile can replace lost teeth throughout its life.

Inside Your Mouth

You have several kinds of teeth in your mouth. Each type of tooth has a special job to do. When you look in the mirror and smile, you see two rows of flat, squared-off teeth right in the front of your mouth. There are four on top and four smaller teeth below. These front teeth are called **incisors.** They are sharp and act like knives to slice and bite off chunks of food. (Look at your "toothprint" after you bite into an apple to see how broad and sharp your teeth are.)

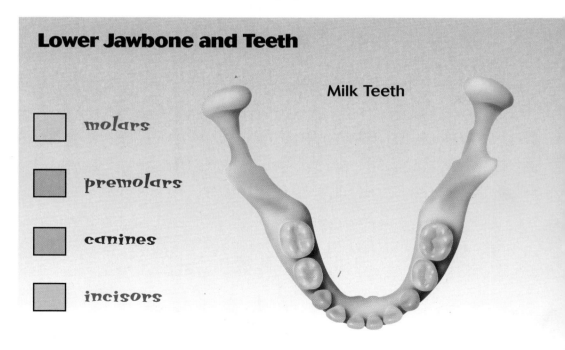

Lower Jawbone and Teeth

Milk Teeth

☐ molars

☐ premolars

☐ canines

☐ incisors

Next to the incisors are teeth called **canines**. The word "canine" comes from the Latin word for "dog." Canine teeth are pointed like the fangs of a dog. We use our canines to tear food into small pieces. You have four canines, two in the upper jaw and two in the lower jaw.

Farther back are the **premolars** and then the **molars**. The premolars have two pointed peaks. They look like two canine teeth put together. The molars are broader and have three pointed peaks. Their tops are flat with raised bumps and ridges. They crush and grind food so that you can swallow it easily.

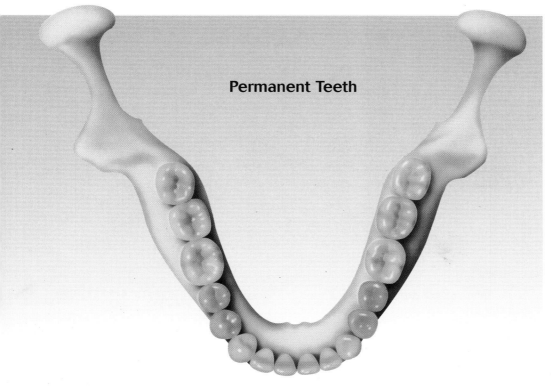

Permanent Teeth

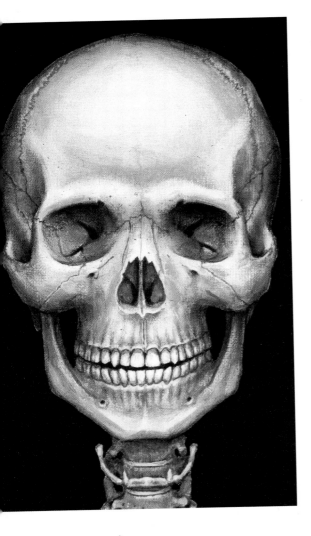

Your teeth are held firmly in place by your **jaws**. Deep inside the upper and lower jaws are **jawbones**. Long roots grow down from each tooth, connecting it to your jawbone. Soft pink gums cover the jawbones and help to hold your teeth in place.

Your upper jawbone cannot move. It is actually a part of your skull, the bony case that forms the shape of your head. Your lower jawbone can move up, down, and even sideways. When you move your jaw, you move your teeth. The muscles that control your jaws are powerful, so your teeth can grind food with great force.

By looking at this human skull, you can see how your teeth are connected to your jawbones.

What's in a Tooth?

What are teeth made of? The whitish covering on the teeth is called **enamel**. It is the hardest substance in your whole body. Only the **crown** of the tooth (the part you can see) and the **neck** (the part at the gum line) are covered with enamel. The **root** is buried deep inside the gum, so it does not need this extra-hard protection.

Under the outer covering of enamel is a hard yellow substance called **dentin**. It is actually harder than bone. Most of the tooth is made up of dentin.

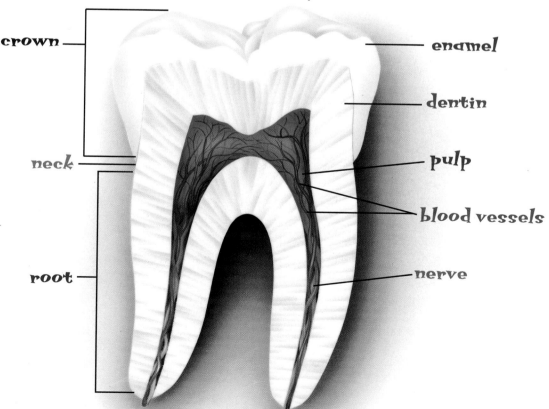

crown

neck

root

enamel

dentin

pulp

blood vessels

nerve

The center of each tooth is filled with soft material called **pulp.** Tiny *blood vessels* and nerves run through the pulp. The blood vessels bring **nutrients** to the dentin and help to keep it healthy and strong. The nerves inside teeth send messages to the brain, so that you always know what your teeth are doing. You can feel it when you bite into something, and know just how hard you are biting.

How White Are Your Teeth?

Toothpaste commercials talk about shining white smiles. But not everyone has bright white teeth. The enamel of some people's teeth is naturally slightly yellow, no matter how much they clean their teeth. In fact, the yellowish enamel may be even stronger than the whiter kind. Stains from foods can also make teeth yellow.

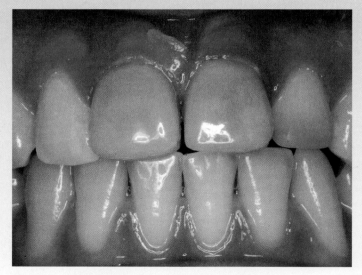

The teeth of adults are sometimes discolored by drinking coffee or tea.

The Microworld Inside Your Mouth

Would you believe that there are millions of tiny creatures living inside your body? These creatures, known as **bacteria,** are so small that you need a microscope to see them.

Many kinds of bacteria live in our bodies. Some are "good," and some are "bad." "Good" bacteria help us. For instance, the bacteria that live in your intestines break down the food you eat so that you can **digest** it more easily. "Bad" bacteria hurt us. Some bacteria make us sick. For instance, you get strep throat because bacteria attack your body and make you ill.

If you could look at your teeth through a microscope, this is what you'd see.

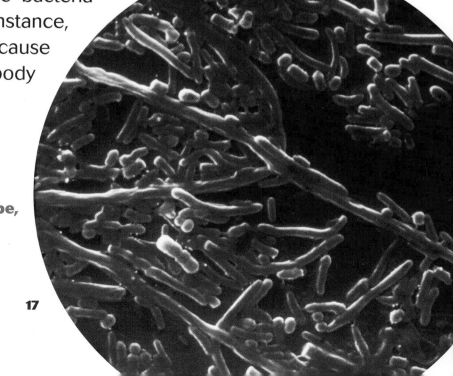

17

If you could look through a microscope at the inside of your own mouth, you might be shocked at what you saw. A tiny world of bacteria is having a party inside your mouth! At this party, you bring the food and the bacteria just eat. When you eat a hamburger, for example, you chew it up into tiny pieces with your teeth, and then you swallow it. Now the hamburger is all gone, right? Well, not exactly. Every time you eat something, tiny bits of food are left on your teeth. Bacteria feed on these little bits of food. And these bacteria are germs that can really harm your teeth.

Did You Know...

Bacteria are not the only things living inside your mouth. Other tiny creatures, called **tooth amoebas,** live there too. They are very much like the amoebas that live in ponds. Under a microscope, they look like shapeless blobs of jelly. Tooth amoebas help to protect your teeth by feeding on bacteria, as well as on the bits of food left in your teeth.

How Cavities Form

Millions of bacteria feast on the food left in your teeth. Bacteria grow and multiply, eventually covering your teeth with a soft, sticky coat of **plaque.** Plaque is a mixture of bits of leftover food, bacteria, and other substances. It forms mainly between the teeth and at the edge of the gums. When you do not clean your teeth regularly, plaque can build up. If left for more than a few days, plaque hardens into **tartar,** which is more difficult to remove.

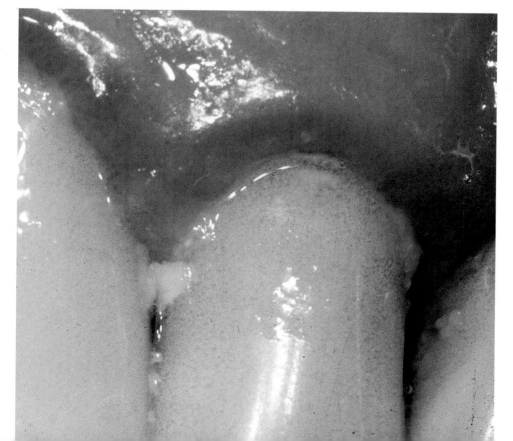

As you can see in this picture, plaque often builds up where the teeth meet the gums.

As bacteria grow on your teeth, they make an acid that slowly eats through the tooth enamel. This is **tooth decay**. And once it gets through the hard enamel into the softer dentin, that acid works fast. Eventually, tooth decay makes a **cavity**—a hole in the tooth. Bacteria make even more acid when you eat sugary foods. That's why people say, "Don't eat so much candy—it will rot your teeth."

Activity 1: How Is an Egg Like a Tooth?

You can try to make an eggshell decay, just like a tooth. You'll need a hard-boiled egg (cooked by an adult) and a bowl of vinegar. Let the egg sit in the vinegar for about a day. Vinegar is acidic, just like the acid that the bacteria make in your mouth. When you check on the egg, you'll see that part of the shell has been eaten away by the vinegar. Tooth decay works the same way.

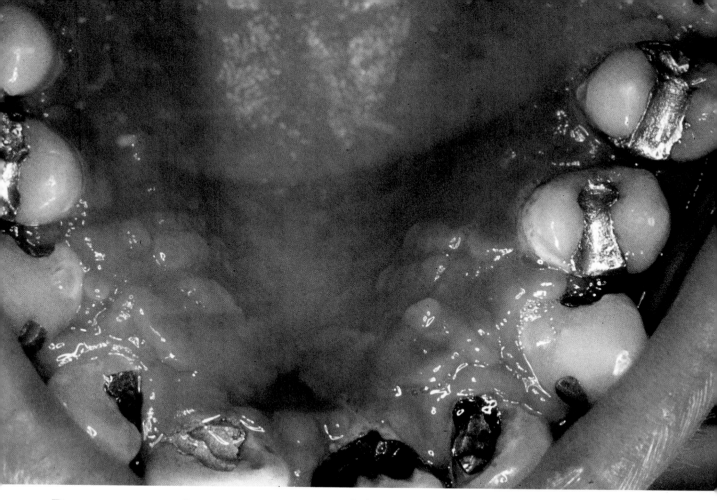

Do your parents have a mouth full of fillings? If they do, you might too one day. Even so, brushing with fluoride toothpaste and flossing can help you have a healthier mouth.

You may get cavities when you are older—no matter how well you take care of your teeth. Studies show that good or bad teeth may be **inherited.** So you could have nice strong teeth like your mom—or get a mouth full of cavities like your dad.

Ice cream cones are usually a treat. But if you have a cavity, eating one can be painful.

Your teeth may give you some clues to let you know that a cavity is forming. If eating hot soup or a cold ice cream cone makes your teeth hurt, you may have a cavity.

When acid from bacteria eats away the tooth enamel and then the dentin, it moves into the pulp. As soon as it comes into contact with a nerve—ouch! You have a toothache. Toothaches can be very painful and should be checked by a dentist. But not all toothaches are that serious. Sometimes, food gets stuck between

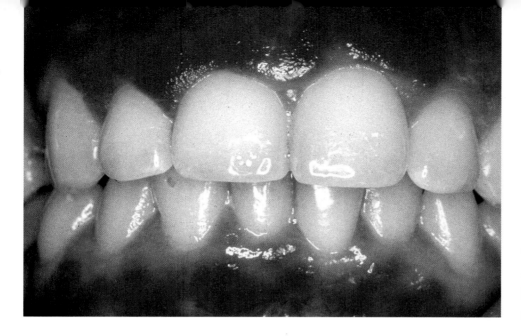

This person has a very bad case of gingivitis.

teeth. This can bother your gums, and cause your tooth to throb with pain. The good news is that you can avoid this pain by making sure your teeth stay clean.

Bacteria can also grow down into the gums and cause **gum disease.** Gum disease usually affects adults. One of the most common types of gum disease is *gingivitis*, or swelling of the gums.

Your body does not let bacteria take over your mouth without a fight. It has a defense called *saliva*— the watery stuff that fills your mouth when you eat, or sometimes even when you think about food. Saliva mixes with your food to make chewing and swallowing easier. Saliva also helps to clean your teeth by washing away food leftovers. It contains substances that help cut down the amount of acid made by the bacteria.

Going to the Dentist

How often do you go to the dentist? You should have a checkup every 6 months. That is the best way to keep from getting cavities.

In a routine visit, the dentist first checks all your teeth, looking for any problems. Holes or cracks in the enamel and dark-colored spots on the teeth are signs of trouble. But sometimes cavities are hard to spot,

This dentist is checking a boy's teeth for cavities.

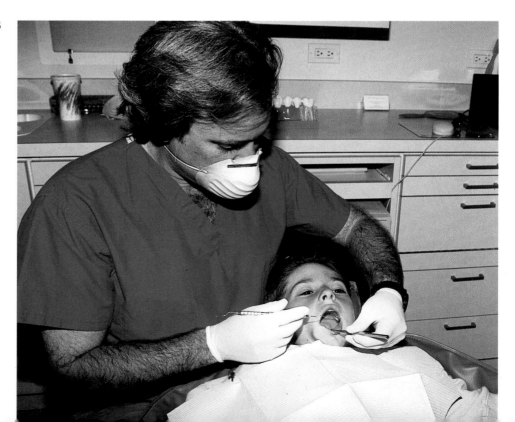

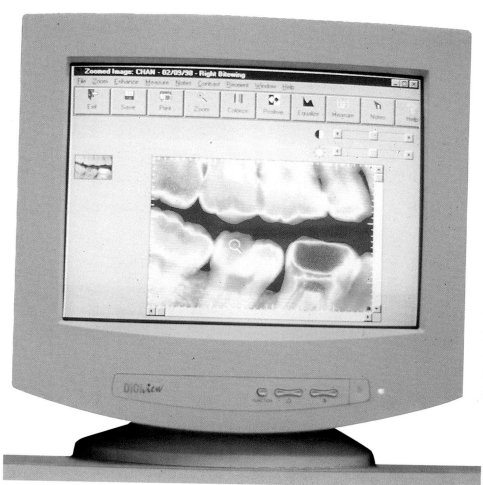

The red area on this computer-enhanced view of an X ray shows a cavity.

especially if they are between teeth or at the edge of the gums.

The dentist can find those cavities by taking X-ray pictures of your teeth. X rays show parts of the teeth and jawbone that are hidden inside the gums. If you are lucky, the X rays will show that you do not have any cavities. But if you do have cavities, the X rays will show the dentist exactly where they are.

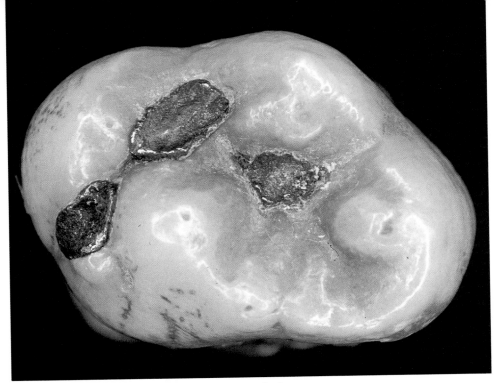

This molar has three amalgam fillings.

Cavities should be fixed as soon as possible so that the tooth decay does not get any worse. To do this, the dentist must put a **filling** in the cavity. Most fillings are made of **amalgam**, a mixture of silver and other metals. But if the cavity is in a tooth that shows when you smile, the dentist may use a mixture of tooth-colored materials called **porcelain**.

The dentist can't just put the filling right into the cavity. Bits of food and bacteria might be hiding there. If they are not removed, the bacteria might continue to grow and multiply, producing more acid and making a bigger hole in your tooth. Dentists use a drill to clean out the hole and get rid of all the bad stuff. (Before the dentist starts to drill, you may be given a shot, or a patch with a pain-killing drug may be placed on your gum. This numbs your mouth so you will not feel any pain.

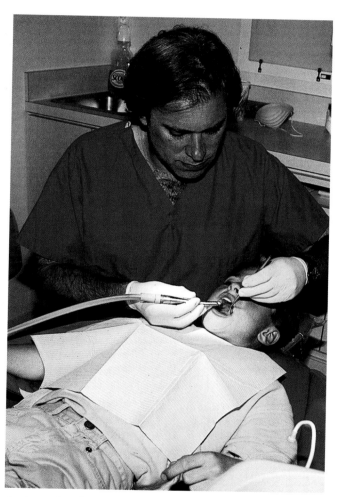

A dentist is drilling a patient's tooth before filling a cavity.

High-Tech Tools

If a cavity is small, today's dentists can use some painless new tools instead of drilling. They may clean out the cavity with a high-speed jet of air. Or they may use a **laser drill**— a pinpoint beam of laser light combined with water— to cool and clean a cavity. Lasers can also be used to remove plaque or to treat gum disease by killing bacteria between the teeth and gums. Some dentists use laser light with a bleaching mixture to make teeth whiter.

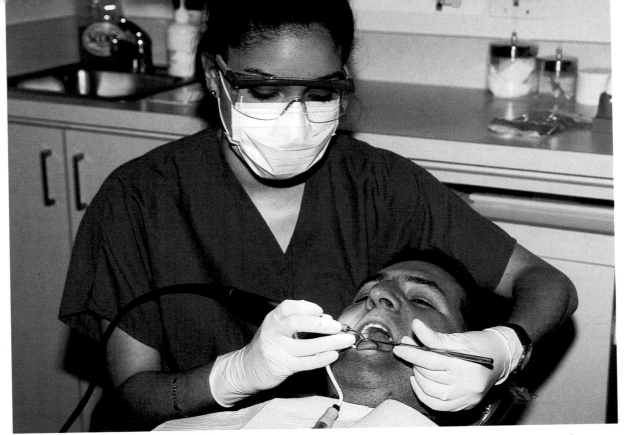

This dental hygienist is scraping tartar off a man's teeth.

When a cavity has been cleaned out and shaped, the dentist packs in the filling material. After it dries and hardens, the filling may need a little drilling and polishing to make it just the right shape to fit with your other teeth when you chew.

After the dentist has examined your teeth and fixed any cavities, it is time for a cleaning that will leave your teeth smooth and healthy. The dentist (or dental hygienist) may use a special tool called a probe to remove any bits of food stuck between your teeth.

Other metal tools may be used to scrape away the plaque that has built up. Or the dentist may use a device that blasts away the plaque with a beam of **ultrasound.** Finally, an electric toothbrush cleans and polishes your teeth. (The dentist may let you choose the flavor of the toothpaste—how about strawberry, orange, cinnamon, or even chocolate?)

Sometimes a tooth is so badly decayed that it can't be saved. In that case, the dentist may have to **extract,** or pull out, the tooth. Usually you will be given **anesthesia** for a tooth extraction, to keep you from feeling any pain. After the tooth is taken out, your gum may feel sore for a while.

Sometimes a badly damaged tooth can be saved by **root canal therapy.** A root canal is a narrow, hollow tunnel in a tooth's root. When the decay spreads down into the tooth, the pulp may become infected. Then a dentist may treat the infection by performing

Early Dentists

Hundreds of years ago, people did not have dentists. There were only "tooth pullers." These tooth pullers had different methods for pulling teeth. Some tied a string to the patient's tooth and pulled. Others used a tool to yank teeth out. Sometimes tooth pullers hired musicians to play loud music so that people in the neighborhood wouldn't be frightened by a patient's screams.

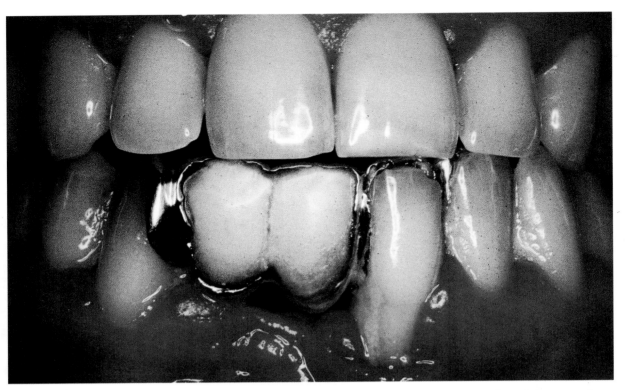

This metal bridge connects two false teeth to healthy teeth on either side of the hole.

root canal therapy to take out the pulp. The pulp is replaced with a solid packing material that helps to hold the tooth in place.

When accidents happen, a tooth may be chipped, broken, or cracked. As long as the root of the tooth is not damaged, it can probably be saved. One way is by putting a crown, or cap, on it. The crown is cemented right over the damaged tooth. It can look as good and work as well as a normal tooth. If the whole tooth is missing, the dentist may make a **bridge.** This is a false tooth that is attached to good teeth on either

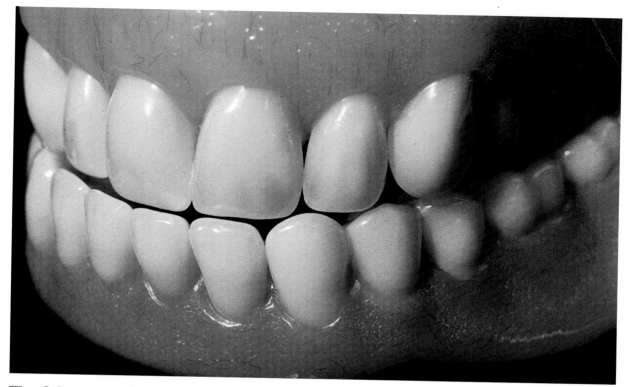

The false teeth in a denture rest in a tough, plastic base that is fitted to the patient's mouth.

side of the empty space. A missing tooth can also be replaced with an **implant**—a false tooth that is set into the gum and permanently attached to the jawbone. Implants work like natural teeth. If all of the teeth are missing or have to be taken out, the dentist can make a complete set of false teeth, which is called a **denture.**

Dentists have many ways to fix teeth, but they'd much rather find no cavities at all when you come in for a checkup. You can help the dentist take care of your teeth by brushing and flossing them regularly at home.

How to Prevent Cavities

Brushing and flossing your teeth and gums makes a big difference in preventing tooth decay. Cleaning your teeth does not have to be a chore. If you do it every day, brushing and flossing becomes a habit, just like taking a shower or combing your hair.

Be sure to use a toothpaste with **fluoride** in it. Fluoride helps protect your teeth from tooth decay by making the enamel even stronger.

Many cities now add fluoride to their drinking water. Thanks to fluoride, children today get only 36 percent as many cavities as children did 40 years ago. The American Dental Association advises that fluoridated water, fluoridated toothpaste, and fluoridated mouthwash are great ways to fight tooth decay.

You should brush your teeth after every meal, but that's not always

Are Your Teeth Clean?

With your fingernail, scrape very gently along some of your teeth, starting at the gums. Did you scrape off some soft, whitish stuff? That is plaque.

easy—especially if you like to have snacks during the day. Be sure to brush your teeth at least twice a day—when you get up in the morning and before you go to bed. Researchers found that if teeth are cleaned at least once within 24 hours, bacteria cannot make enough acid to damage them.

Brush at least twice a day to keep your teeth healthy.

How to Brush Your Teeth

How do you brush your teeth? Here are some general rules for a complete cleaning:

1. Move your toothbrush up and down and in circles.

2. Brush the top teeth downward from the gums.

3. Brush the bottom teeth upward from the gums.

4. Brush the backs of the top and bottom teeth.

5. Remember to brush the top and bottom rows of your teeth, too. Also, brush the flat surfaces and the sides of these teeth.

6. Rinse thoroughly—and smile.

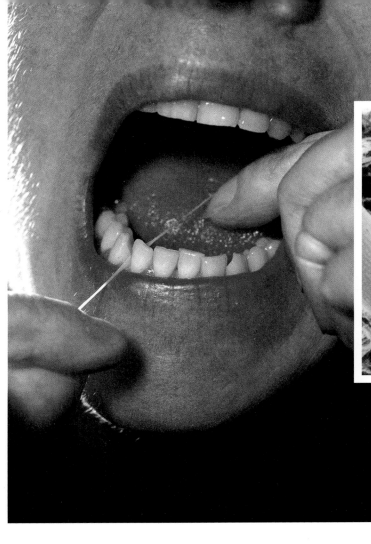

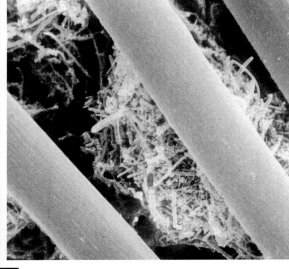

▲ A picture taken through a microscope can show bacteria on a piece of dental floss.

◄ Flossing can remove the bacteria and food particles that brushing misses.

You should get a new toothbrush every 2 to 3 months. Bacteria can grow in a toothbrush, so you put germs into your mouth when you use it.

You should also floss at least once a day. Bacteria feed on food that is left between your teeth. Moving a strand of dental floss back and forth between your teeth will remove the bits of food you missed while you were brushing.

Activity 2: How Clean Are Your Teeth?

You can find out by using disclosing tablets or a special mouthwash that colors the plaque on your teeth with a bright vegetable dye. You can buy the tablets from the drugstore, or your dentist may give you some samples.

Chew a tablet for 30 seconds but do not swallow it. Wash your mouth out with water and look in a mirror. Where are the darkest plaque stains? These places show you where you need to brush your teeth better next time.

What kinds of foods do you eat? Do you eat a lot of vegetables and fruits? What about candy? We're told to stay away from sweets like cookies and candy. But you might be surprised to learn that foods like corn-flakes and raisins may be to blame for the holes in your teeth. Starches like potato chips and crackers may not taste sweet, but to bacteria, they're just like lollipops. Saliva breaks starches down into a sugar called maltose, and bacteria really love maltose. Starches are especially bad for your teeth because they actually stick around longer than sugars do. This gives bacteria more time to cause cavities.

You probably have heard the popular saying in milk commercials: "Milk does a body good." It's true. Milk, cheese, and green vegetables contain **calcium,** which helps keep your bones and teeth strong and healthy. Other substances in these foods are also good for your teeth.

Foods that Stick

Barely Sticky

Apples

Bananas

Hot fudge sundaes

Chocolate candy bars

Moderately Sticky

White bread

Caramels

Cream-filled sponge cakes

Very Sticky

Granola bars

Oatmeal cookies

Potato chips

Salted crackers

Raisins

Cream-filled sandwich cookies

Peanut butter crackers

Have Some Cheese Please!

Have a piece of cheddar cheese for a snack. Cheese somehow increases the amount of saliva that flows in your mouth. As you know, saliva decreases the amount of acid that is produced by bacteria. So, when you eat cheese, you are actually helping to protect your teeth.

Cheese is a good source of calcium. It also increases the amount of saliva in your mouth.

If you watch what you eat and brush and floss your teeth after meals, you will help make your teeth the best that they can be.

Would you believe that there could be a vaccine for tooth decay by the year 2000? That's what some researchers say. In addition, dentists are finding better methods to identify people who are more likely to have tooth decay. This means that young children will have an even better chance to keep their teeth healthy and strong all their lives.

Glossary

amalgam—a mixture of silver and other metals used for filling cavities.

anesthesia—a drug used to stop a person from feeling pain.

bacteria—tiny living things that are too small to see without a microscope.

blood vessel—one of the tubes that carries blood throughout the body.

bridge—one or more false teeth used to replace a missing tooth or teeth. It is attached to the good teeth on each side of the empty space.

calcium—a chemical element found in teeth and bones.

canines—pointed teeth on each side of the incisors. They are used to tear food.

cavity—a hole in a tooth, produced by tooth decay.

crown—the top part of a tooth, above the gums. It can also refer to an artificial cap placed over a broken or damaged tooth.

dentin—a hard, yellowish substance that makes up most of a tooth.

denture—a complete set of false teeth that can be removed from the mouth.

digest—to break down food so that it can be used by the body.

enamel—the outer covering of a tooth; the hardest material in the body.

extract—to pull out a tooth.

filling—a substance that a dentist puts into a cavity to stop tooth decay.

fluoride—a mineral that helps to make teeth stronger. It may be added to toothpaste or drinking water or applied to the teeth by a dentist.

gingivitis—inflammation (painful swelling) of the gums.

gum disease—damage to the gums caused by trapped food or bacteria.

gums—the soft pink tissue inside the mouth that surrounds the teeth.

implant—a false tooth that is set into the gum and permanently attached to the jawbone.

incisors—front teeth with flat, squared-off shape. These teeth are used for cutting.

inherited—passed from parent to child.

jawbones—the bones of the upper and lower jaws, to which the roots of the teeth are attached. Only the lower jawbone can move.

jaws—bony structures between the nose and the chin that hold the teeth.

laser drill—a pinpoint-sized beam of laser light that is combined with water and used to clean out cavities before filling them.

milk teeth—a child's first set of teeth.

molars—broad teeth with three points, the farthest back in the mouth. They crush and grind food.

neck—the middle part of a tooth, at the gum line.

nerve—a structure that carries messages to the brain

nutrients—vitamins and minerals needed for good health.

permanent teeth—teeth that replace the milk teeth.

plaque—a mixture of leftover food, bacteria, and other substances that forms on teeth, especially between teeth and at the edge of the gums.

porcelain—a hard, tooth-colored substance used for filling cavities.

premolars—teeth with two points, on each side of the canines. They can tear and grind food.

pulp—a soft substance that fills the center of a tooth. It contains nerves and blood vessels.

root—the lower part of a tooth, which holds it in the gums and attaches it to the jawbone.

root canal therapy—replacement of the pulp in the root of an infected tooth with solid packing material.

saliva—the watery fluid that forms in the mouth and helps in chewing and swallowing food.

tartar—another name for plaque; plaque that has been hardened by calcium deposits

tooth amoeba—a microscopic jelly-like creature that lives in the gums and feeds on bacteria.

tooth decay—the effects of acid, produced by bacteria in the mouth, which eats through the outer layers of a tooth, producing a hole or cavity.

ultrasound—very high-pitched sound used in a tool for cleaning teeth.

Learning More

Books
Bridget and Neil Ardley, *Skin, Hair, and Teeth*. Englewood Cliffs,
  NJ: Silver Burdett, 1988.

Roger Diévart, *Teeth, Tusks and Fangs*. Ossining, NY: Young
  Discovery Library, 1991.

Jennifer Storey Gillis, *Tooth Truth: Fun Facts & Projects*.
  Pownal, VT: Storey Communications, 1996.

Organizations and Online Sites
Academy of General Dentistry
211 East Chicago Ave., Suite 1200
Chicago, IL 60611-2670
http://www.agd.org/consumer

American Dental Association
211 East Chicago Ave.
Chicago, IL 60611
E-mail: online@ada.org
http://www.ada.org/tc-cons.html
ADA "Kids' Corner" with coloring sheets and movies
http://www.ada.org/consumer/kids/index.html

The Dental Consumer Advisor
http://www.toothinfo.com/
This site has a variety of useful information.

Dental Health Fact Sheets
http://www.pe.net/~iddpc1/facts.htm
This has all kinds of interesting information about teeth and keeping them healthy.

Lessons for a Lifetime of Healthy Smiles
http://www.floridadental.org/fda/dentallines/teaching
This site explains how to care for your teeth.

Organized Dentistry Associations
http://www.dental-resources.com/assoc2.html
This site can help you find a dentist in your area.

Tooth Fairy Links to Fun and Dental Health
http://members.tripod.com/~toothfairytales/
This site has a variety of links to fun facts, activities, songs, and products.

Index

Page numbers in *italics* indicate illustrations.

About the Authors

Dr. Alvin Silverstein is a Professor of Biology at the College of Staten Island of the City University of New York. **Virginia Silverstein** is a translator of Russian scientific literature. The Silversteins first worked together on a research project at the University of Pennsylvania. Since then, they have produced six children and more than 150 published books for young people.

Laura Silverstein Nunn, a graduate of Kean College, has been helping with her parents' books since her high-school days. She is the coauthor of more than twenty books on diseases and health, science concepts, endangered species, and pets. Laura lives with her husband Matt and their young son Cory in a rural New Jersey town not far from her childhood home.

Sourcebook of HVAC Details

Frank E. Beaty, Jr., P.E.

McGraw-Hill Book Company

New York St. Louis San Francisco Auckland Bogotá
Hamburg Johannesburg London Madrid Mexico
Milan Montreal New Delhi Panama
Paris São Paulo Singapore
Sydney Tokyo Toronto

Library of Congress Cataloging-in-Publication Data

Beaty, Frank E.
    Sourcebook of HVAC details.

    Companion volume to the Sourcebook of HVAC specifications.
    Includes index.
    1. Heating—Equipment and supplies. 2. Ventilation—
Equipment and supplies. 3. Air conditioning—Equipment
and supplies. I. Title. II. Title: Source book of HVAC
details.

TH7345.B43 1986   697   85-24045
ISBN 0-07-004193-8

1234567890 SEM/BKP 8932109876

ISBN 0-07-004193-8

The editors for this book were Betty Sun and Geraldine Fahey
and the production supervisor was Teresa F. Leaden.

Printed by Semline, Inc. and bound by The Book Press.

Contents

Preface

SUGGESTED USE OF STANDARD DETAILS

Standard details, as included in this *Sourcebook of HVAC Details,* are seldom complete or exactly what is needed by a design engineer preparing a set of working drawings. However, they can be very helpful when their role is understood.

Standard details should be used as a guide, or a starting point, for the designer in the preparation of the details needed for a particular situation. Such details should be considered as a "road map" drawn by someone who has been to a location before. It will probably lead you into the area in which you want to go, but not necessarily to the particular destination.

The details included in this book are related to, and numbered to match, the companion volume, *Sourcebook of HVAC Specifications,* which is also published by McGraw-Hill. While the two volumes complement each other, they are not dependent on each other. The numbers of the details reflect the various specification sections of *Sourcebook of HVAC Specifications.*

WHY USE STANDARD DETAILS?

Standard details can save *time* and *money!* When properly used, standard details eliminate the need to redraw the same detail time and time again—a task that drafters find frustrating because they are repeating the same detail drawn last week or yesterday and management finds expensive because they are paying for this repetitive work.

Standard details can often save both time and money by reminding the designer of some small point that might be overlooked. Omission of such small items often means an incomplete project at worst or several phone calls and letters at best.

Most offices do accumulate details, but they are very seldom standardized or organized in a way that makes them easily available to anyone other than the individual accumulating them.

USE OF THIS SOURCEBOOK

Sourcebook of HVAC Details has been prepared with the idea that these details can be photocopied and revised as needed. The type used in the written portion is Prestige Elite 12 which is available on most typewriters. The judicial use of "whiteout" can remove any unwanted portion of the written material or drawing, and of course additions can be drawn in with a dark pencil or even typed in.

The author has made extensive use of "adhesive-backed transparent film" and the normal office copy machine for the application of such details to tracings. Exhibit 1, which appears at the end of this preface, is a composite drawing produced for a small project made up using this method.

Where do details go on project documents? This is a question that every designer (or office) must answer. The author has been placing details on one or more detail sheets for larger projects and organizing them on one end of a sheet for small projects. (See Exhibit 1 for an example.)

The author's experience is that the left end of a roll of drawings is more difficult to view in the field so items such as details that do not require repeated or continuous references are placed on the far left-hand side of the drawings. Information referred to repeatedly is placed on the right-hand portion of the sheets where possible.

Details are prepared with their own borders and notes so that they stand alone and can be amended or revised without being confused with other details or information on the sheet.

Details in this *Sourcebook* can of course be traced or redrawn, but this prevents the drafter from attending to other duties. Someone with less knowledge of mechanical systems, such as a secretary or a junior drafter, can make the changes on the photocopy, thus leaving the drafter free for more important tasks.

Frank E. Beaty, Jr.

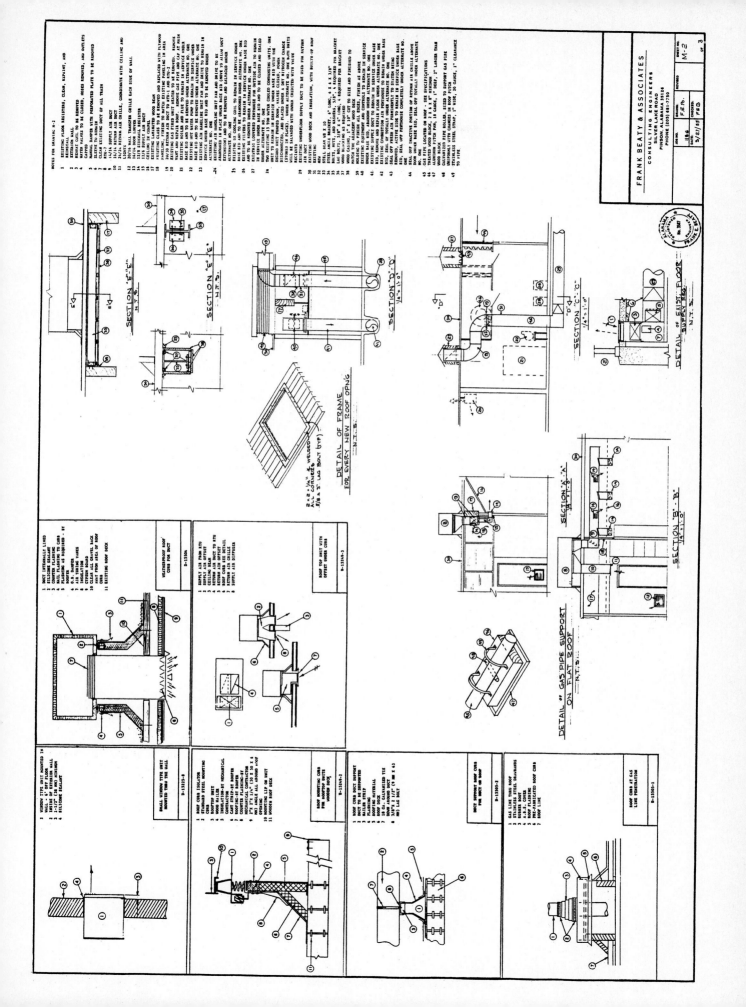

NOTES FOR DRAWING M-2

1. EXISTING FLOOR REGISTERS, CLEAN, REPAINT, AND REINSTALL.
2. EXTERIOR WALL.
3. EXISTING COIL TO BE REMOVED.
4. WATER VALVES TO BE CLOSED, HOSES REMOVED, AND OUTLETS CAPPED.
5. SLEEVE TO REMAIN.
6. CLEAR EXISTING DUCT OF ALL TRASH.
7. 14/14 SUPPLY AIR DUCT
8. 10/14 RETURN AIR DUCT
9. 20/16 WALL TRANSFER GRILLE EACH SIDE OF WALL.

FRANK BEATY & ASSOCIATES
CONSULTING ENGINEERS
SILVER LAKE ROAD
PINSON, ALABAMA 35126
PHONE (205) 681-7750

M-2

CHAPTER 1

Central Station Refrigeration Equipment

1 COMPRESSOR – UNLOADING TYPE
2 CANTED LOOP FOR VIBRATION
3 ISOLATORS – SPRING OR PAD TYPE AS SPECIFIED
4 HOT GAS RISER – DOUBLE WITH OIL SEAL
5 SUCTION LINE FROM EVAPORATOR
6 SUCTION LINE OIL TRAP IF RISE IS 8' (2.5 M) OR GREATER; PROVIDE ADDITIONAL TRAPS IF RISE EXCEEDS 20' (6 M)
7 BACKSEATED REFRIGERANT VALVE
8 PIPE ANCHOR
9 HOT GAS UP TO CONDENSER SEE D–15250–3

RECIPROCATING COMPRESSOR REFRIGERANT PIPING

D–15150–1

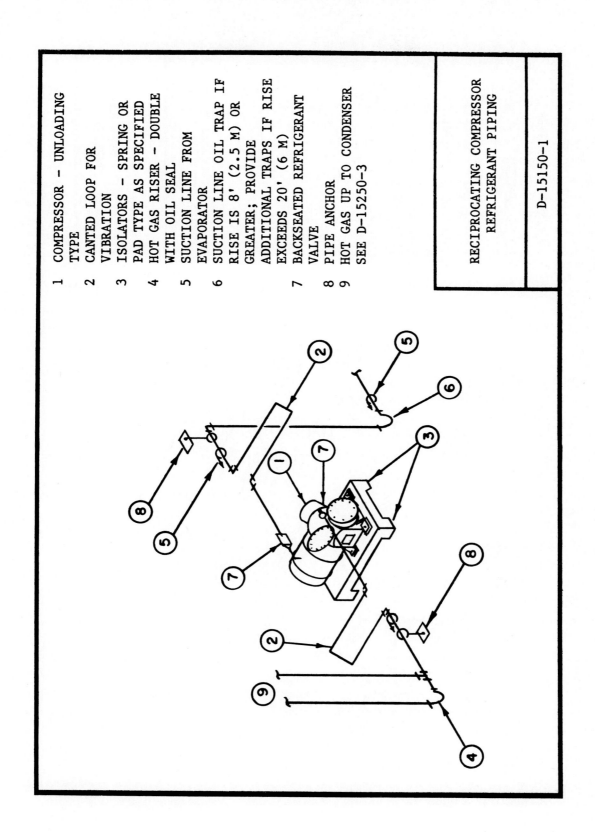

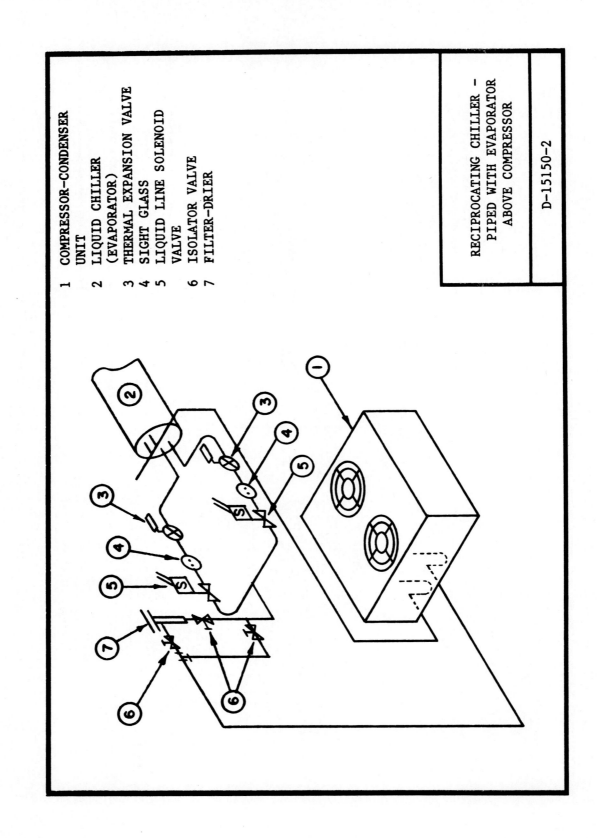

1 COMPRESSOR-CONDENSER UNIT
2 LIQUID CHILLER (EVAPORATOR)
3 THERMAL EXPANSION VALVE
4 SIGHT GLASS
5 LIQUID LINE SOLENOID VALVE
6 ISOLATOR VALVE
7 FILTER-DRIER

RECIPROCATING CHILLER - PIPED WITH EVAPORATOR ABOVE COMPRESSOR

D-15150-2

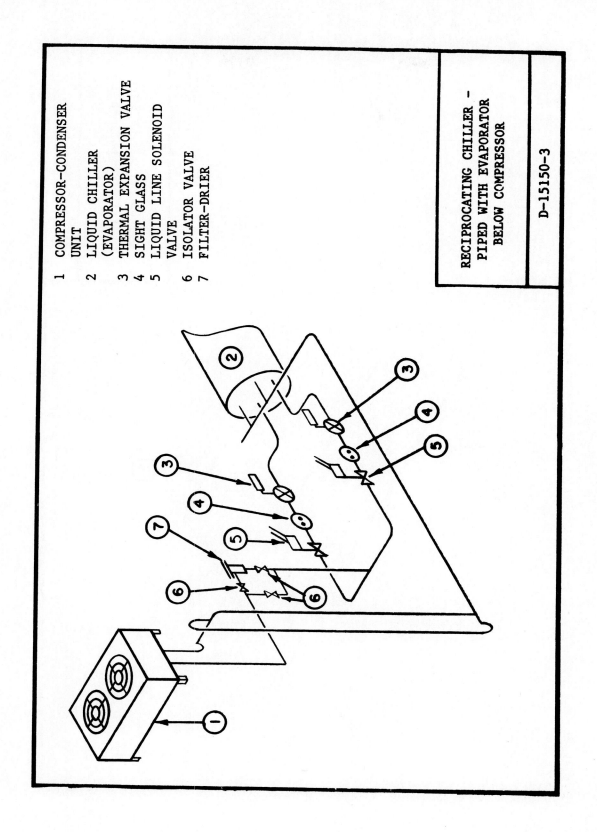

1 COMPRESSOR—CONDENSER UNIT
2 LIQUID CHILLER (EVAPORATOR)
3 THERMAL EXPANSION VALVE
4 SIGHT GLASS
5 LIQUID LINE SOLENOID VALVE
6 ISOLATOR VALVE
7 FILTER—DRIER

RECIPROCATING CHILLER – PIPED WITH EVAPORATOR BELOW COMPRESSOR

D–15150–3

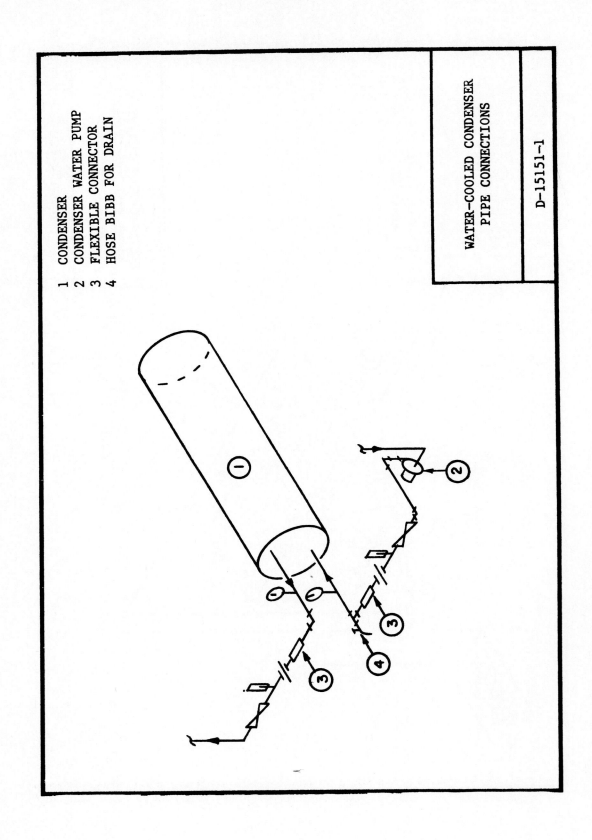

1 CONDENSER
2 CONDENSER WATER PUMP
3 FLEXIBLE CONNECTOR
4 HOSE BIBB FOR DRAIN

WATER-COOLED CONDENSER
PIPE CONNECTIONS

D-15151-1

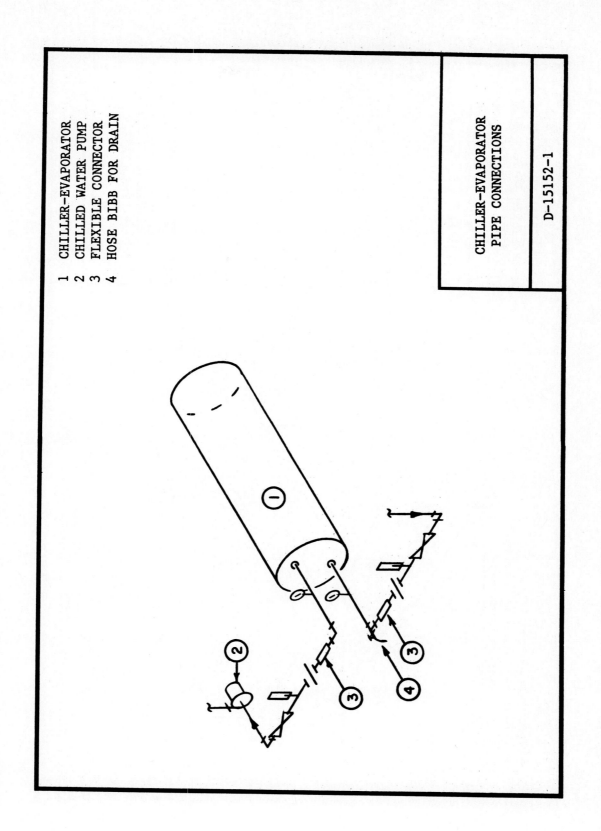

1 CHILLER–EVAPORATOR
2 CHILLED WATER PUMP
3 FLEXIBLE CONNECTOR
4 HOSE BIBB FOR DRAIN

CHILLER–EVAPORATOR
PIPE CONNECTIONS

D–15152–1

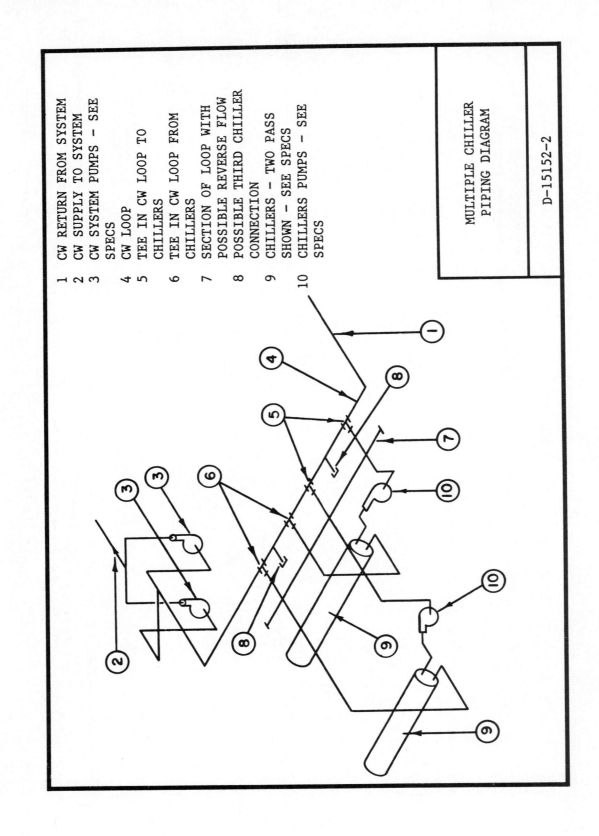

1 CW RETURN FROM SYSTEM
2 CW SUPPLY TO SYSTEM
3 CW SYSTEM PUMPS – SEE
   SPECS
4 CW LOOP
5 TEE IN CW LOOP TO
   CHILLERS
6 TEE IN CW LOOP FROM
   CHILLERS
7 SECTION OF LOOP WITH
   POSSIBLE REVERSE FLOW
8 POSSIBLE THIRD CHILLER
   CONNECTION
9 CHILLERS – TWO PASS
   SHOWN – SEE SPECS
10 CHILLERS PUMPS – SEE
   SPECS

MULTIPLE CHILLER
PIPING DIAGRAM

D–15152–2

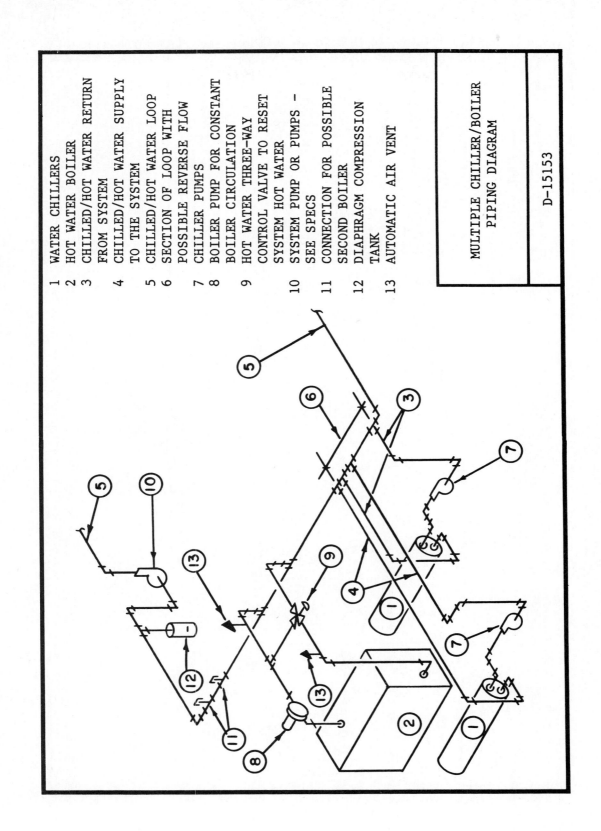

1 WATER CHILLERS
2 HOT WATER BOILER
3 CHILLED/HOT WATER RETURN FROM SYSTEM
4 CHILLED/HOT WATER SUPPLY TO THE SYSTEM
5 CHILLED/HOT WATER LOOP
6 SECTION OF LOOP WITH POSSIBLE REVERSE FLOW
7 CHILLER PUMPS
8 BOILER PUMP FOR CONSTANT BOILER CIRCULATION
9 HOT WATER THREE-WAY CONTROL VALVE TO RESET SYSTEM HOT WATER
10 SYSTEM PUMP OR PUMPS – SEE SPECS
11 CONNECTION FOR POSSIBLE SECOND BOILER
12 DIAPHRAGM COMPRESSION TANK
13 AUTOMATIC AIR VENT

MULTIPLE CHILLER/BOILER PIPING DIAGRAM

D-15153

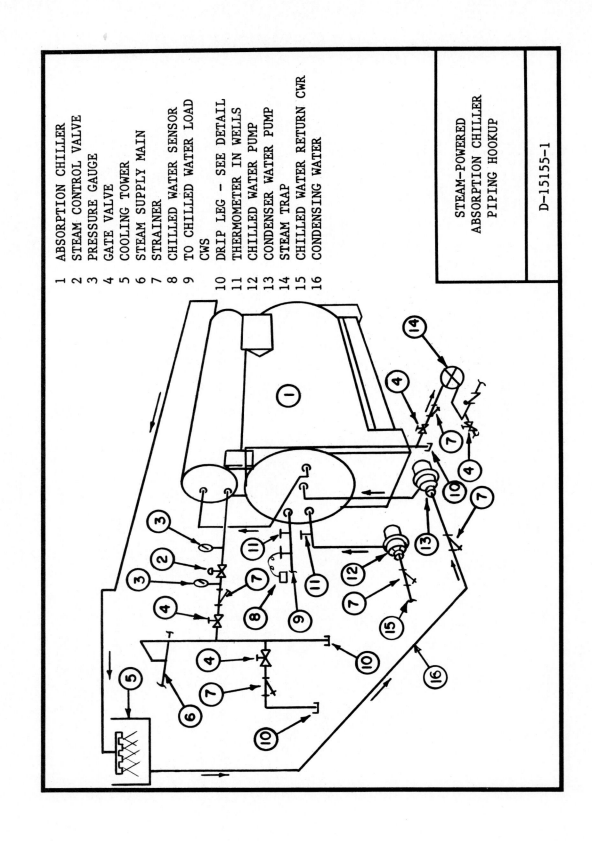

1   ABSORPTION CHILLER
2   STEAM CONTROL VALVE
3   PRESSURE GAUGE
4   GATE VALVE
5   COOLING TOWER
6   STEAM SUPPLY MAIN
7   STRAINER
8   CHILLED WATER SENSOR
9   TO CHILLED WATER LOAD
     CWS
10 DRIP LEG – SEE DETAIL
11 THERMOMETER IN WELLS
12 CHILLED WATER PUMP
13 CONDENSER WATER PUMP
14 STEAM TRAP
15 CHILLED WATER RETURN CWR
16 CONDENSING WATER

STEAM–POWERED
ABSORPTION CHILLER
PIPING HOOKUP

D–15155–1

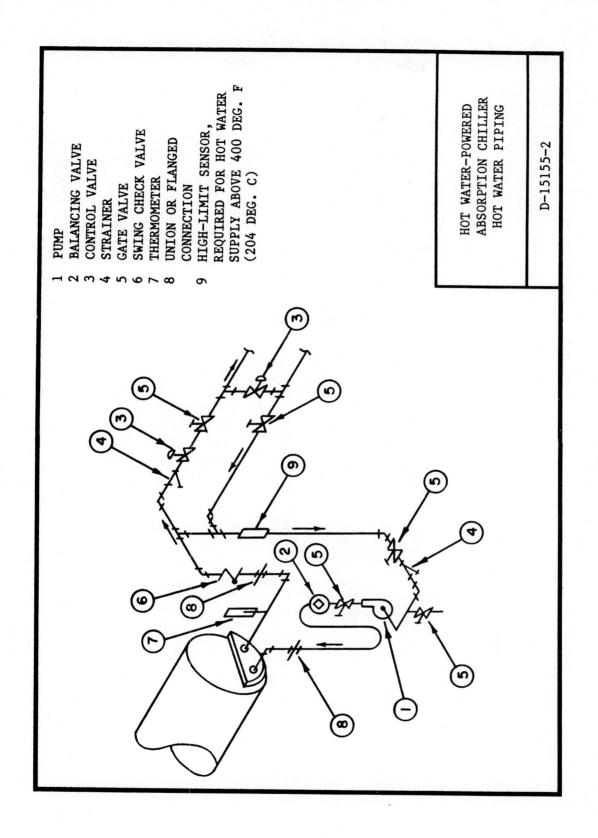

1 PUMP
2 BALANCING VALVE
3 CONTROL VALVE
4 STRAINER
5 GATE VALVE
6 SWING CHECK VALVE
7 THERMOMETER
8 UNION OR FLANGED
  CONNECTION
9 HIGH-LIMIT SENSOR,
  REQUIRED FOR HOT WATER
  SUPPLY ABOVE 400 DEG. F
  (204 DEG. C)

HOT WATER-POWERED
ABSORPTION CHILLER
HOT WATER PIPING

D-15155-2

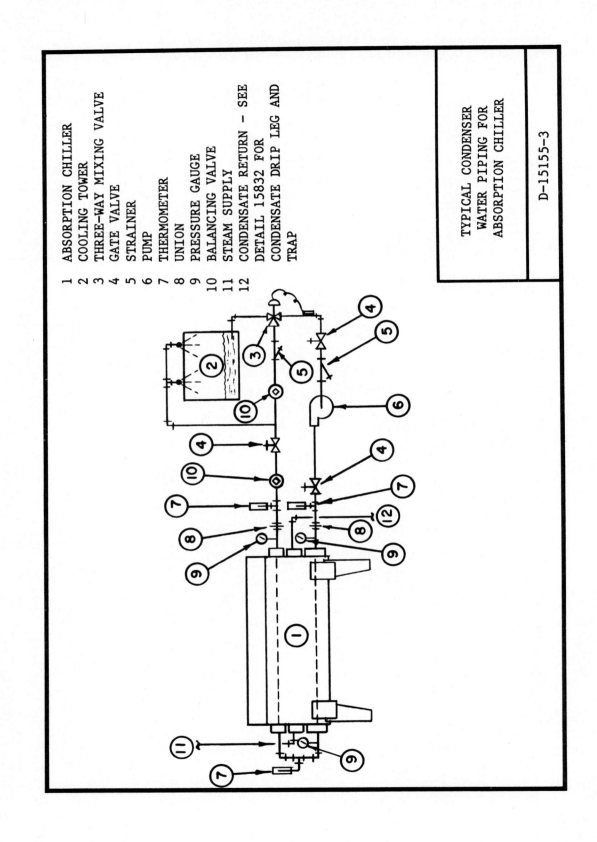

1 ABSORPTION CHILLER
2 COOLING TOWER
3 THREE-WAY MIXING VALVE
4 GATE VALVE
5 STRAINER
6 PUMP
7 THERMOMETER
8 UNION
9 PRESSURE GAUGE
10 BALANCING VALVE
11 STEAM SUPPLY
12 CONDENSATE RETURN – SEE
   DETAIL 15832 FOR
   CONDENSATE DRIP LEG AND
   TRAP

TYPICAL CONDENSER
WATER PIPING FOR
ABSORPTION CHILLER

D–15155–3

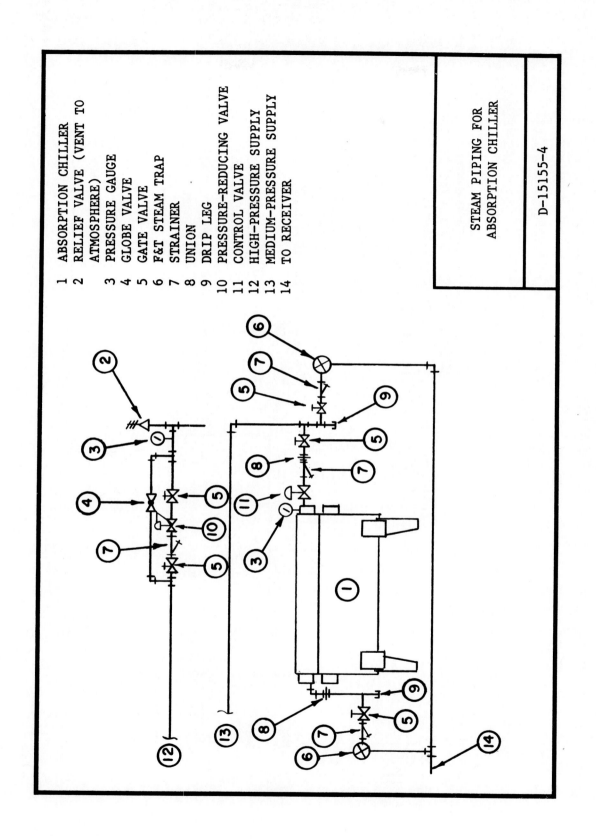

1 ABSORPTION CHILLER
2 RELIEF VALVE (VENT TO
   ATMOSPHERE)
3 PRESSURE GAUGE
4 GLOBE VALVE
5 GATE VALVE
6 F&T STEAM TRAP
7 STRAINER
8 UNION
9 DRIP LEG
10 PRESSURE-REDUCING VALVE
11 CONTROL VALVE
12 HIGH-PRESSURE SUPPLY
13 MEDIUM-PRESSURE SUPPLY
14 TO RECEIVER

STEAM PIPING FOR
ABSORPTION CHILLER

D-15155-4

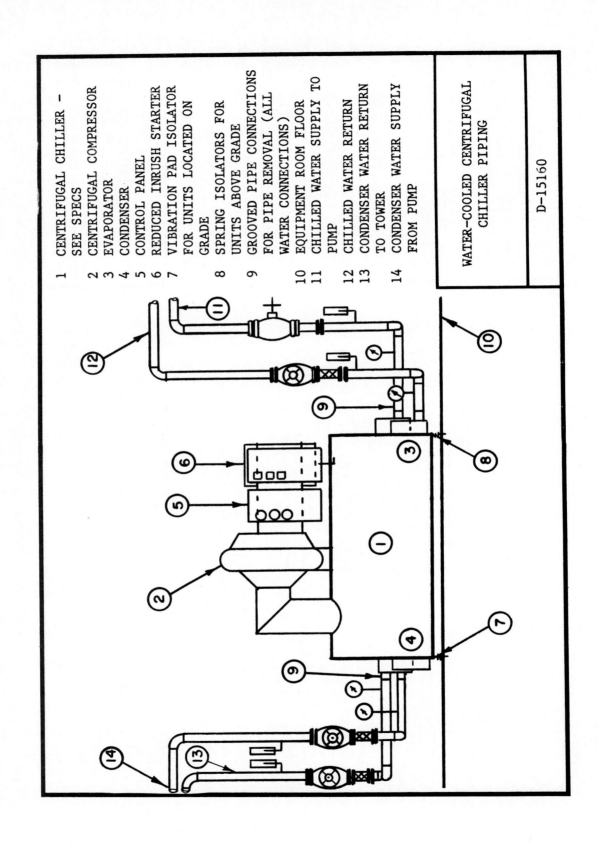

1   CENTRIFUGAL CHILLER –
       SEE SPECS
2   CENTRIFUGAL COMPRESSOR
3   EVAPORATOR
4   CONDENSER
5   CONTROL PANEL
6   REDUCED INRUSH STARTER
7   VIBRATION PAD ISOLATOR
       FOR UNITS LOCATED ON
       GRADE
8   SPRING ISOLATORS FOR
       UNITS ABOVE GRADE
9   GROOVED PIPE CONNECTIONS
       FOR PIPE REMOVAL (ALL
       WATER CONNECTIONS)
10   EQUIPMENT ROOM FLOOR
11   CHILLED WATER SUPPLY TO
       PUMP
12   CHILLED WATER RETURN
13   CONDENSER WATER RETURN
       TO TOWER
14   CONDENSER WATER SUPPLY
       FROM PUMP

WATER–COOLED CENTRIFUGAL
CHILLER PIPING

D–15160

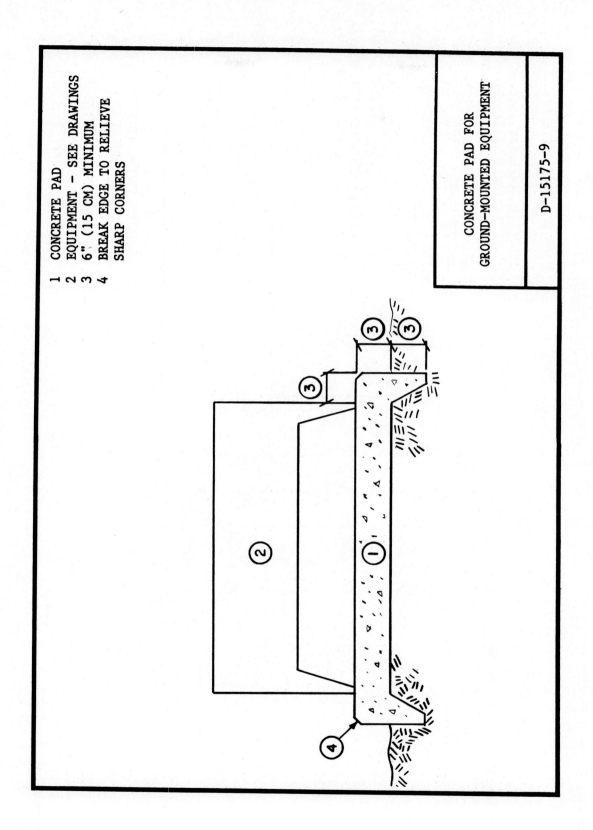

1 CONCRETE PAD
2 EQUIPMENT – SEE DRAWINGS
3 6" (15 CM) MINIMUM
4 BREAK EDGE TO RELIEVE
  SHARP CORNERS

CONCRETE PAD FOR
GROUND–MOUNTED EQUIPMENT

D–15175–9

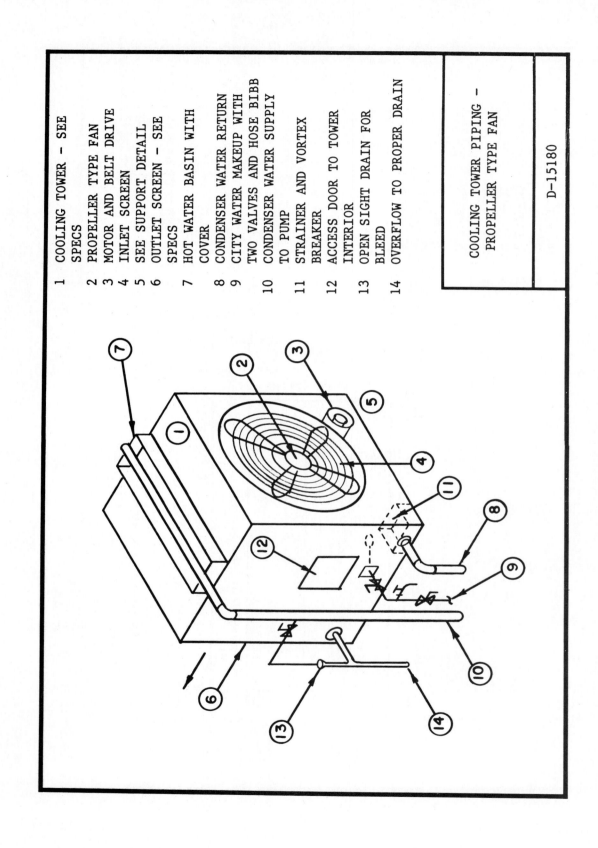

1   COOLING TOWER – SEE SPECS
2   PROPELLER TYPE FAN
3   MOTOR AND BELT DRIVE
4   INLET SCREEN
5   SEE SUPPORT DETAIL
6   OUTLET SCREEN – SEE SPECS
7   HOT WATER BASIN WITH COVER
8   CONDENSER WATER RETURN
9   CITY WATER MAKEUP WITH TWO VALVES AND HOSE BIBB
10 CONDENSER WATER SUPPLY TO PUMP
11 STRAINER AND VORTEX BREAKER
12 ACCESS DOOR TO TOWER INTERIOR
13 OPEN SIGHT DRAIN FOR BLEED
14 OVERFLOW TO PROPER DRAIN

COOLING TOWER PIPING – PROPELLER TYPE FAN

D–15180

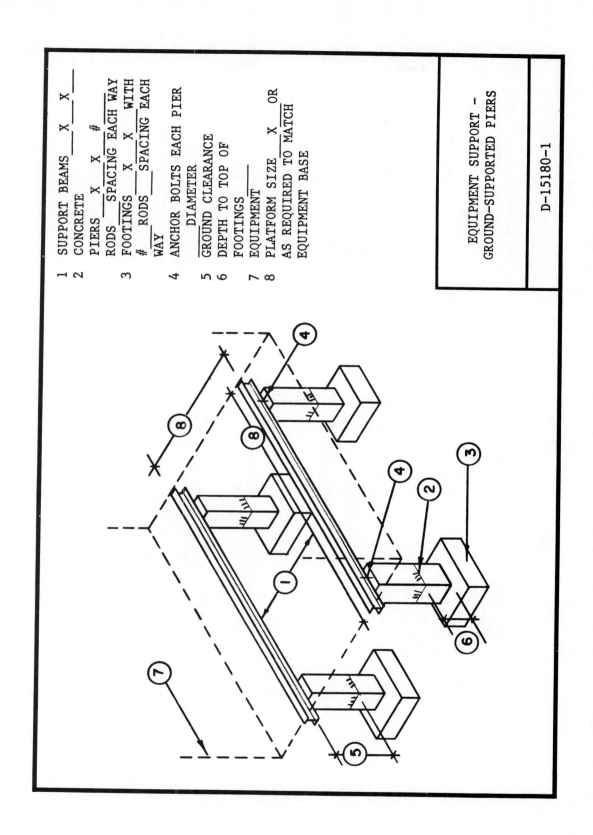

1 SUPPORT BEAMS ___ X ___ X ___

2 CONCRETE
  PIERS ___ X ___ X ___ #
  RODS ___ SPACING EACH WAY WITH

3 FOOTINGS ___ X ___ X ___ WITH
  # ___ RODS ___ SPACING EACH
  WAY

4 ANCHOR BOLTS EACH PIER
  ___ DIAMETER

5 GROUND CLEARANCE

6 DEPTH TO TOP OF
  FOOTINGS

7 EQUIPMENT

8 PLATFORM SIZE ___ X ___ OR
  AS REQUIRED TO MATCH
  EQUIPMENT BASE

EQUIPMENT SUPPORT –
GROUND–SUPPORTED PIERS

D–15180–1

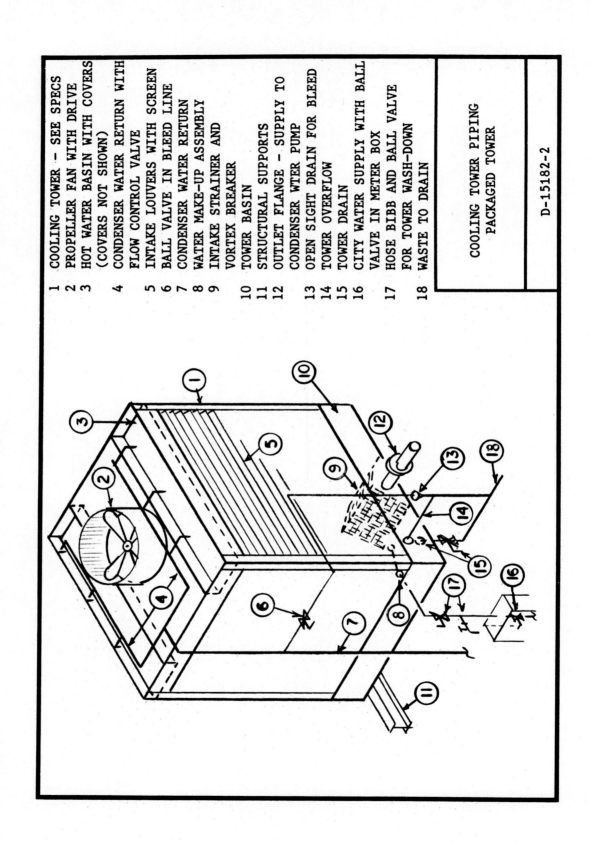

1 COOLING TOWER - SEE SPECS
2 PROPELLER FAN WITH DRIVE
3 HOT WATER BASIN WITH COVERS
   (COVERS NOT SHOWN)
4 CONDENSER WATER RETURN WITH
   FLOW CONTROL VALVE
5 INTAKE LOUVERS WITH SCREEN
6 BALL VALVE IN BLEED LINE
7 CONDENSER WATER RETURN
8 WATER MAKE-UP ASSEMBLY
9 INTAKE STRAINER AND
   VORTEX BREAKER
10 TOWER BASIN
11 STRUCTURAL SUPPORTS
12 OUTLET FLANGE - SUPPLY TO
   CONDENSER WTER PUMP
13 OPEN SIGHT DRAIN FOR BLEED
14 TOWER OVERFLOW
15 TOWER DRAIN
16 CITY WATER SUPPLY WITH BALL
   VALVE IN METER BOX
17 HOSE BIBB AND BALL VALVE
   FOR TOWER WASH-DOWN
18 WASTE TO DRAIN

COOLING TOWER PIPING
PACKAGED TOWER

D-15182-2

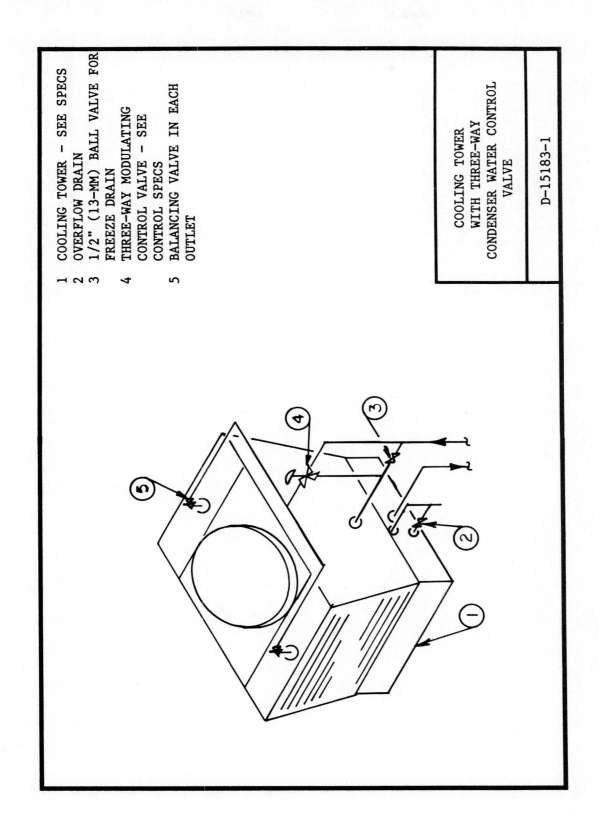

1 COOLING TOWER – SEE SPECS
2 OVERFLOW DRAIN
3 1/2" (13-MM) BALL VALVE FOR
  FREEZE DRAIN
4 THREE-WAY MODULATING
  CONTROL VALVE – SEE
  CONTROL SPECS
5 BALANCING VALVE IN EACH
  OUTLET

COOLING TOWER
WITH THREE-WAY
CONDENSER WATER CONTROL
VALVE

D-15183-1

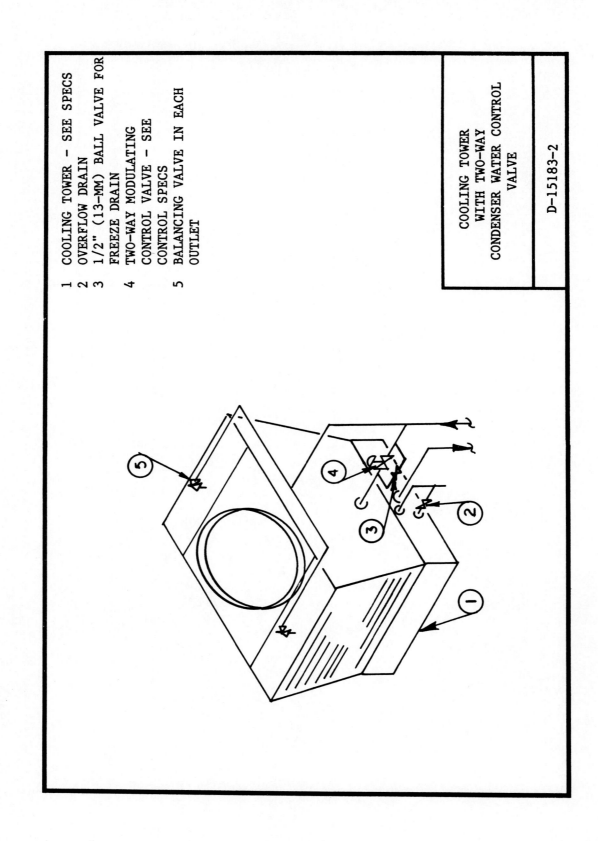

1 COOLING TOWER - SEE SPECS
2 OVERFLOW DRAIN
3 1/2" (13-MM) BALL VALVE FOR
   FREEZE DRAIN
4 TWO-WAY MODULATING
   CONTROL VALVE - SEE
   CONTROL SPECS
5 BALANCING VALVE IN EACH
   OUTLET

COOLING TOWER
WITH TWO-WAY
CONDENSER WATER CONTROL
VALVE

D-15183-2

1-20

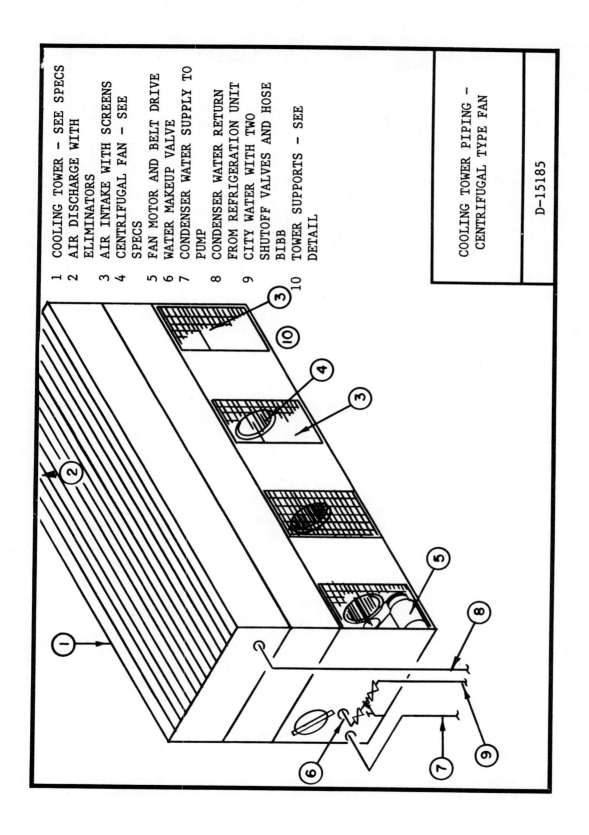

1 COOLING TOWER – SEE SPECS
2 AIR DISCHARGE WITH
   ELIMINATORS
3 AIR INTAKE WITH SCREENS
4 CENTRIFUGAL FAN – SEE
   SPECS
5 FAN MOTOR AND BELT DRIVE
6 WATER MAKEUP VALVE
7 CONDENSER WATER SUPPLY TO
   PUMP
8 CONDENSER WATER RETURN
   FROM REFRIGERATION UNIT
9 CITY WATER WITH TWO
   SHUTOFF VALVES AND HOSE
   BIBB
10 TOWER SUPPORTS – SEE
   DETAIL

COOLING TOWER PIPING –
CENTRIFUGAL TYPE FAN

D–15185

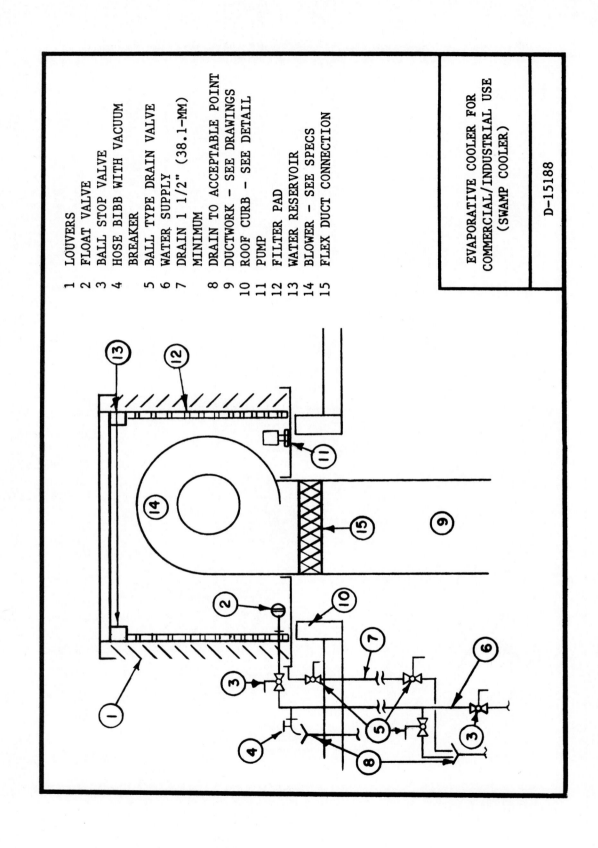

1 LOUVERS
2 FLOAT VALVE
3 BALL STOP VALVE
4 HOSE BIBB WITH VACUUM
  BREAKER
5 BALL TYPE DRAIN VALVE
6 WATER SUPPLY
7 DRAIN 1 1/2" (38.1-MM)
  MINIMUM
8 DRAIN TO ACCEPTABLE POINT
9 DUCTWORK – SEE DRAWINGS
10 ROOF CURB – SEE DETAIL
11 PUMP
12 FILTER PAD
13 WATER RESERVOIR
14 BLOWER – SEE SPECS
15 FLEX DUCT CONNECTION

EVAPORATIVE COOLER FOR
COMMERCIAL/INDUSTRIAL USE
(SWAMP COOLER)

D–15188

CHAPTER 2

Packaged Equipment

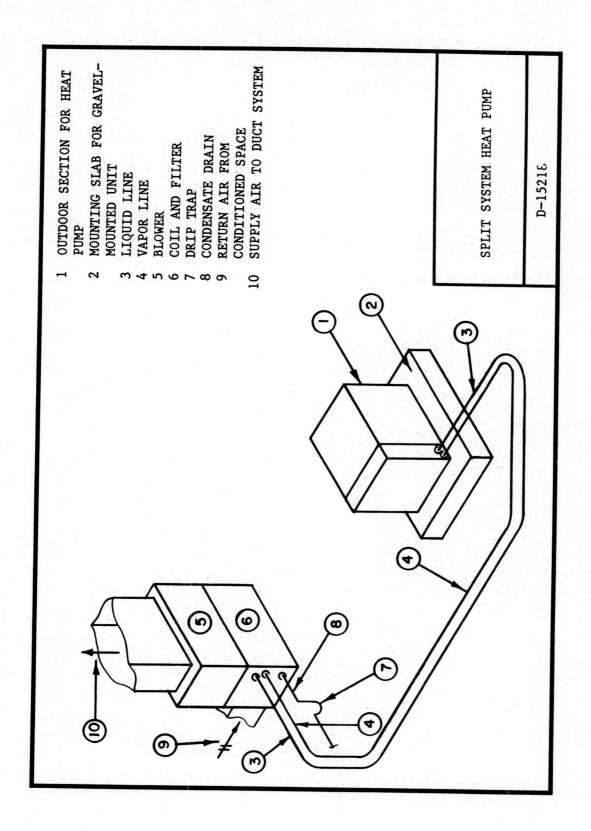

1 OUTDOOR SECTION FOR HEAT PUMP
2 MOUNTING SLAB FOR GRAVEL-MOUNTED UNIT
3 LIQUID LINE
4 VAPOR LINE
5 BLOWER
6 COIL AND FILTER
7 DRIP TRAP
8 CONDENSATE DRAIN
9 RETURN AIR FROM CONDITIONED SPACE
10 SUPPLY AIR TO DUCT SYSTEM

SPLIT SYSTEM HEAT PUMP

D-15218

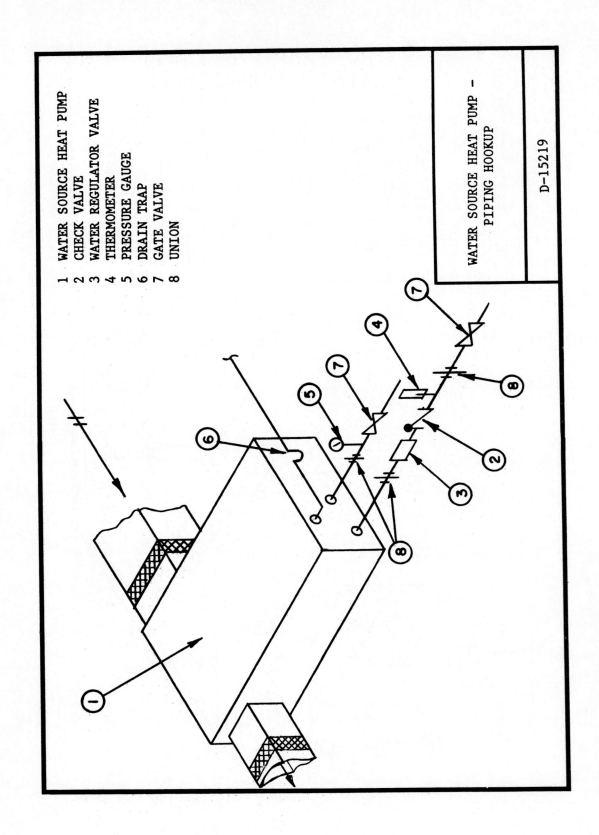

WATER SOURCE HEAT PUMP –
PIPING HOOKUP

D-15219

1 WATER SOURCE HEAT PUMP
2 CHECK VALVE
3 WATER REGULATOR VALVE
4 THERMOMETER
5 PRESSURE GAUGE
6 DRAIN TRAP
7 GATE VALVE
8 UNION

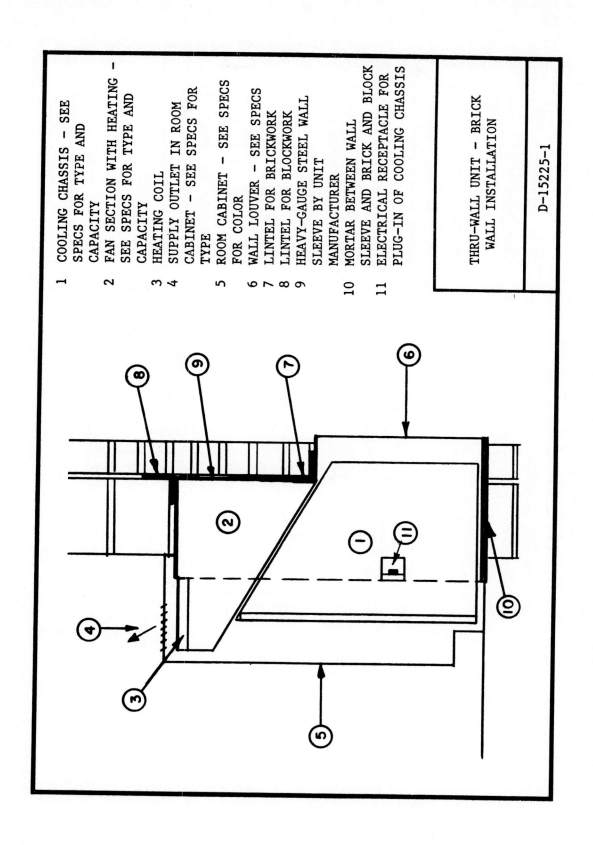

1 COOLING CHASSIS – SEE SPECS FOR TYPE AND CAPACITY
2 FAN SECTION WITH HEATING – SEE SPECS FOR TYPE AND CAPACITY
3 HEATING COIL
4 SUPPLY OUTLET IN ROOM CABINET – SEE SPECS FOR TYPE
5 ROOM CABINET – SEE SPECS FOR COLOR
6 WALL LOUVER – SEE SPECS
7 LINTEL FOR BRICKWORK
8 LINTEL FOR BLOCKWORK
9 HEAVY-GAUGE STEEL WALL SLEEVE BY UNIT MANUFACTURER
10 MORTAR BETWEEN WALL SLEEVE AND BRICK AND BLOCK
11 ELECTRICAL RECEPTACLE FOR PLUG-IN OF COOLING CHASSIS

THRU-WALL UNIT – BRICK WALL INSTALLATION

D-15225-1

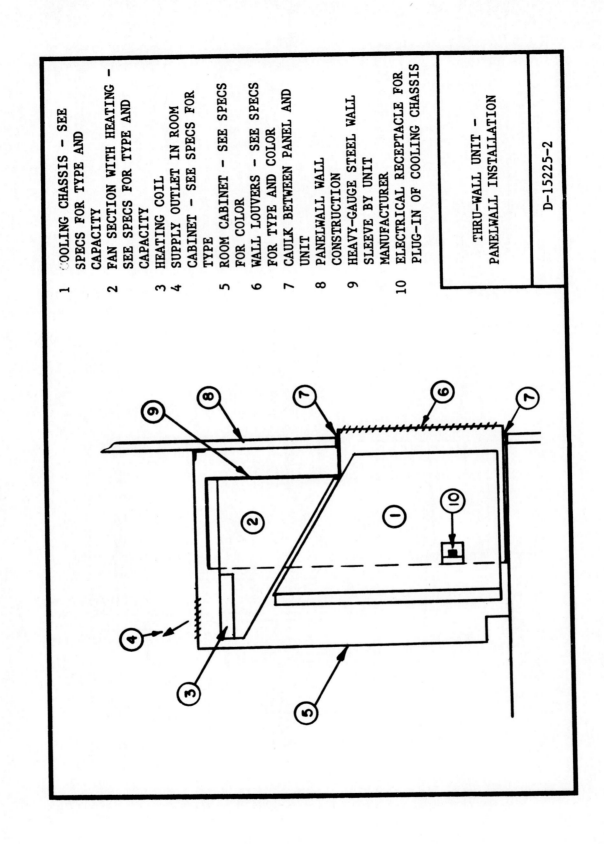

1 COOLING CHASSIS – SEE SPECS FOR TYPE AND CAPACITY

2 FAN SECTION WITH HEATING – SEE SPECS FOR TYPE AND CAPACITY

3 HEATING COIL

4 SUPPLY OUTLET IN ROOM CABINET – SEE SPECS FOR TYPE

5 ROOM CABINET – SEE SPECS FOR COLOR

6 WALL LOUVERS – SEE SPECS FOR TYPE AND COLOR

7 CAULK BETWEEN PANEL AND UNIT

8 PANELWALL WALL CONSTRUCTION

9 HEAVY-GAUGE STEEL WALL SLEEVE BY UNIT MANUFACTURER

10 ELECTRICAL RECEPTACLE FOR PLUG-IN OF COOLING CHASSIS

THRU-WALL UNIT – PANELWALL INSTALLATION

D-15225-2

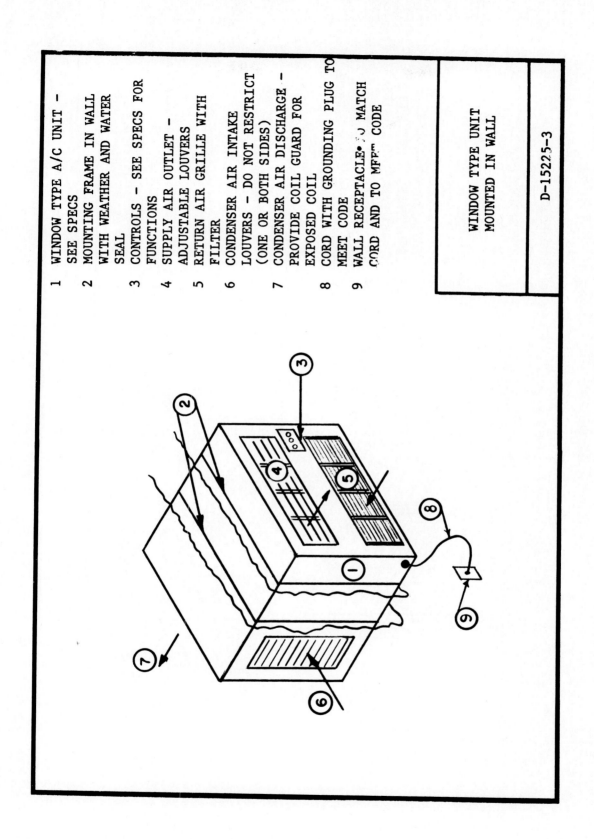

1 WINDOW TYPE A/C UNIT –
  SEE SPECS
2 MOUNTING FRAME IN WALL
  WITH WEATHER AND WATER
  SEAL
3 CONTROLS – SEE SPECS FOR
  FUNCTIONS
4 SUPPLY AIR OUTLET –
  ADJUSTABLE LOUVERS
5 RETURN AIR GRILLE WITH
  FILTER
6 CONDENSER AIR INTAKE
  LOUVERS – DO NOT RESTRICT
  (ONE OR BOTH SIDES)
7 CONDENSER AIR DISCHARGE –
  PROVIDE COIL GUARD FOR
  EXPOSED COIL
8 CORD WITH GROUNDING PLUG TO
  MEET CODE
9 WALL RECEPTACLE TO MATCH
  CORD AND TO MEET CODE

WINDOW TYPE UNIT
MOUNTED IN WALL

D-15225-3

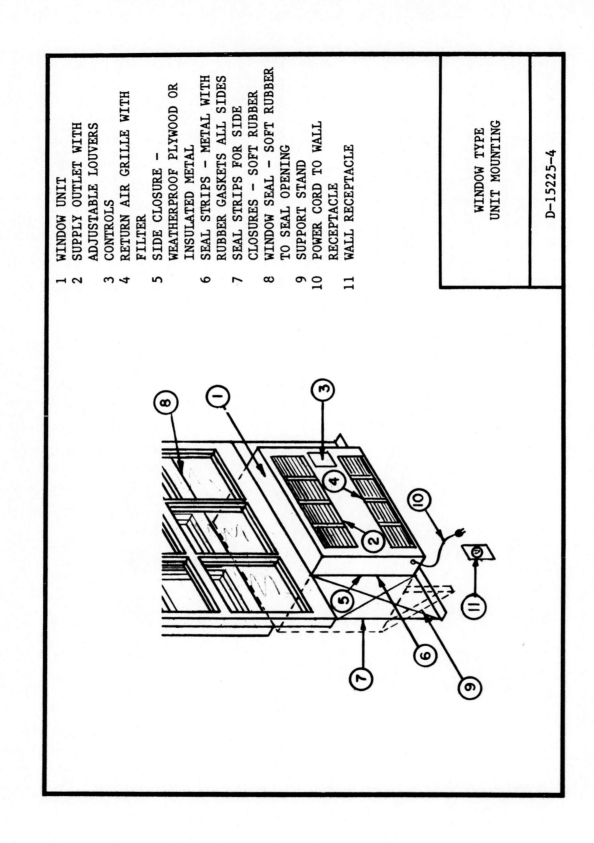

1 WINDOW UNIT
2 SUPPLY OUTLET WITH
  ADJUSTABLE LOUVERS
3 CONTROLS
4 RETURN AIR GRILLE WITH
  FILTER
5 SIDE CLOSURE –
  WEATHERPROOF PLYWOOD OR
  INSULATED METAL
6 SEAL STRIPS – METAL WITH
  RUBBER GASKETS ALL SIDES
7 SEAL STRIPS FOR SIDE
  CLOSURES – SOFT RUBBER
8 WINDOW SEAL – SOFT RUBBER
  TO SEAL OPENING
9 SUPPORT STAND
10 POWER CORD TO WALL
   RECEPTACLE
11 WALL RECEPTACLE

WINDOW TYPE
UNIT MOUNTING

D–15225–4

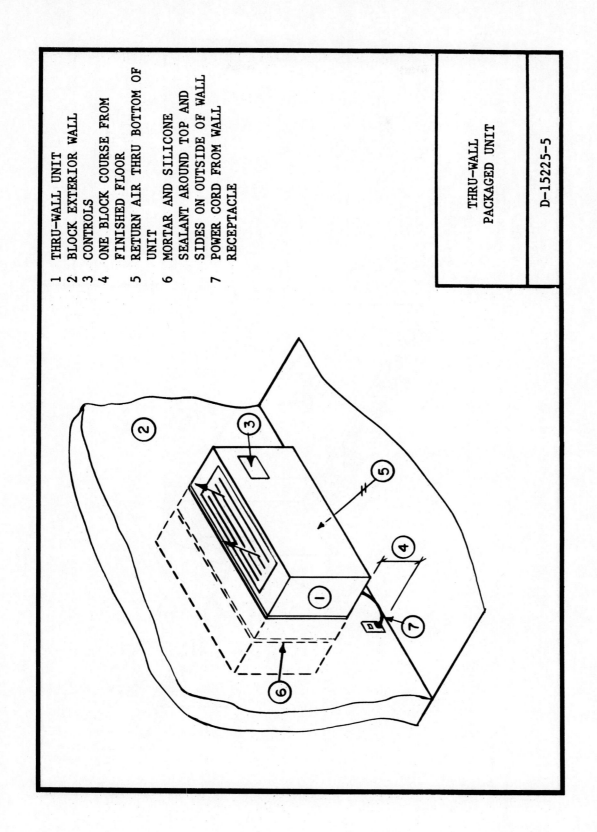

1 THRU-WALL UNIT
2 BLOCK EXTERIOR WALL
3 CONTROLS
4 ONE BLOCK COURSE FROM FINISHED FLOOR
5 RETURN AIR THRU BOTTOM OF UNIT
6 MORTAR AND SILICONE SEALANT AROUND TOP AND SIDES ON OUTSIDE OF WALL
7 POWER CORD FROM WALL RECEPTACLE

THRU-WALL
PACKAGED UNIT

D-15225-5

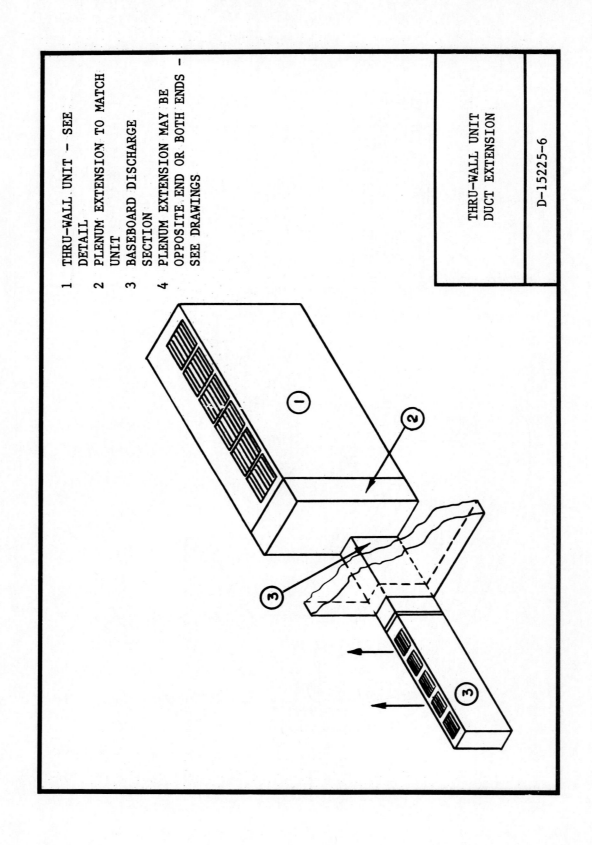

1 THRU-WALL UNIT - SEE
   DETAIL
2 PLENUM EXTENSION TO MATCH
   UNIT
3 BASEBOARD DISCHARGE
   SECTION
4 PLENUM EXTENSION MAY BE
   OPPOSITE END OR BOTH ENDS -
   SEE DRAWINGS

THRU-WALL UNIT
DUCT EXTENSION

D-15225-6

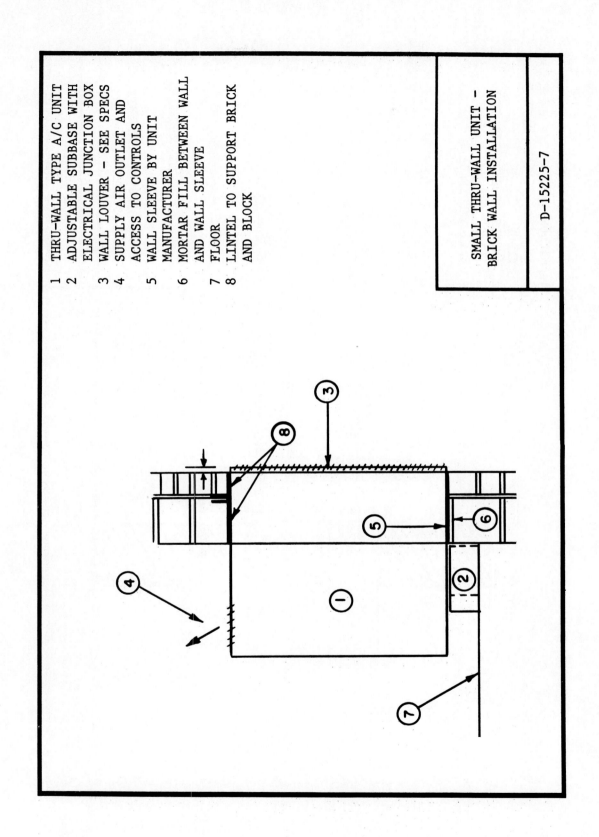

1 THRU-WALL TYPE A/C UNIT
2 ADJUSTABLE SUBBASE WITH ELECTRICAL JUNCTION BOX
3 WALL LOUVER – SEE SPECS
4 SUPPLY AIR OUTLET AND ACCESS TO CONTROLS
5 WALL SLEEVE BY UNIT MANUFACTURER
6 MORTAR FILL BETWEEN WALL AND WALL SLEEVE
7 FLOOR
8 LINTEL TO SUPPORT BRICK AND BLOCK

SMALL THRU-WALL UNIT – BRICK WALL INSTALLATION

D-15225-7

2-11

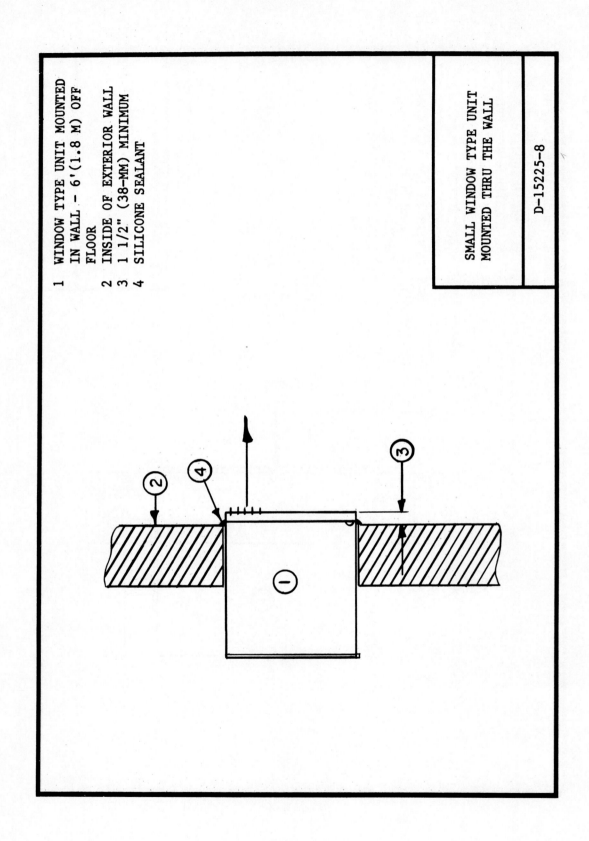

1 WINDOW TYPE UNIT MOUNTED IN WALL - 6'(1.8 M) OFF FLOOR
2 INSIDE OF EXTERIOR WALL
3 1 1/2" (38-MM) MINIMUM
4 SILICONE SEALANT

SMALL WINDOW TYPE UNIT MOUNTED THRU THE WALL

D-15225-8

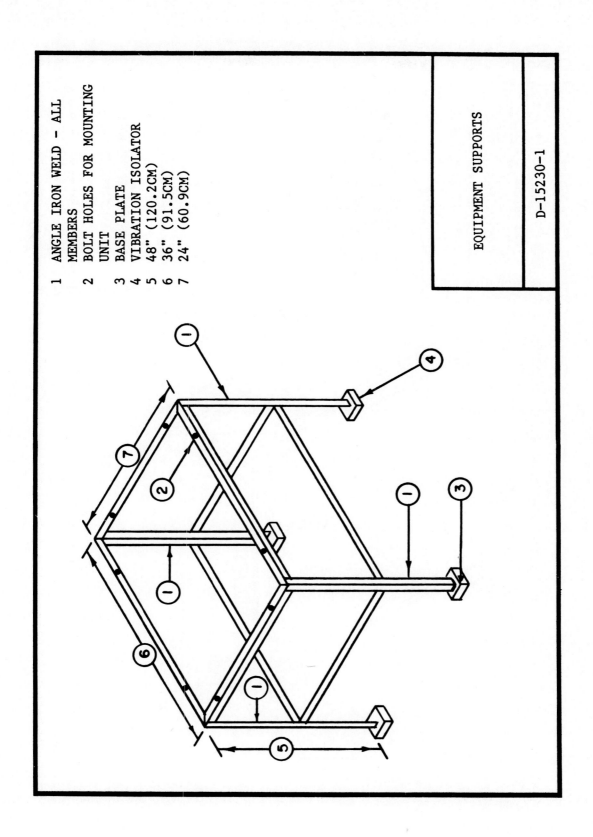

1 ANGLE IRON WELD – ALL
  MEMBERS
2 BOLT HOLES FOR MOUNTING
  UNIT
3 BASE PLATE
4 VIBRATION ISOLATOR
5 48" (120.2CM)
6 36" (91.5CM)
7 24" (60.9CM)

EQUIPMENT SUPPORTS

D–15230–1

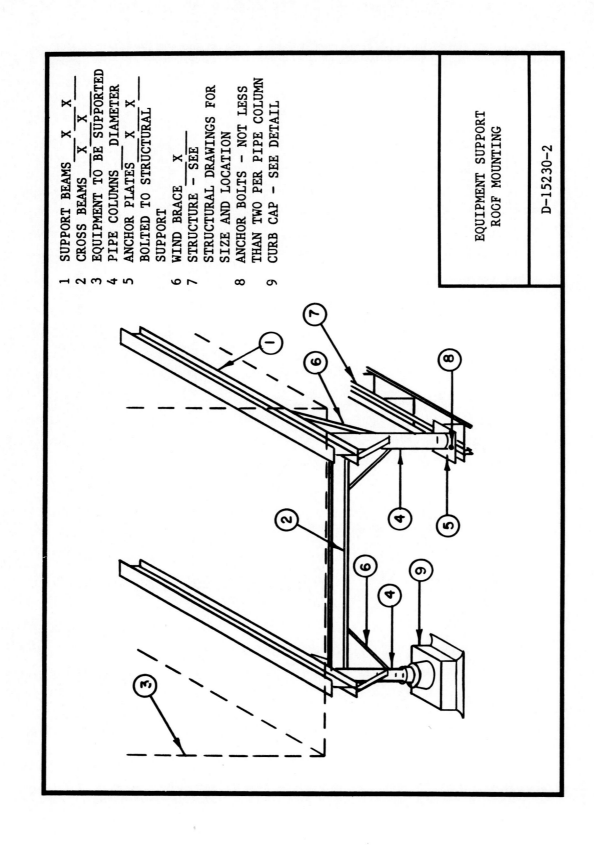

1 SUPPORT BEAMS   X   X
2 CROSS BEAMS   X   X
3 EQUIPMENT TO BE SUPPORTED
4 PIPE COLUMNS   DIAMETER
5 ANCHOR PLATES   X   X
   BOLTED TO STRUCTURAL
   SUPPORT
6 WIND BRACE   X
7 STRUCTURE - SEE
   STRUCTURAL DRAWINGS FOR
   SIZE AND LOCATION
8 ANCHOR BOLTS - NOT LESS
   THAN TWO PER PIPE COLUMN
9 CURB CAP - SEE DETAIL

EQUIPMENT SUPPORT
ROOF MOUNTING

D-15230-2

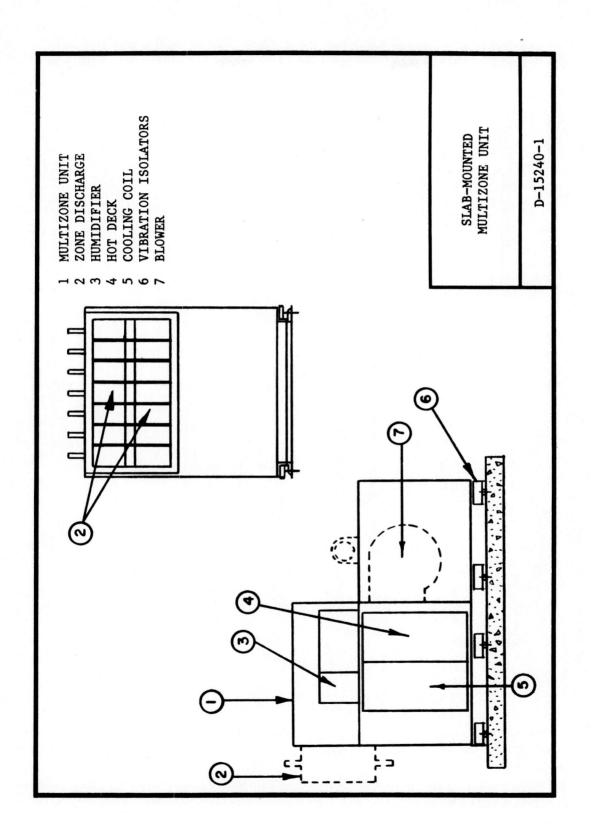

1 MULTIZONE UNIT
2 ZONE DISCHARGE
3 HUMIDIFIER
4 HOT DECK
5 COOLING COIL
6 VIBRATION ISOLATORS
7 BLOWER

SLAB-MOUNTED
MULTIZONE UNIT

D-15240-1

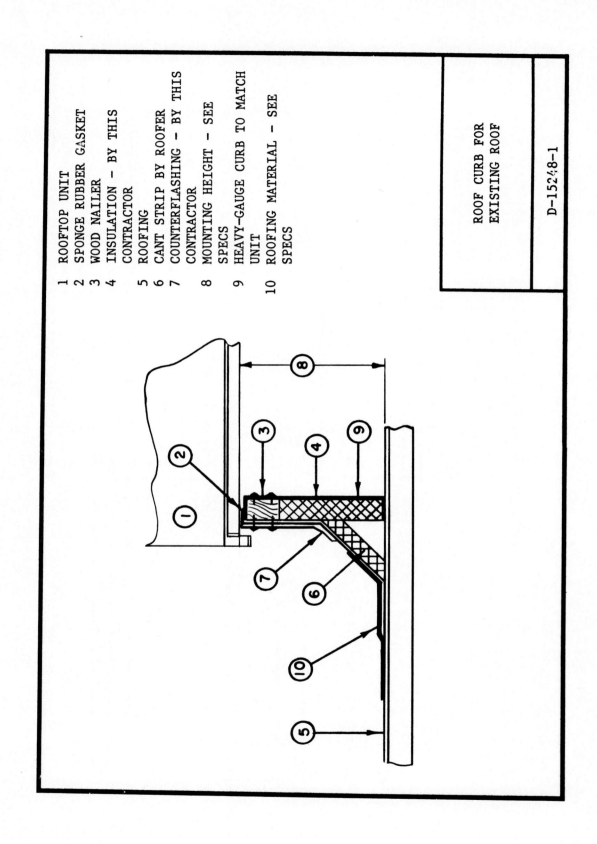

1 ROOFTOP UNIT
2 SPONGE RUBBER GASKET
3 WOOD NAILER
4 INSULATION – BY THIS
 CONTRACTOR
5 ROOFING
6 CANT STRIP BY ROOFER
7 COUNTERFLASHING – BY THIS
 CONTRACTOR
8 MOUNTING HEIGHT – SEE
 SPECS
9 HEAVY-GAUGE CURB TO MATCH
 UNIT
10 ROOFING MATERIAL – SEE
 SPECS

ROOF CURB FOR
EXISTING ROOF

D–15248–1

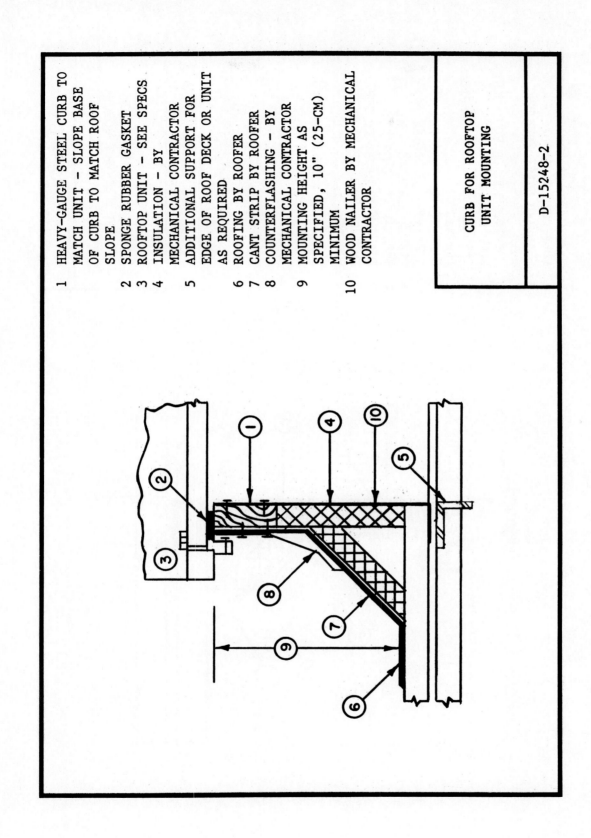

1 HEAVY-GAUGE STEEL CURB TO MATCH UNIT – SLOPE BASE OF CURB TO MATCH ROOF SLOPE
2 SPONGE RUBBER GASKET
3 ROOFTOP UNIT – SEE SPECS
4 INSULATION – BY MECHANICAL CONTRACTOR
5 ADDITIONAL SUPPORT FOR EDGE OF ROOF DECK OR UNIT AS REQUIRED
6 ROOFING BY ROOFER
7 CANT STRIP BY ROOFER
8 COUNTERFLASHING – BY MECHANICAL CONTRACTOR
9 MOUNTING HEIGHT AS SPECIFIED, 10" (25-CM) MINIMUM
10 WOOD NAILER BY MECHANICAL CONTRACTOR

CURB FOR ROOFTOP UNIT MOUNTING

D-15248-2

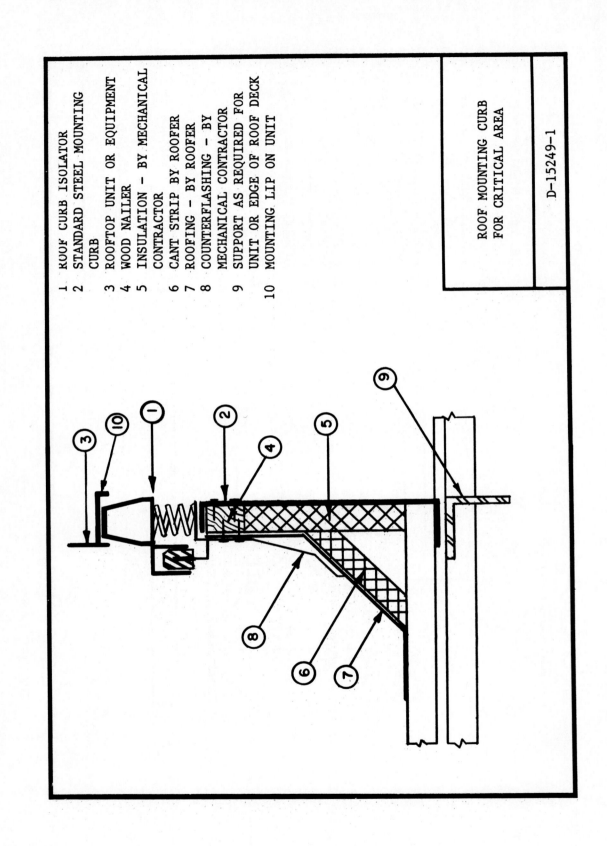

1 ROOF CURB ISOLATOR
2 STANDARD STEEL MOUNTING CURB
3 ROOFTOP UNIT OR EQUIPMENT
4 WOOD NAILER
5 INSULATION – BY MECHANICAL CONTRACTOR
6 CANT STRIP BY ROOFER
7 ROOFING – BY ROOFER
8 COUNTERFLASHING – BY MECHANICAL CONTRACTOR
9 SUPPORT AS REQUIRED FOR UNIT OR EDGE OF ROOF DECK
10 MOUNTING LIP ON UNIT

ROOF MOUNTING CURB FOR CRITICAL AREA

D–15249–1

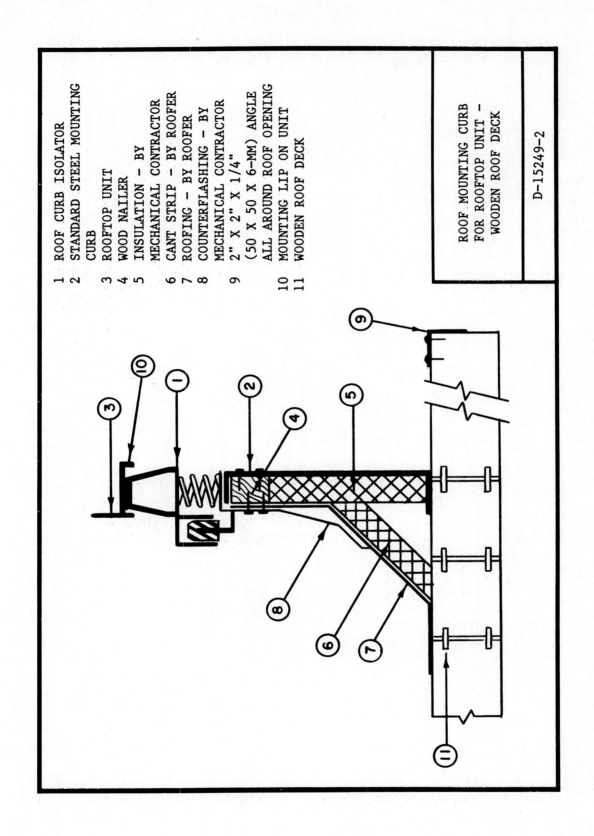

1 ROOF CURB ISOLATOR
2 STANDARD STEEL MOUNTING
   CURB
3 ROOFTOP UNIT
4 WOOD NAILER
5 INSULATION – BY
   MECHANICAL CONTRACTOR
6 CANT STRIP – BY ROOFER
7 ROOFING – BY ROOFER
8 COUNTERFLASHING – BY
   MECHANICAL CONTRACTOR
9 2" X 2" X 1/4"
   (50 X 50 X 6–MM) ANGLE
   ALL AROUND ROOF OPENING
10 MOUNTING LIP ON UNIT
11 WOODEN ROOF DECK

ROOF MOUNTING CURB
FOR ROOFTOP UNIT –
WOODEN ROOF DECK

D–15249–2

2–19

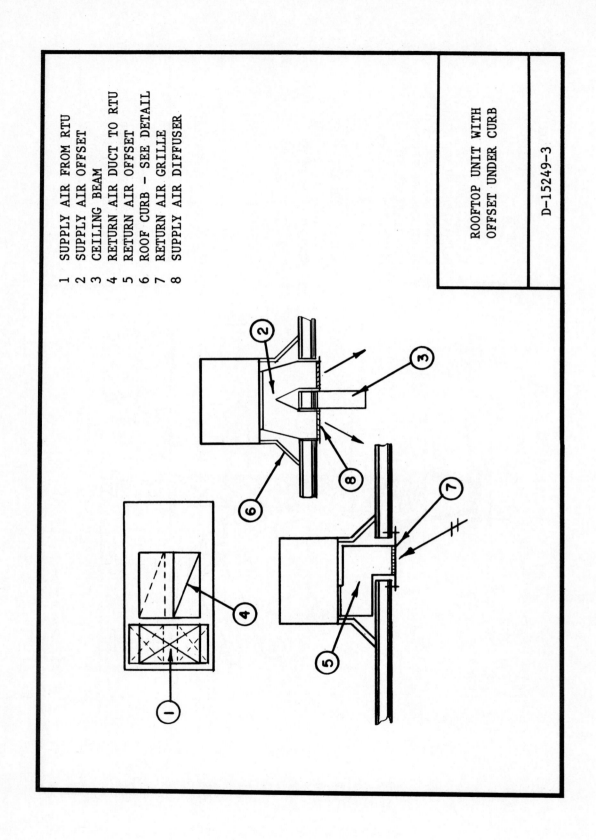

1 SUPPLY AIR FROM RTU
2 SUPPLY AIR OFFSET
3 CEILING BEAM
4 RETURN AIR DUCT TO RTU
5 RETURN AIR OFFSET
6 ROOF CURB - SEE DETAIL
7 RETURN AIR GRILLE
8 SUPPLY AIR DIFFUSER

ROOFTOP UNIT WITH
OFFSET UNDER CURB

D-15249-3

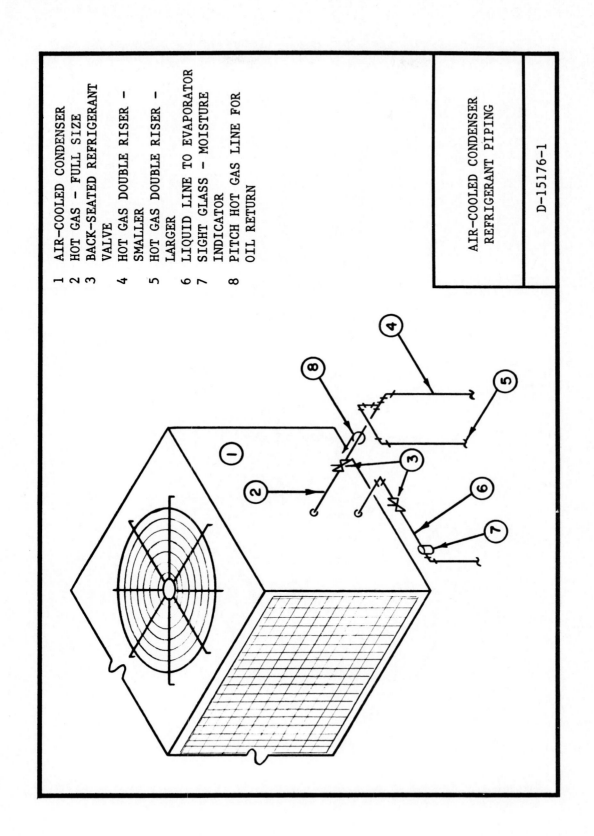

1 AIR-COOLED CONDENSER
2 HOT GAS - FULL SIZE
3 BACK-SEATED REFRIGERANT VALVE
4 HOT GAS DOUBLE RISER - SMALLER
5 HOT GAS DOUBLE RISER - LARGER
6 LIQUID LINE TO EVAPORATOR
7 SIGHT GLASS - MOISTURE INDICATOR
8 PITCH HOT GAS LINE FOR OIL RETURN

AIR-COOLED CONDENSER
REFRIGERANT PIPING

D-15176-1

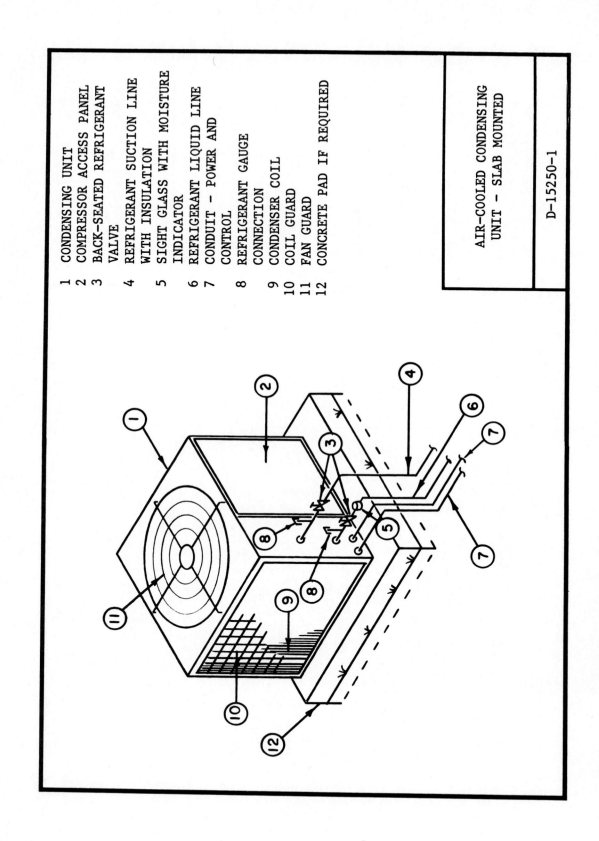

1 CONDENSING UNIT
2 COMPRESSOR ACCESS PANEL
3 BACK-SEATED REFRIGERANT VALVE
4 REFRIGERANT SUCTION LINE WITH INSULATION
5 SIGHT GLASS WITH MOISTURE INDICATOR
6 REFRIGERANT LIQUID LINE
7 CONDUIT – POWER AND CONTROL
8 REFRIGERANT GAUGE CONNECTION
9 CONDENSER COIL
10 COIL GUARD
11 FAN GUARD
12 CONCRETE PAD IF REQUIRED

AIR-COOLED CONDENSING UNIT – SLAB MOUNTED

D–15250–1

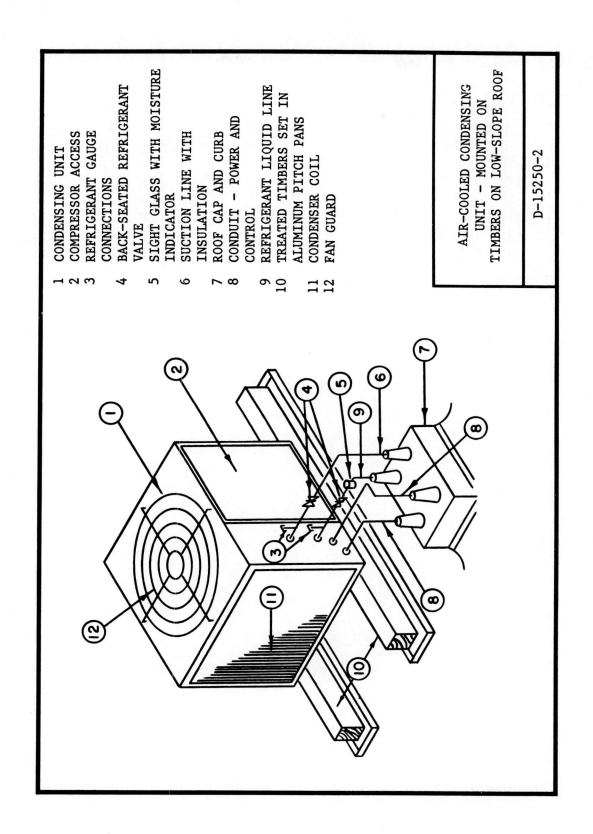

1 CONDENSING UNIT
2 COMPRESSOR ACCESS
3 REFRIGERANT GAUGE CONNECTIONS
4 BACK-SEATED REFRIGERANT VALVE
5 SIGHT GLASS WITH MOISTURE INDICATOR
6 SUCTION LINE WITH INSULATION
7 ROOF CAP AND CURB
8 CONDUIT – POWER AND CONTROL
9 REFRIGERANT LIQUID LINE
10 TREATED TIMBERS SET IN ALUMINUM PITCH PANS
11 CONDENSER COIL
12 FAN GUARD

AIR-COOLED CONDENSING UNIT – MOUNTED ON TIMBERS ON LOW-SLOPE ROOF

D-15250-2

1 CONDENSING UNIT – SEE SPECS
2 TREATED WOOD TIMBERS
3 16-GAUGE ALUMINUM PAN EMBEDDED IN ROOFING
4 REFRIGERANT LINES AND CONDUIT FOR POWER AND CONTROLS
5 ROOF CURB CAP – SEE DETAIL

NOTE: ON EXISTING ROOF REMOVE ALL GRAVEL UNDER PAN AREA AND SEAT PAN IN MASTIC COMPATIBLE WITH THE EXISTING ROOF.

AIR-COOLED
CONDENSING UNIT –
CIRCULAR UNIT MOUNTED ON
TIMBERS ON ROOF

D-15250-3

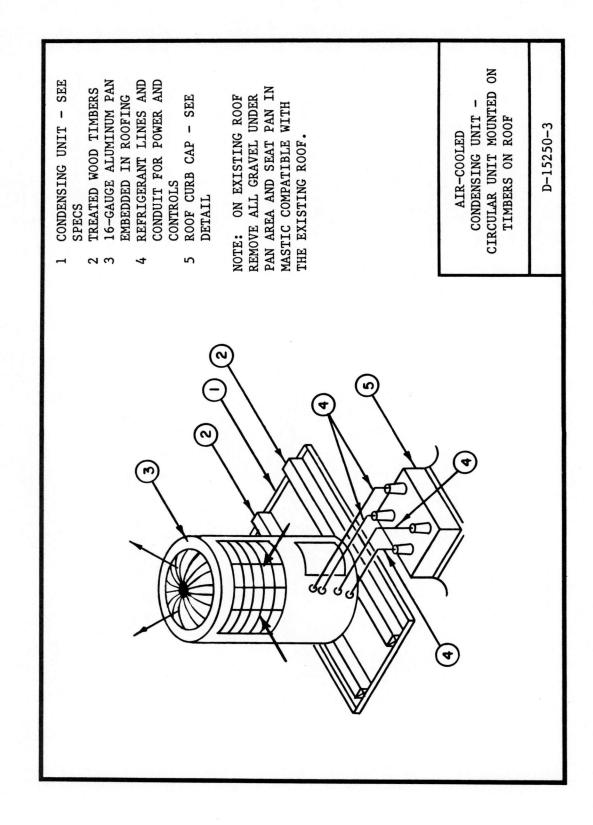

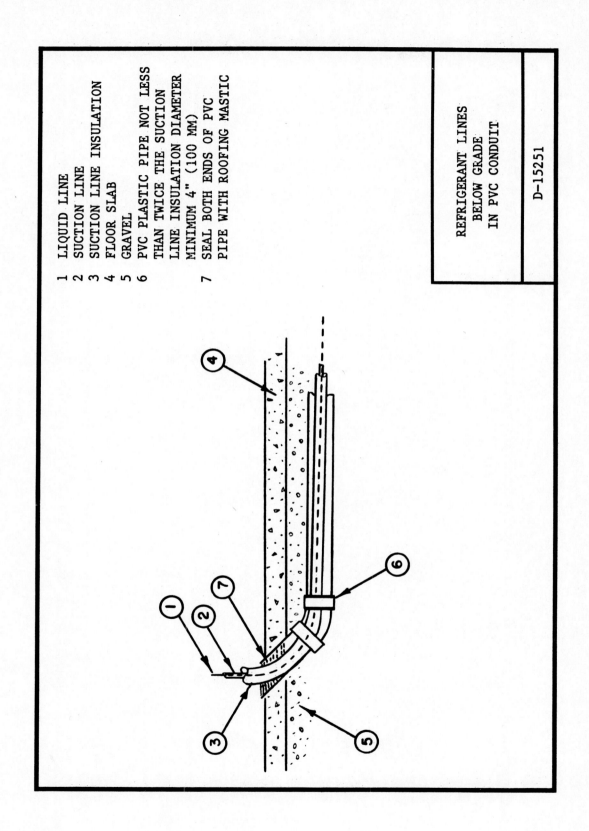

1 LIQUID LINE
2 SUCTION LINE
3 SUCTION LINE INSULATION
4 FLOOR SLAB
5 GRAVEL
6 PVC PLASTIC PIPE NOT LESS
  THAN TWICE THE SUCTION
  LINE INSULATION DIAMETER
  MINIMUM 4" (100 MM)
7 SEAL BOTH ENDS OF PVC
  PIPE WITH ROOFING MASTIC

REFRIGERANT LINES
BELOW GRADE
IN PVC CONDUIT

D-15251

CHAPTER **3**

Air Moving and Conditioning Equipment

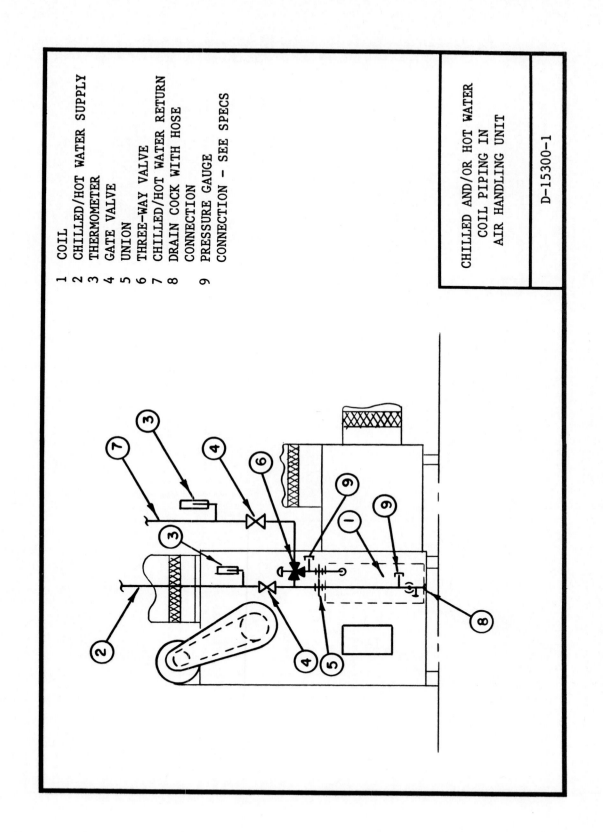

1 COIL
2 CHILLED/HOT WATER SUPPLY
3 THERMOMETER
4 GATE VALVE
5 UNION
6 THREE-WAY VALVE
7 CHILLED/HOT WATER RETURN
8 DRAIN COCK WITH HOSE
  CONNECTION
9 PRESSURE GAUGE
  CONNECTION - SEE SPECS

CHILLED AND/OR HOT WATER
COIL PIPING IN
AIR HANDLING UNIT

D-15300-1

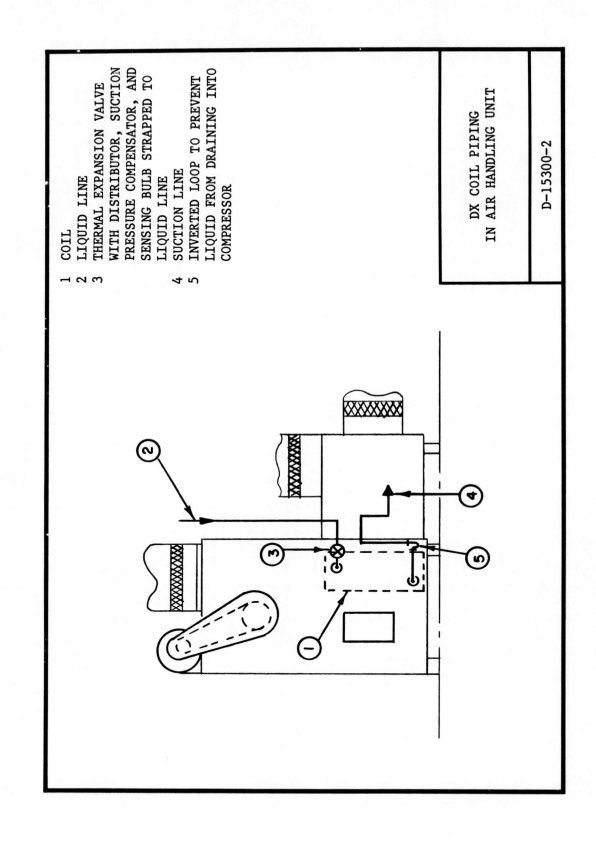

1 COIL
2 LIQUID LINE
3 THERMAL EXPANSION VALVE
  WITH DISTRIBUTOR, SUCTION
  PRESSURE COMPENSATOR, AND
  SENSING BULB STRAPPED TO
  LIQUID LINE
4 SUCTION LINE
5 INVERTED LOOP TO PREVENT
  LIQUID FROM DRAINING INTO
  COMPRESSOR

DX COIL PIPING
IN AIR HANDLING UNIT

D-15300-2

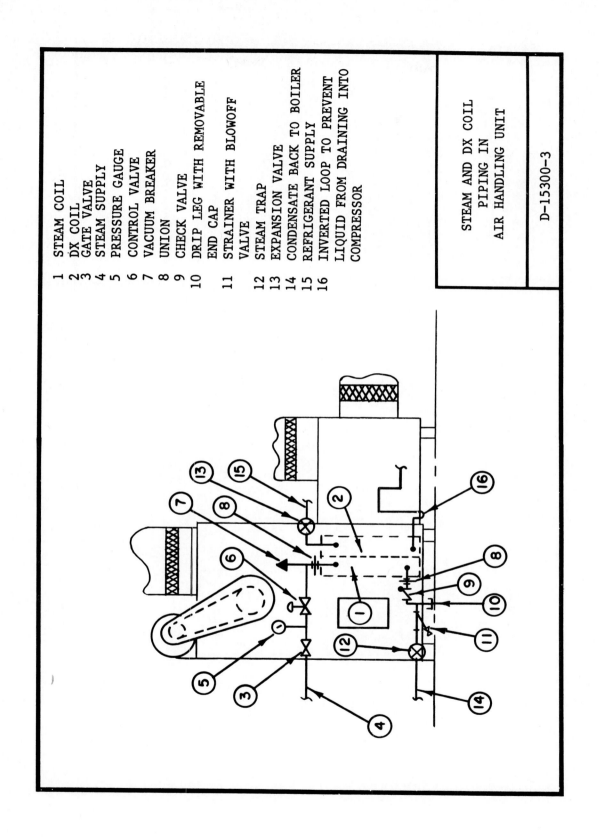

1 STEAM COIL
2 DX COIL
3 GATE VALVE
4 STEAM SUPPLY
5 PRESSURE GAUGE
6 CONTROL VALVE
7 VACUUM BREAKER
8 UNION
9 CHECK VALVE
10 DRIP LEG WITH REMOVABLE
   END CAP
11 STRAINER WITH BLOWOFF
   VALVE
12 STEAM TRAP
13 EXPANSION VALVE
14 CONDENSATE BACK TO BOILER
15 REFRIGERANT SUPPLY
16 INVERTED LOOP TO PREVENT
   LIQUID FROM DRAINING INTO
   COMPRESSOR

STEAM AND DX COIL
PIPING IN
AIR HANDLING UNIT

D-15300-3

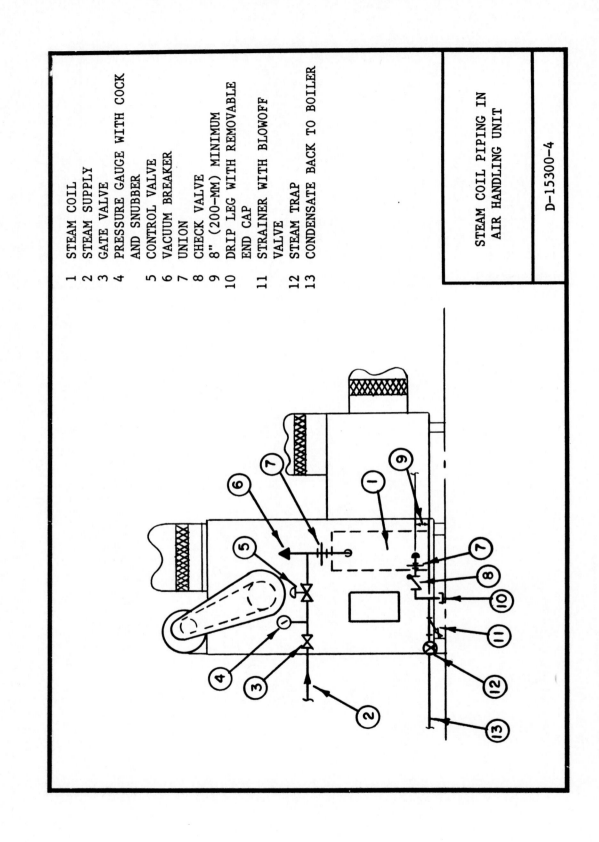

1 STEAM COIL
2 STEAM SUPPLY
3 GATE VALVE
4 PRESSURE GAUGE WITH COCK
  AND SNUBBER
5 CONTROL VALVE
6 VACUUM BREAKER
7 UNION
8 CHECK VALVE
9 8" (200-MM) MINIMUM
10 DRIP LEG WITH REMOVABLE
   END CAP
11 STRAINER WITH BLOWOFF
   VALVE
12 STEAM TRAP
13 CONDENSATE BACK TO BOILER

STEAM COIL PIPING IN
AIR HANDLING UNIT

D-15300-4

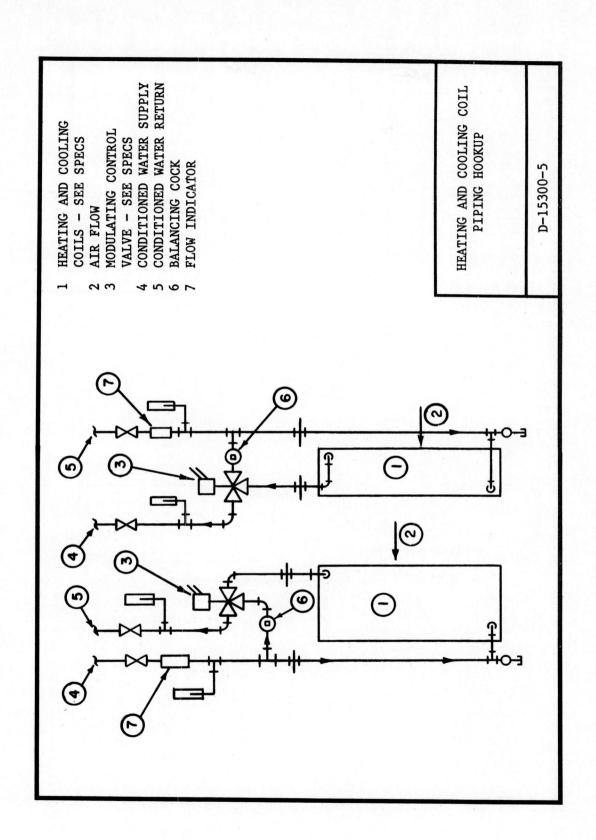

1 HEATING AND COOLING
  COILS - SEE SPECS
2 AIR FLOW
3 MODULATING CONTROL
  VALVE - SEE SPECS
4 CONDITIONED WATER SUPPLY
5 CONDITIONED WATER RETURN
6 BALANCING COCK
7 FLOW INDICATOR

HEATING AND COOLING COIL
PIPING HOOKUP

D-15300-5

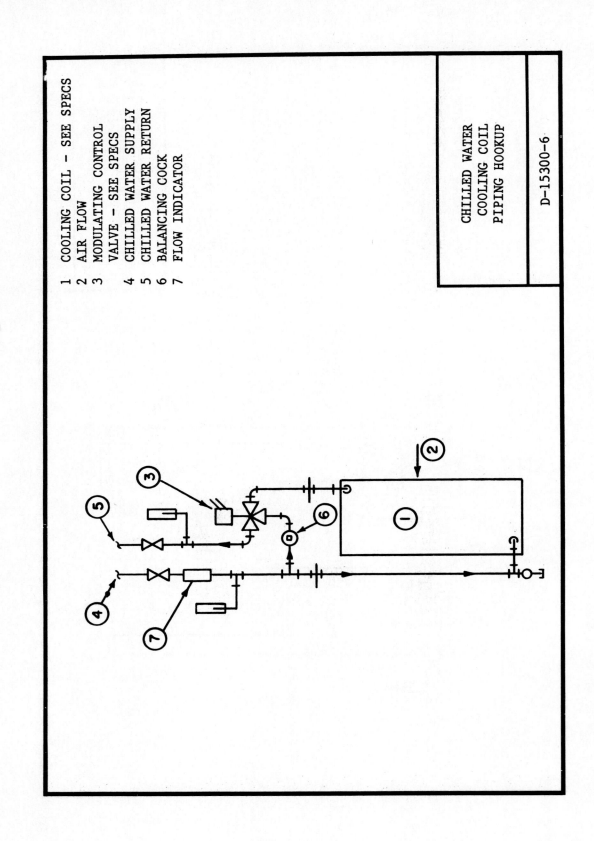

1 COOLING COIL – SEE SPECS
2 AIR FLOW
3 MODULATING CONTROL
   VALVE – SEE SPECS
4 CHILLED WATER SUPPLY
5 CHILLED WATER RETURN
6 BALANCING COCK
7 FLOW INDICATOR

CHILLED WATER
COOLING COIL
PIPING HOOKUP

D-15300-6

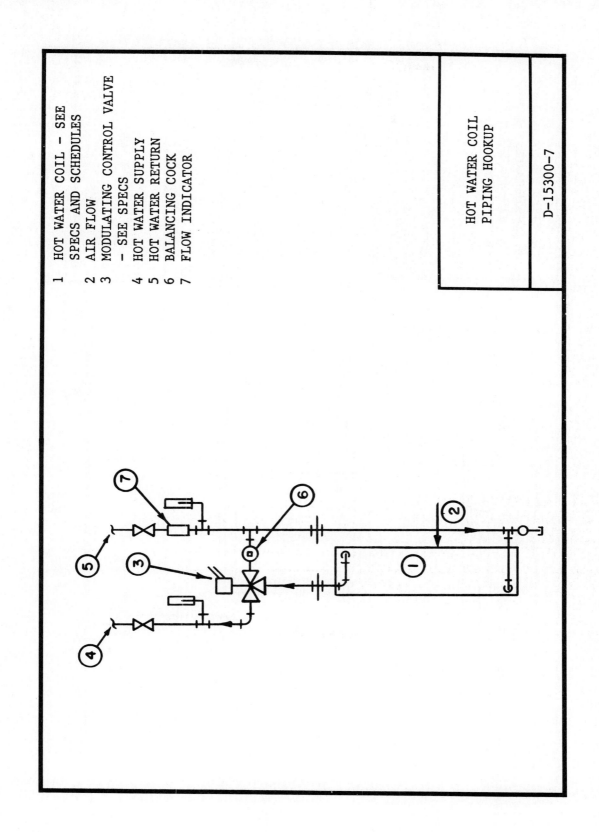

1 HOT WATER COIL – SEE
  SPECS AND SCHEDULES
2 AIR FLOW
3 MODULATING CONTROL VALVE
  – SEE SPECS
4 HOT WATER SUPPLY
5 HOT WATER RETURN
6 BALANCING COCK
7 FLOW INDICATOR

HOT WATER COIL
PIPING HOOKUP

D-15300-7

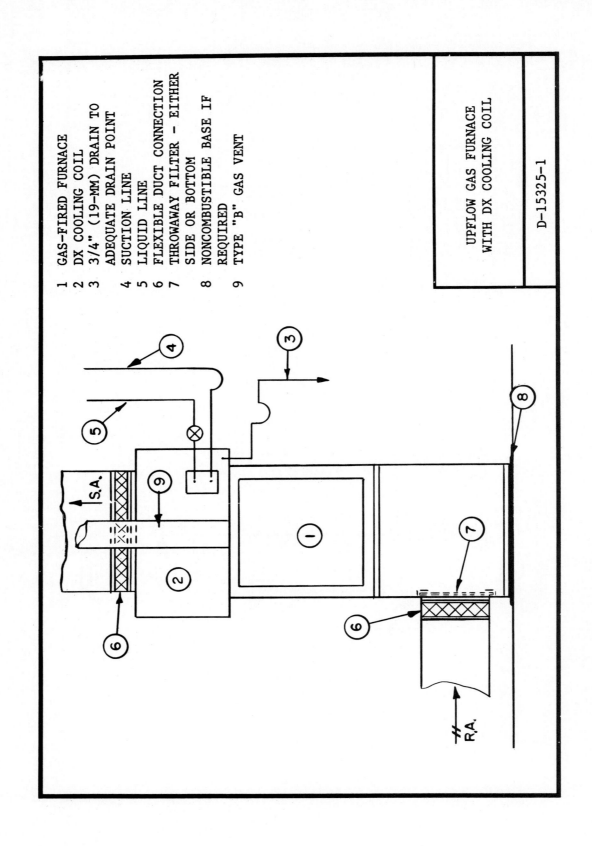

1 GAS-FIRED FURNACE
2 DX COOLING COIL
3 3/4" (19-MM) DRAIN TO
  ADEQUATE DRAIN POINT
4 SUCTION LINE
5 LIQUID LINE
6 FLEXIBLE DUCT CONNECTION
7 THROWAWAY FILTER - EITHER
  SIDE OR BOTTOM
8 NONCOMBUSTIBLE BASE IF
  REQUIRED
9 TYPE "B" GAS VENT

UPFLOW GAS FURNACE
WITH DX COOLING COIL

D-15325-1

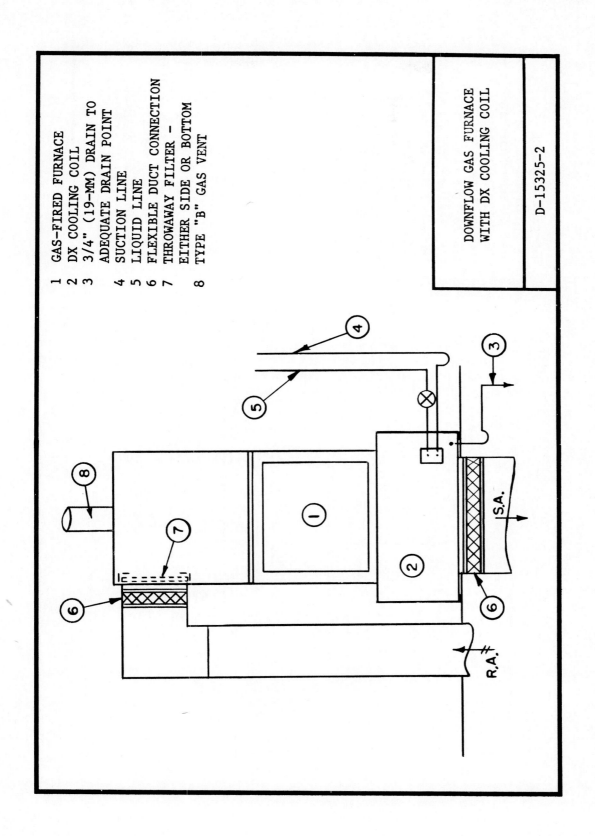

1 GAS-FIRED FURNACE
2 DX COOLING COIL
3 3/4" (19-MM) DRAIN TO
   ADEQUATE DRAIN POINT
4 SUCTION LINE
5 LIQUID LINE
6 FLEXIBLE DUCT CONNECTION
7 THROWAWAY FILTER –
   EITHER SIDE OR BOTTOM
8 TYPE "B" GAS VENT

DOWNFLOW GAS FURNACE
WITH DX COOLING COIL

D-15325-2

S.A.

R.A.

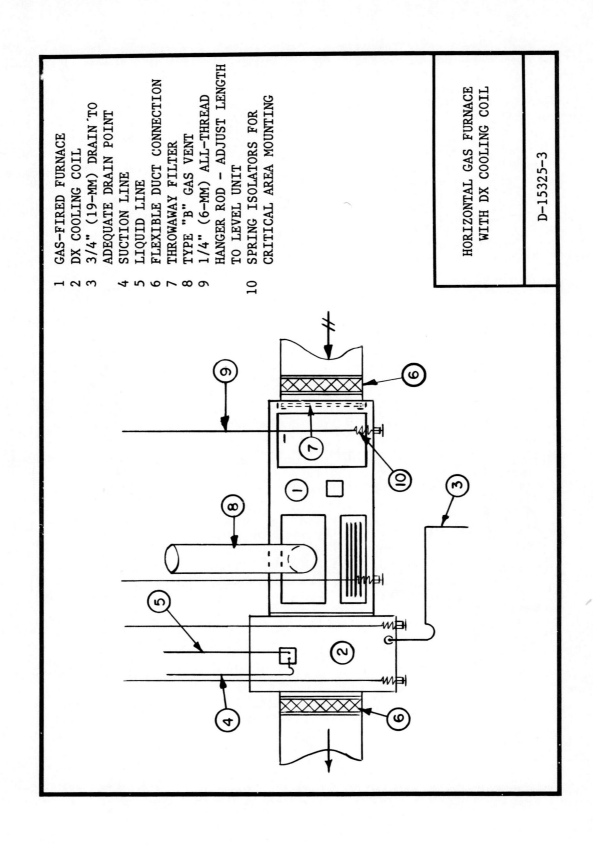

1 GAS-FIRED FURNACE
2 DX COOLING COIL
3 3/4" (19-MM) DRAIN TO
   ADEQUATE DRAIN POINT
4 SUCTION LINE
5 LIQUID LINE
6 FLEXIBLE DUCT CONNECTION
7 THROWAWAY FILTER
8 TYPE "B" GAS VENT
9 1/4" (6-MM) ALL-THREAD
   HANGER ROD – ADJUST LENGTH
   TO LEVEL UNIT
10 SPRING ISOLATORS FOR
   CRITICAL AREA MOUNTING

HORIZONTAL GAS FURNACE
WITH DX COOLING COIL

D-15325-3

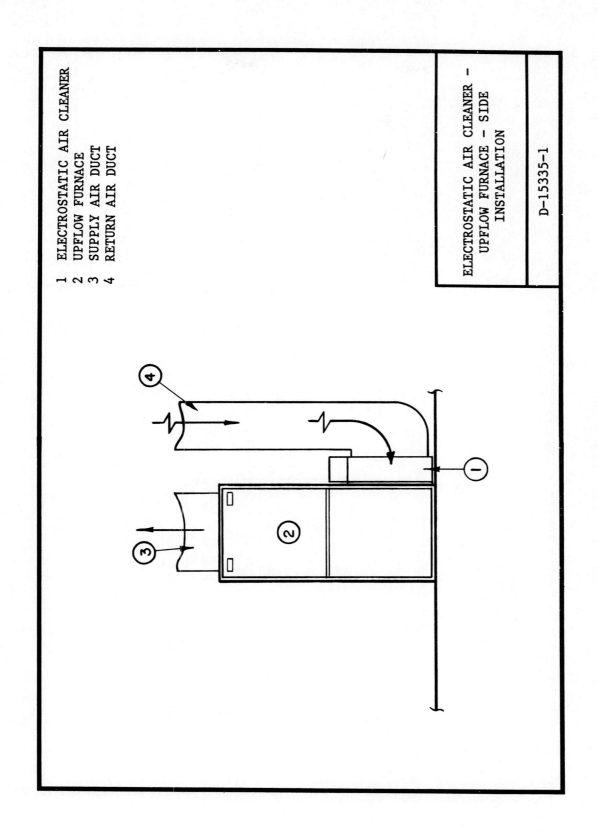

1 ELECTROSTATIC AIR CLEANER
2 UPFLOW FURNACE
3 SUPPLY AIR DUCT
4 RETURN AIR DUCT

ELECTROSTATIC AIR CLEANER –
UPFLOW FURNACE – SIDE
INSTALLATION

D–15335–1

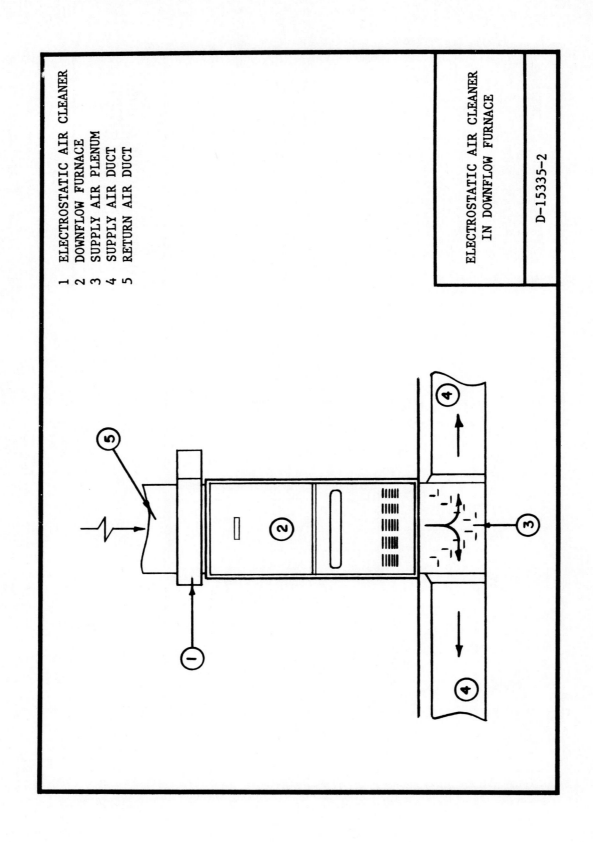

1 ELECTROSTATIC AIR CLEANER
2 DOWNFLOW FURNACE
3 SUPPLY AIR PLENUM
4 SUPPLY AIR DUCT
5 RETURN AIR DUCT

ELECTROSTATIC AIR CLEANER
IN DOWNFLOW FURNACE

D-15335-2

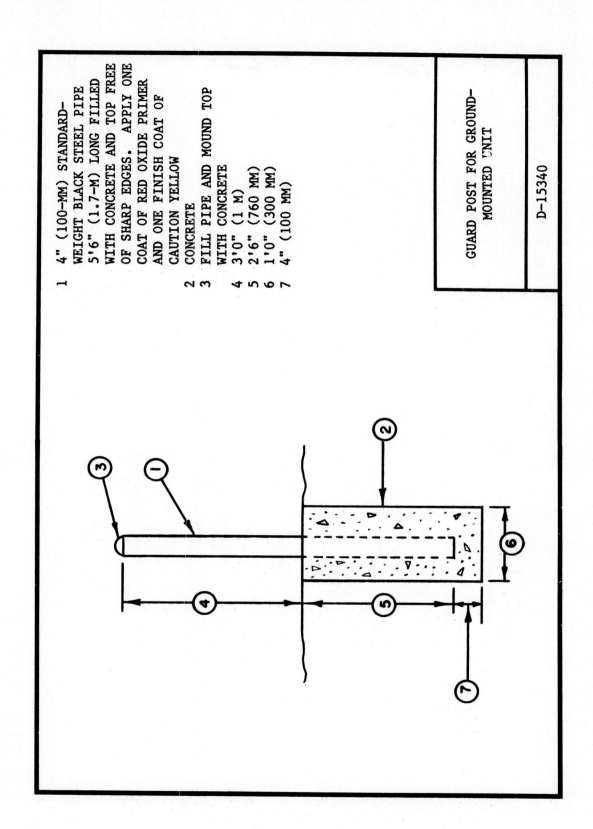

1 4" (100-MM) STANDARD-
   WEIGHT BLACK STEEL PIPE
   5'6" (1.7-M) LONG FILLED
   WITH CONCRETE AND TOP FREE
   OF SHARP EDGES. APPLY ONE
   COAT OF RED OXIDE PRIMER
   AND ONE FINISH COAT OF
   CAUTION YELLOW
2 CONCRETE
3 FILL PIPE AND MOUND TOP
   WITH CONCRETE
4 3'0" (1 M)
5 2'6" (760 MM)
6 1'0" (300 MM)
7 4" (100 MM)

GUARD POST FOR GROUND-
MOUNTED UNIT

D-15340

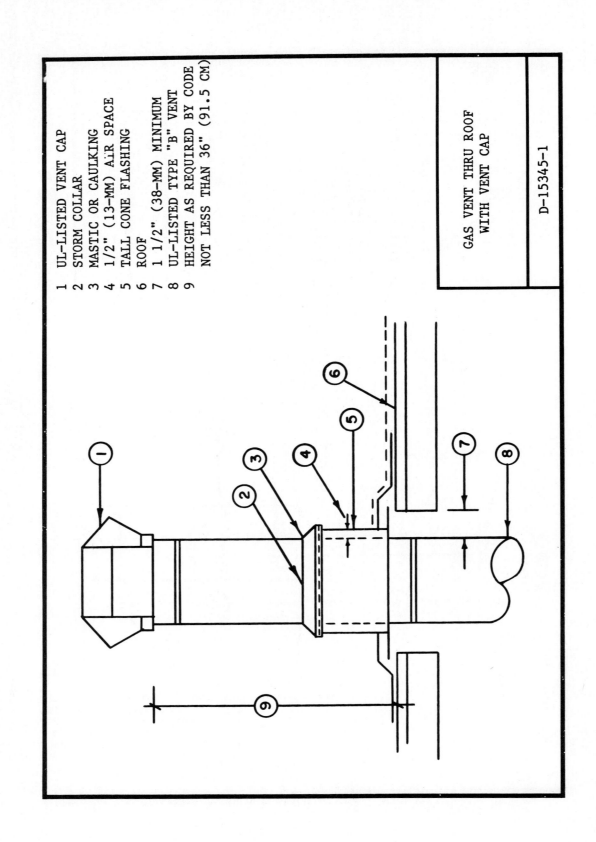

1 UL-LISTED VENT CAP
2 STORM COLLAR
3 MASTIC OR CAULKING
4 1/2" (13-MM) AIR SPACE
5 TALL CONE FLASHING
6 ROOF
7 1 1/2" (38-MM) MINIMUM
8 UL-LISTED TYPE "B" VENT
9 HEIGHT AS REQUIRED BY CODE
  NOT LESS THAN 36" (91.5 CM)

GAS VENT THRU ROOF
WITH VENT CAP

D-15345-1

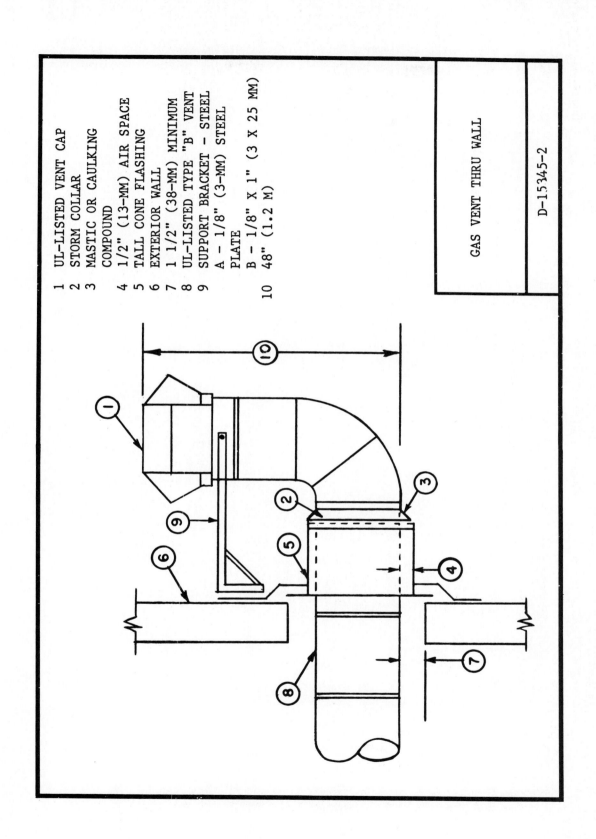

1 UL-LISTED VENT CAP
2 STORM COLLAR
3 MASTIC OR CAULKING
   COMPOUND
4 1/2" (13-MM) AIR SPACE
5 TALL CONE FLASHING
6 EXTERIOR WALL
7 1 1/2" (38-MM) MINIMUM
8 UL-LISTED TYPE "B" VENT
9 SUPPORT BRACKET - STEEL
   A - 1/8" (3-MM) STEEL
   PLATE
   B - 1/8" X 1" (3 X 25 MM)
10 48" (1.2 M)

GAS VENT THRU WALL

D-15345-2

Ventilation Equipment

4-14	D-15416-2	DIRECT-DRIVE CENTRIFUGAL DOME EXHAUST FAN WITH SOUND CONTROL CURB
4-15	D-15420	ROOF-MOUNTED EXHAUST FAN - DOME TYPE - REFER TO SCHEDULE FOR TYPE OF FAN
4-16	D-15421-1	DOME TYPE BELT-DRIVEN CENTRIFUGAL ROOF EXHAUSTER
4-17	D-15421-2	DOME TYPE BELT-DRIVEN CENTRIFUGAL ROOF EXHAUSTER WITH SOUND CURB
4-18	D-15423	KITCHEN EXHAUST HOOD WITH MAKEUP AIR - NO HEAT IN MAKEUP AIR - NO DETAIL ON HOOD
4-19	D-15427-1	PROPELLER WALL EXHAUST FAN - DIRECT DRIVE - LIGHT DUTY
4-20	D-15427-2	PROPELLER WALL FAN - DIRECT DRIVE - HEAVY DUTY - INTAKE WITH FIXED LOUVER - DUCT CONNECTION
4-21	D-15428	PROPELLER TYPE WALL FAN - BELT DRIVE - EXHAUST SHUTTER
4-22	D-15428-1	PROPELLER TYPE WALL FAN - NO LOUVER OR SHUTTER SHOWN
4-23	D-15428-2	PROPELLER TYPE WALL FAN WITH INSULATED MOVABLE LOUVERS
4-24	D-15450-1	RIDGE-MOUNTED VENTILATOR - GRAVITY TYPE
4-25	D-15450-2	VENTILATOR ON FLAT ROOF - GRAVITY TYPE - MANUAL DAMPER - CEILING RING GRILLE
4-26	D-15450-3	VENTILATOR ON PITCHED ROOF - GRAVITY TYPE - MANUAL DAMPER
4-27	D-15450-4	HORIZONTAL RELIEF CAP - ROOF MOUNTED
4-28	D-15455-1	SHUTTER TYPE RELIEF DAMPER - WALL DISCHARGE
4-29	D-15455-2	WALL RELIEF DAMPER WITH BIRD SCREEN

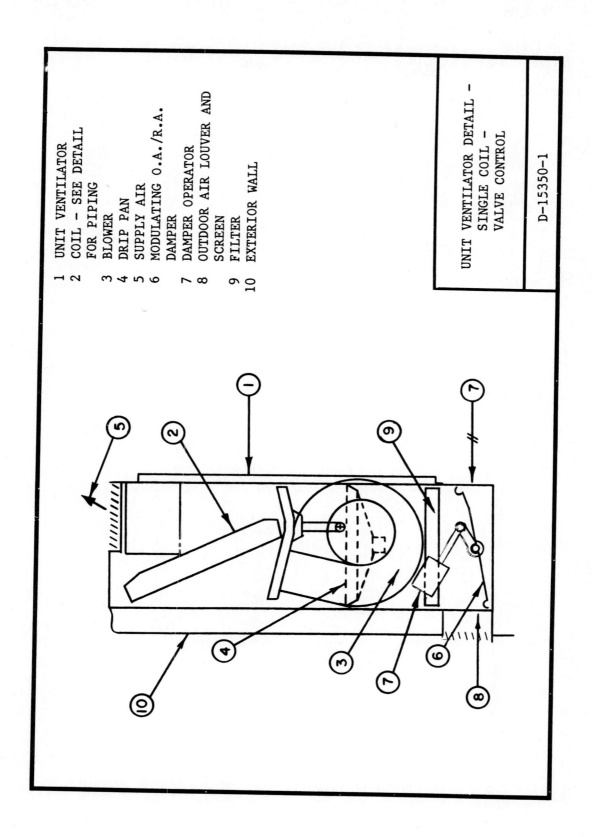

1 UNIT VENTILATOR
2 COIL – SEE DETAIL
   FOR PIPING
3 BLOWER
4 DRIP PAN
5 SUPPLY AIR
6 MODULATING O.A./R.A.
   DAMPER
7 DAMPER OPERATOR
8 OUTDOOR AIR LOUVER AND
   SCREEN
9 FILTER
10 EXTERIOR WALL

UNIT VENTILATOR DETAIL –
SINGLE COIL –
VALVE CONTROL

D–15350–1

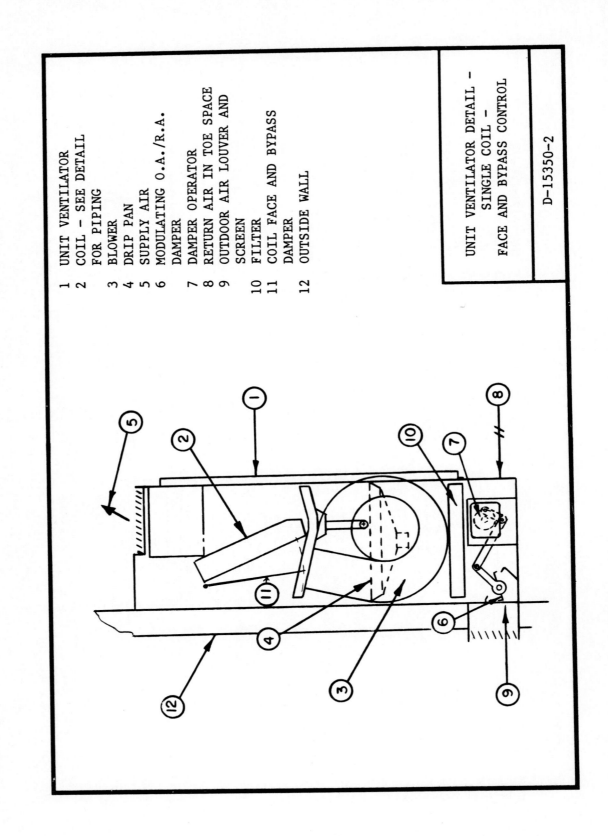

1 UNIT VENTILATOR
2 COIL – SEE DETAIL FOR PIPING
3 BLOWER
4 DRIP PAN
5 SUPPLY AIR
6 MODULATING O.A./R.A. DAMPER
7 DAMPER OPERATOR
8 RETURN AIR IN TOE SPACE
9 OUTDOOR AIR LOUVER AND SCREEN
10 FILTER
11 COIL FACE AND BYPASS DAMPER
12 OUTSIDE WALL

UNIT VENTILATOR DETAIL –
SINGLE COIL –
FACE AND BYPASS CONTROL

D–15350–2

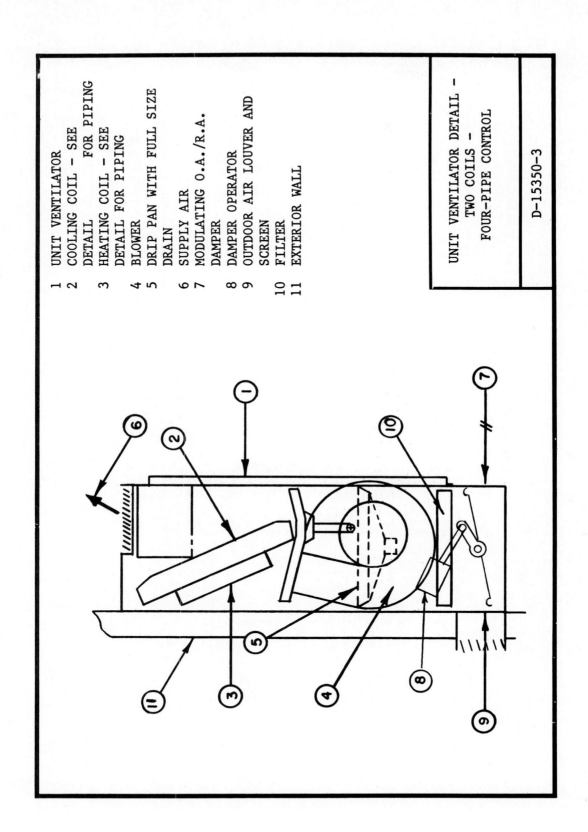

1 UNIT VENTILATOR
2 COOLING COIL – SEE DETAIL FOR PIPING
3 HEATING COIL – SEE DETAIL FOR PIPING
4 BLOWER
5 DRIP PAN WITH FULL SIZE DRAIN
6 SUPPLY AIR
7 MODULATING O.A./R.A. DAMPER
8 DAMPER OPERATOR
9 OUTDOOR AIR LOUVER AND SCREEN
10 FILTER
11 EXTERIOR WALL

UNIT VENTILATOR DETAIL –
TWO COILS –
FOUR–PIPE CONTROL

D–15350–3

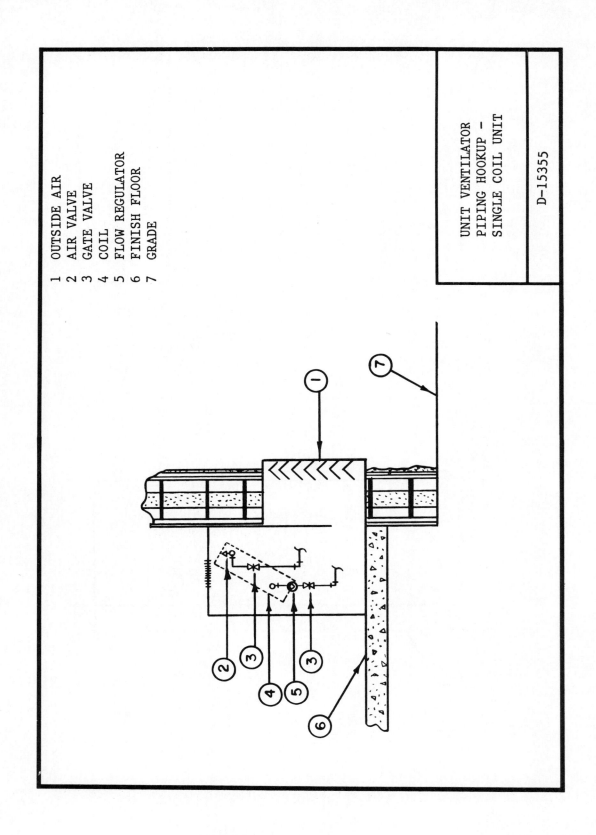

1 OUTSIDE AIR
2 AIR VALVE
3 GATE VALVE
4 COIL
5 FLOW REGULATOR
6 FINISH FLOOR
7 GRADE

UNIT VENTILATOR
PIPING HOOKUP —
SINGLE COIL UNIT

D–15355

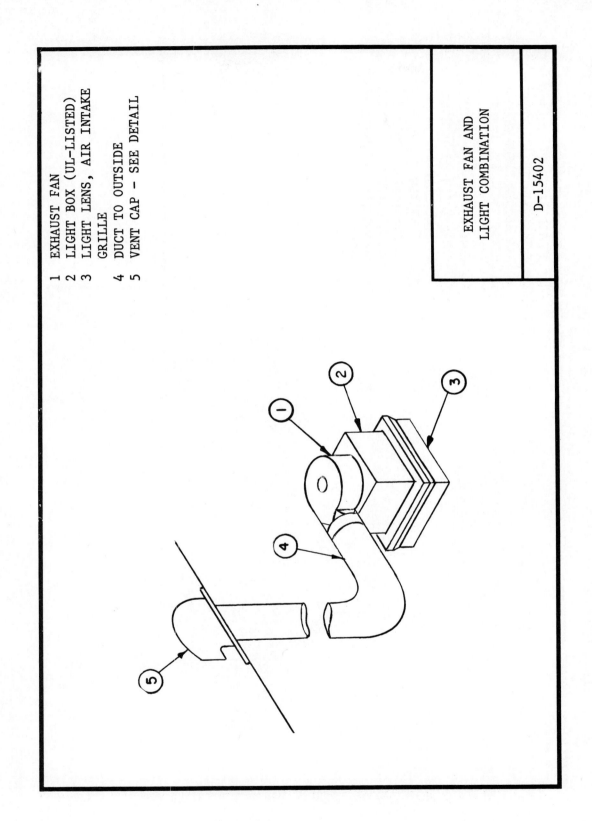

1 EXHAUST FAN
2 LIGHT BOX (UL-LISTED)
3 LIGHT LENS, AIR INTAKE
  GRILLE
4 DUCT TO OUTSIDE
5 VENT CAP – SEE DETAIL

EXHAUST FAN AND
LIGHT COMBINATION

D–15402

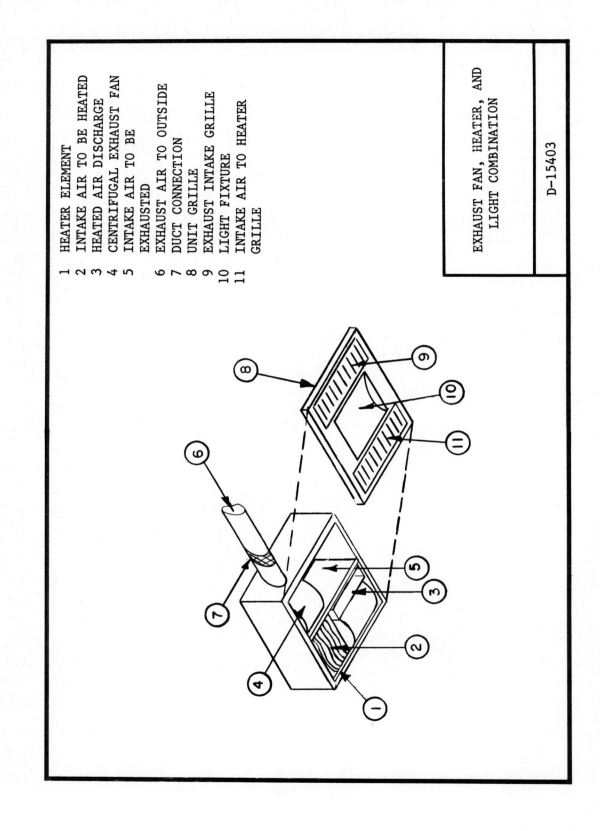

1 HEATER ELEMENT
2 INTAKE AIR TO BE HEATED
3 HEATED AIR DISCHARGE
4 CENTRIFUGAL EXHAUST FAN
5 INTAKE AIR TO BE
  EXHAUSTED
6 EXHAUST AIR TO OUTSIDE
7 DUCT CONNECTION
8 UNIT GRILLE
9 EXHAUST INTAKE GRILLE
10 LIGHT FIXTURE
11 INTAKE AIR TO HEATER
  GRILLE

EXHAUST FAN, HEATER, AND
LIGHT COMBINATION

D-15403

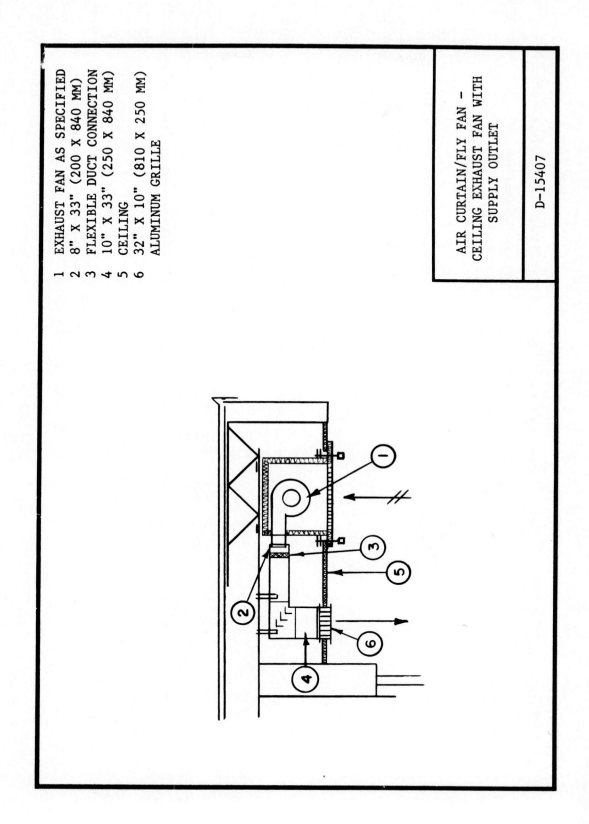

1 EXHAUST FAN AS SPECIFIED
2 8" X 33" (200 X 840 MM)
3 FLEXIBLE DUCT CONNECTION
4 10" X 33" (250 X 840 MM)
5 CEILING
6 32" X 10" (810 X 250 MM)
   ALUMINUM GRILLE

AIR CURTAIN/FLY FAN –
CEILING EXHAUST FAN WITH
SUPPLY OUTLET

D-15407

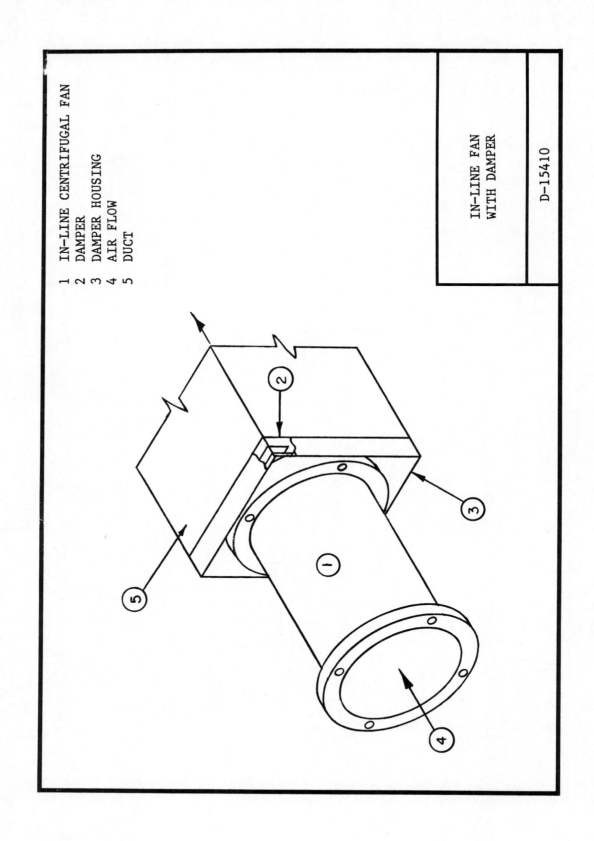

1 IN-LINE CENTRIFUGAL FAN
2 DAMPER
3 DAMPER HOUSING
4 AIR FLOW
5 DUCT

IN-LINE FAN
WITH DAMPER

D-15410

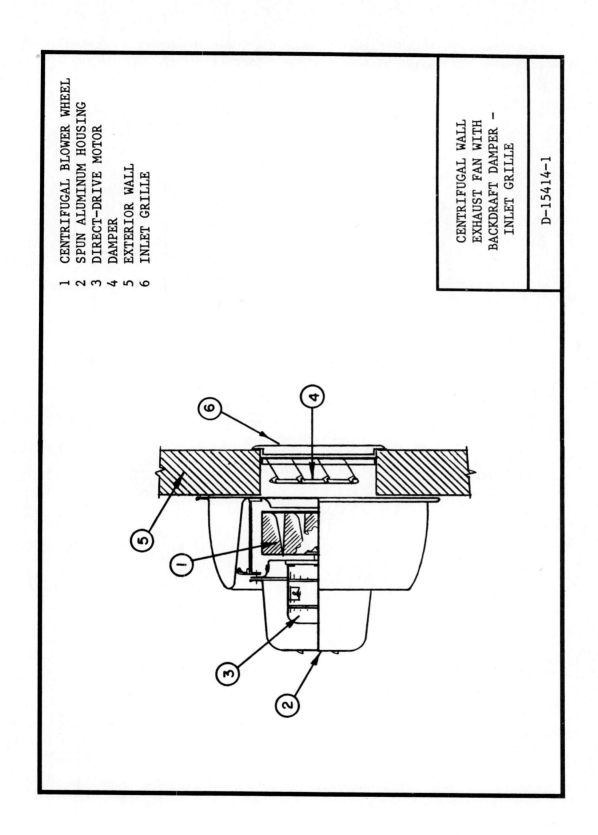

1 CENTRIFUGAL BLOWER WHEEL
2 SPUN ALUMINUM HOUSING
3 DIRECT-DRIVE MOTOR
4 DAMPER
5 EXTERIOR WALL
6 INLET GRILLE

CENTRIFUGAL WALL
EXHAUST FAN WITH
BACKDRAFT DAMPER –
INLET GRILLE

D-15414-1

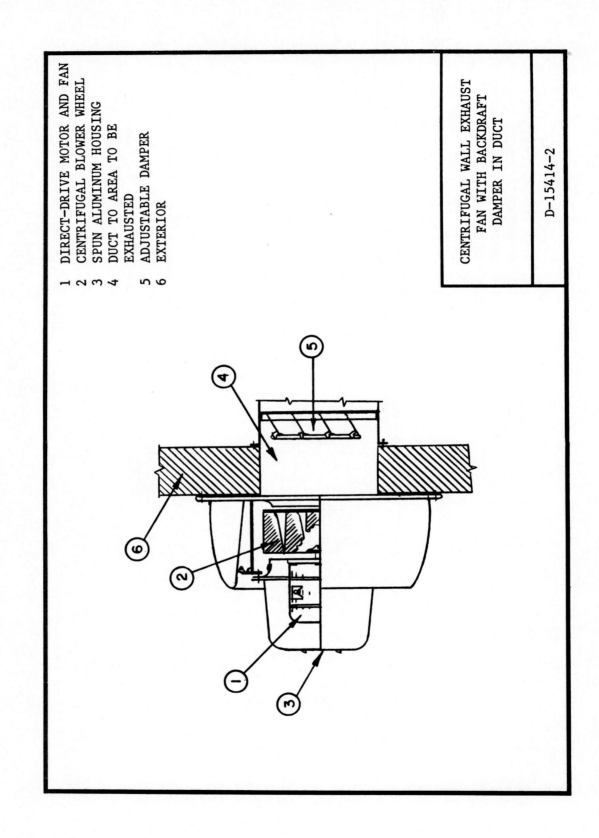

1 DIRECT-DRIVE MOTOR AND FAN
2 CENTRIFUGAL BLOWER WHEEL
3 SPUN ALUMINUM HOUSING
4 DUCT TO AREA TO BE
  EXHAUSTED
5 ADJUSTABLE DAMPER
6 EXTERIOR

CENTRIFUGAL WALL EXHAUST
FAN WITH BACKDRAFT
DAMPER IN DUCT

D-15414-2

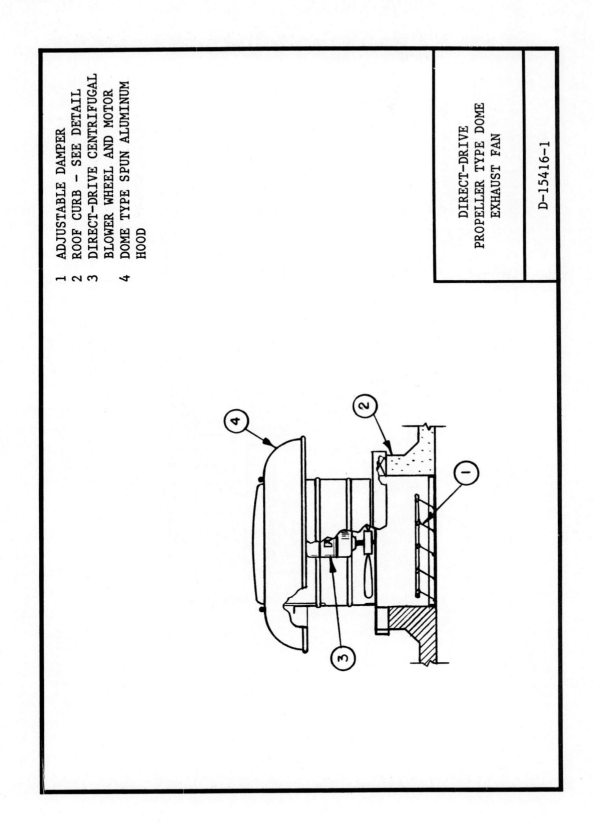

1 ADJUSTABLE DAMPER
2 ROOF CURB – SEE DETAIL
3 DIRECT-DRIVE CENTRIFUGAL
  BLOWER WHEEL AND MOTOR
4 DOME TYPE SPUN ALUMINUM
  HOOD

DIRECT-DRIVE
PROPELLER TYPE DOME
EXHAUST FAN

D-15416-1

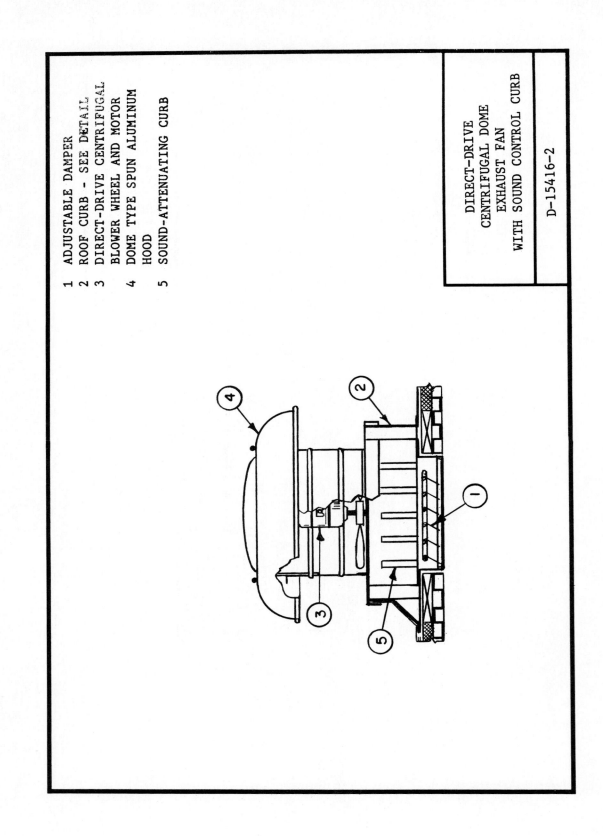

1 ADJUSTABLE DAMPER
2 ROOF CURB - SEE DETAIL
3 DIRECT-DRIVE CENTRIFUGAL BLOWER WHEEL AND MOTOR
4 DOME TYPE SPUN ALUMINUM HOOD
5 SOUND-ATTENUATING CURB

DIRECT-DRIVE
CENTRIFUGAL DOME
EXHAUST FAN
WITH SOUND CONTROL CURB

D-15416-2

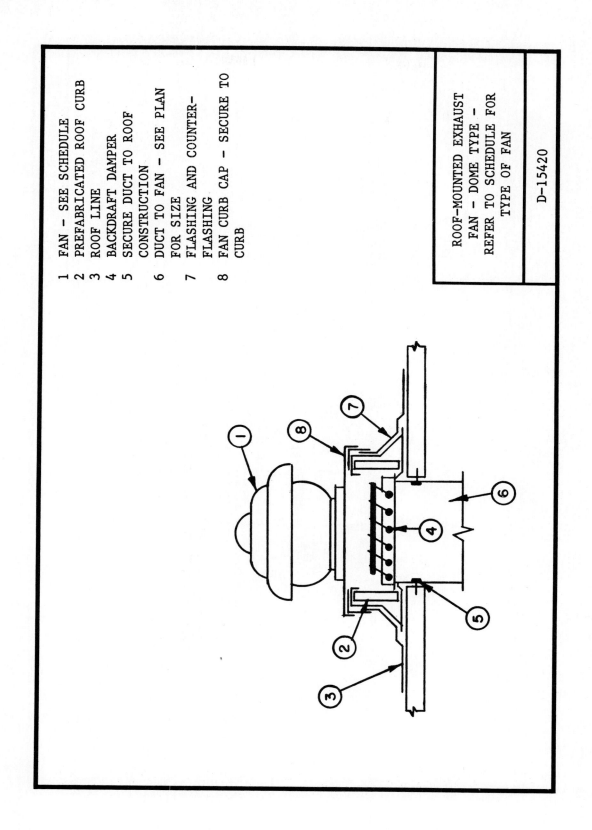

1 FAN – SEE SCHEDULE
2 PREFABRICATED ROOF CURB
3 ROOF LINE
4 BACKDRAFT DAMPER
5 SECURE DUCT TO ROOF
  CONSTRUCTION
6 DUCT TO FAN – SEE PLAN
  FOR SIZE
7 FLASHING AND COUNTER–
  FLASHING
8 FAN CURB CAP – SECURE TO
  CURB

ROOF–MOUNTED EXHAUST
FAN – DOME TYPE –
REFER TO SCHEDULE FOR
TYPE OF FAN

D–15420

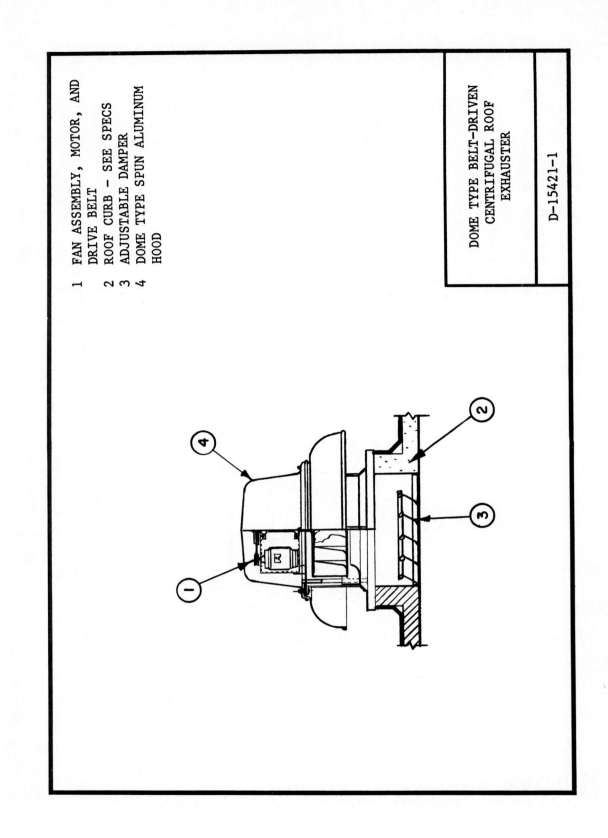

1 FAN ASSEMBLY, MOTOR, AND
  DRIVE BELT
2 ROOF CURB – SEE SPECS
3 ADJUSTABLE DAMPER
4 DOME TYPE SPUN ALUMINUM
  HOOD

DOME TYPE BELT-DRIVEN
CENTRIFUGAL ROOF
EXHAUSTER

D-15421-1

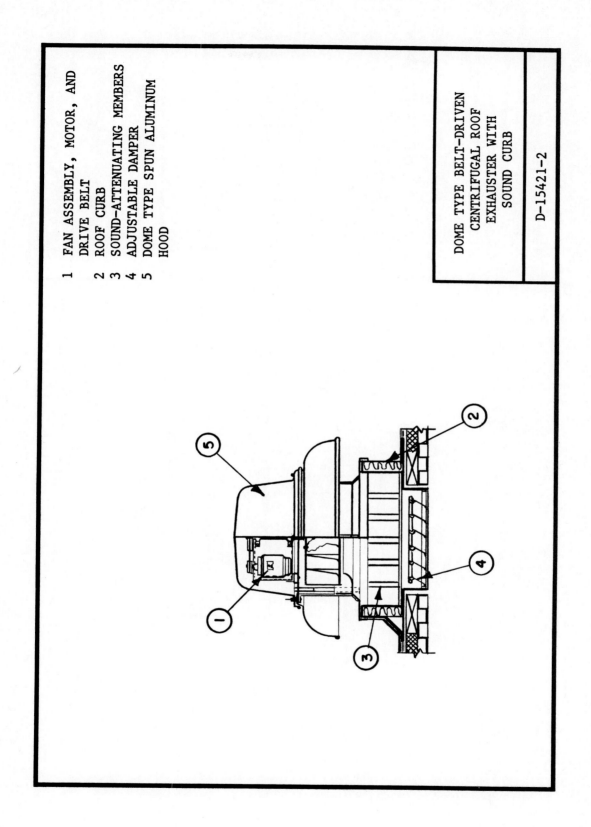

1 FAN ASSEMBLY, MOTOR, AND
   DRIVE BELT
2 ROOF CURB
3 SOUND-ATTENUATING MEMBERS
4 ADJUSTABLE DAMPER
5 DOME TYPE SPUN ALUMINUM
   HOOD

DOME TYPE BELT-DRIVEN
CENTRIFUGAL ROOF
EXHAUSTER WITH
SOUND CURB

D-15421-2

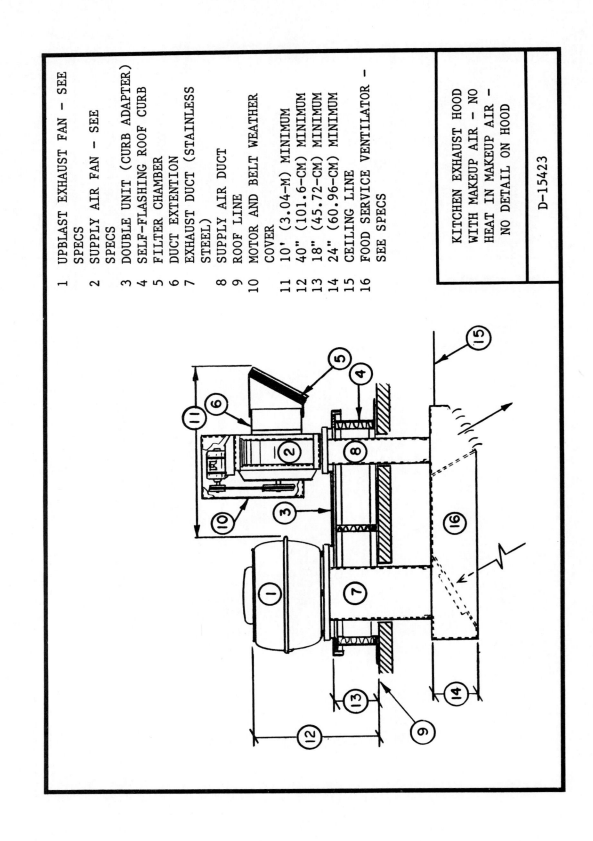

1 UPBLAST EXHAUST FAN – SEE SPECS
2 SUPPLY AIR FAN – SEE SPECS
3 DOUBLE UNIT (CURB ADAPTER)
4 SELF-FLASHING ROOF CURB
5 FILTER CHAMBER
6 DUCT EXTENTION
7 EXHAUST DUCT (STAINLESS STEEL)
8 SUPPLY AIR DUCT
9 ROOF LINE
10 MOTOR AND BELT WEATHER COVER
11 10' (3.04–M) MINIMUM
12 40" (101.6–CM) MINIMUM
13 18" (45.72–CM) MINIMUM
14 24" (60.96–CM) MINIMUM
15 CEILING LINE
16 FOOD SERVICE VENTILATOR – SEE SPECS

KITCHEN EXHAUST HOOD
WITH MAKEUP AIR – NO
HEAT IN MAKEUP AIR –
NO DETAIL ON HOOD

D–15423

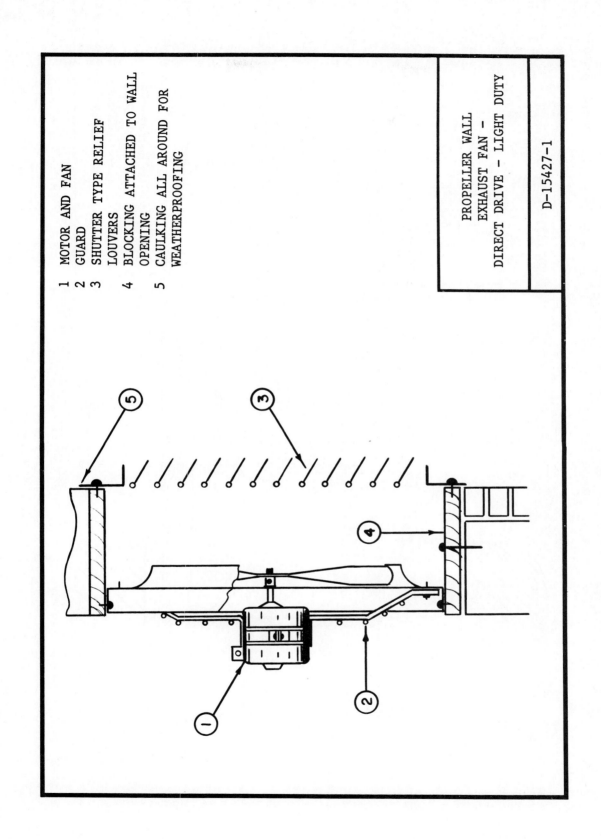

1 MOTOR AND FAN
2 GUARD
3 SHUTTER TYPE RELIEF LOUVERS
4 BLOCKING ATTACHED TO WALL OPENING
5 CAULKING ALL AROUND FOR WEATHERPROOFING

PROPELLER WALL
EXHAUST FAN –
DIRECT DRIVE – LIGHT DUTY

D-15427-1

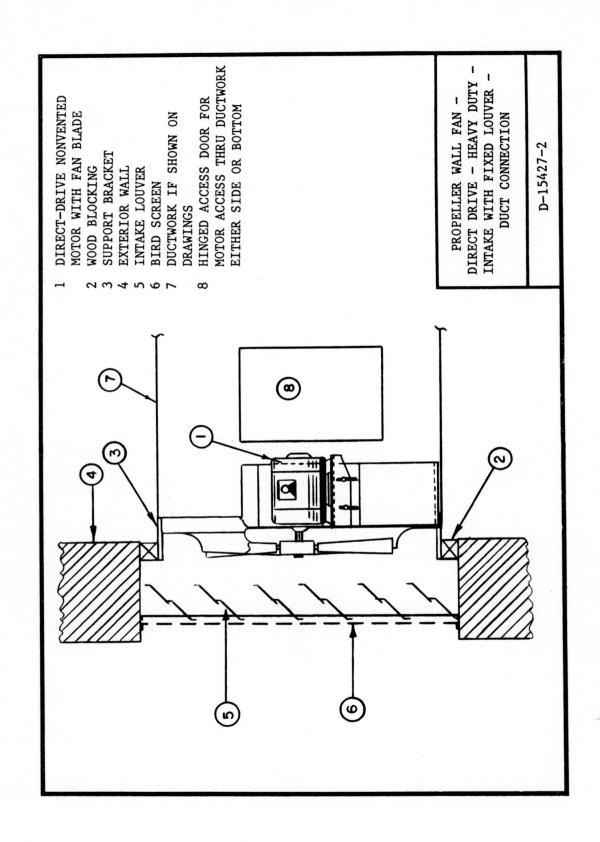

1 DIRECT-DRIVE NONVENTED
   MOTOR WITH FAN BLADE
2 WOOD BLOCKING
3 SUPPORT BRACKET
4 EXTERIOR WALL
5 INTAKE LOUVER
6 BIRD SCREEN
7 DUCTWORK IF SHOWN ON
   DRAWINGS
8 HINGED ACCESS DOOR FOR
   MOTOR ACCESS THRU DUCTWORK
   EITHER SIDE OR BOTTOM

PROPELLER WALL FAN –
DIRECT DRIVE – HEAVY DUTY –
INTAKE WITH FIXED LOUVER –
DUCT CONNECTION

D–15427–2

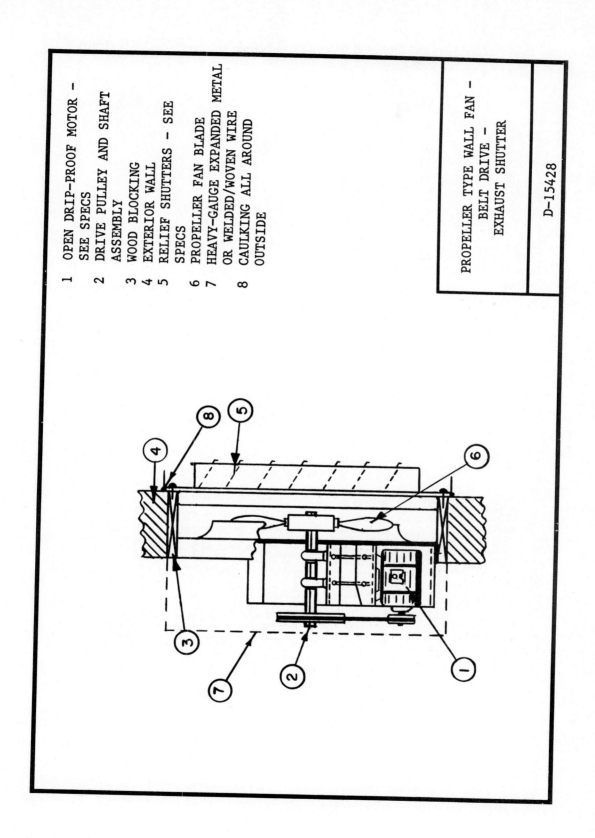

1 OPEN DRIP–PROOF MOTOR –
  SEE SPECS
2 DRIVE PULLEY AND SHAFT
  ASSEMBLY
3 WOOD BLOCKING
4 EXTERIOR WALL
5 RELIEF SHUTTERS – SEE
  SPECS
6 PROPELLER FAN BLADE
7 HEAVY–GAUGE EXPANDED METAL
  OR WELDED/WOVEN WIRE
8 CAULKING ALL AROUND
  OUTSIDE

PROPELLER TYPE WALL FAN –
BELT DRIVE –
EXHAUST SHUTTER

D–15428

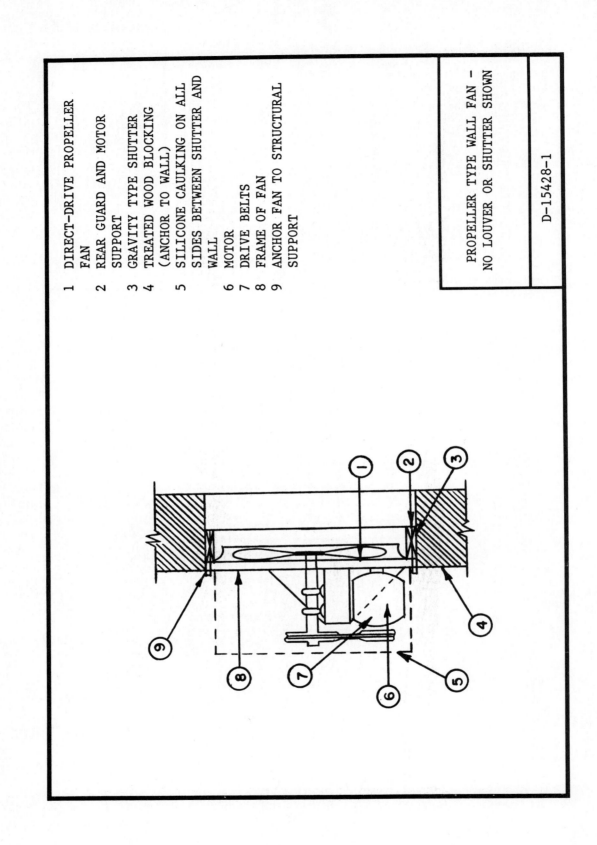

1 DIRECT-DRIVE PROPELLER FAN
2 REAR GUARD AND MOTOR SUPPORT
3 GRAVITY TYPE SHUTTER
4 TREATED WOOD BLOCKING (ANCHOR TO WALL)
5 SILICONE CAULKING ON ALL SIDES BETWEEN SHUTTER AND WALL
6 MOTOR
7 DRIVE BELTS
8 FRAME OF FAN
9 ANCHOR FAN TO STRUCTURAL SUPPORT

PROPELLER TYPE WALL FAN – NO LOUVER OR SHUTTER SHOWN

D-15428-1

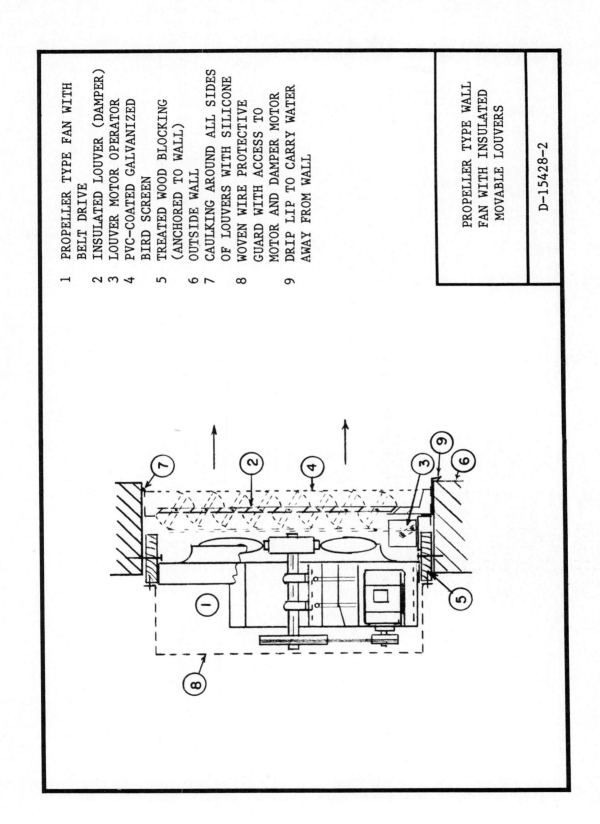

1 PROPELLER TYPE FAN WITH BELT DRIVE
2 INSULATED LOUVER (DAMPER)
3 LOUVER MOTOR OPERATOR
4 PVC-COATED GALVANIZED BIRD SCREEN
5 TREATED WOOD BLOCKING (ANCHORED TO WALL)
6 OUTSIDE WALL
7 CAULKING AROUND ALL SIDES OF LOUVERS WITH SILICONE
8 WOVEN WIRE PROTECTIVE GUARD WITH ACCESS TO MOTOR AND DAMPER MOTOR
9 DRIP LIP TO CARRY WATER AWAY FROM WALL

PROPELLER TYPE WALL FAN WITH INSULATED MOVABLE LOUVERS

D-15428-2

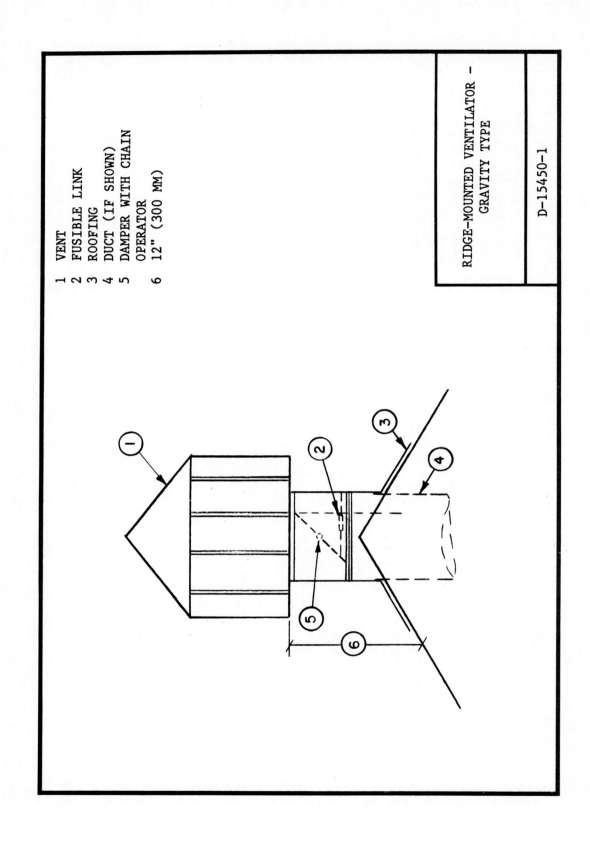

1 VENT
2 FUSIBLE LINK
3 ROOFING
4 DUCT (IF SHOWN)
5 DAMPER WITH CHAIN
  OPERATOR
6 12" (300 MM)

RIDGE-MOUNTED VENTILATOR -
GRAVITY TYPE

D-15450-1

4-24

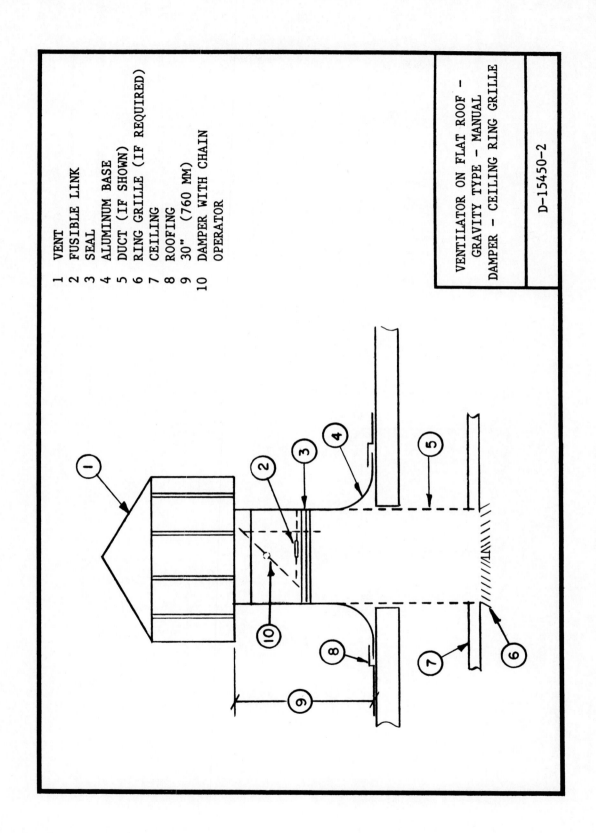

1 VENT
2 FUSIBLE LINK
3 SEAL
4 ALUMINUM BASE
5 DUCT (IF SHOWN)
6 RING GRILLE (IF REQUIRED)
7 CEILING
8 ROOFING
9 30" (760 MM)
10 DAMPER WITH CHAIN
   OPERATOR

VENTILATOR ON FLAT ROOF –
GRAVITY TYPE – MANUAL
DAMPER – CEILING RING GRILLE

D–15450–2

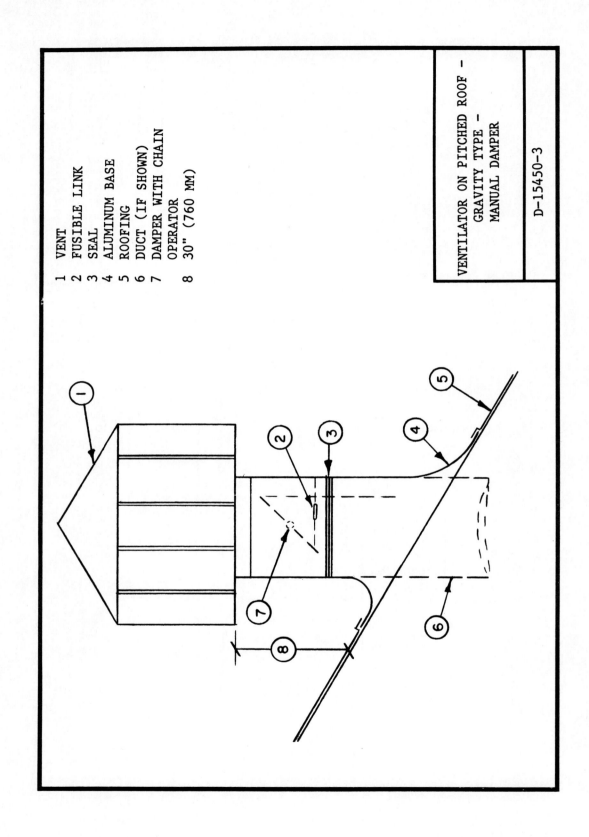

1 VENT
2 FUSIBLE LINK
3 SEAL
4 ALUMINUM BASE
5 ROOFING
6 DUCT (IF SHOWN)
7 DAMPER WITH CHAIN
  OPERATOR
8 30" (760 MM)

VENTILATOR ON PITCHED ROOF -
GRAVITY TYPE -
MANUAL DAMPER

D-15450-3

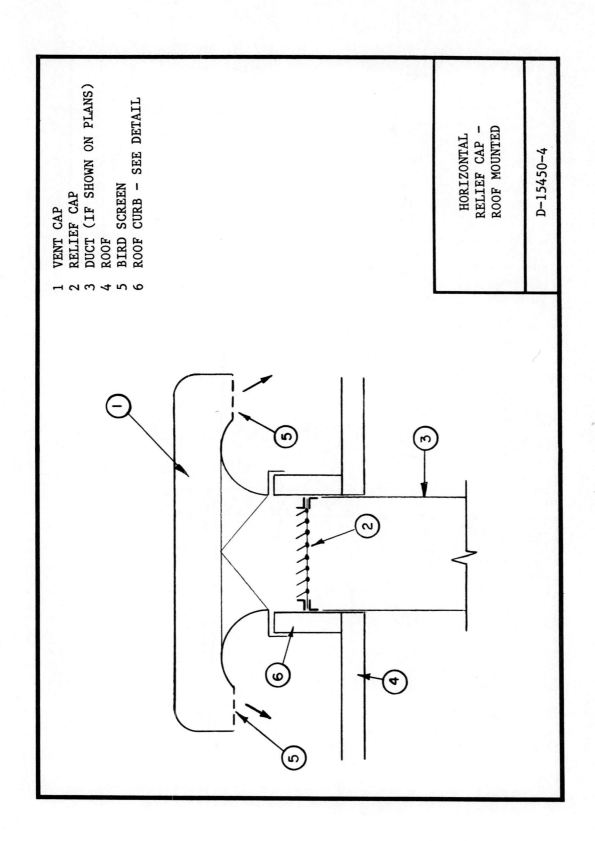

1 VENT CAP
2 RELIEF CAP
3 DUCT (IF SHOWN ON PLANS)
4 ROOF
5 BIRD SCREEN
6 ROOF CURB – SEE DETAIL

HORIZONTAL
RELIEF CAP –
ROOF MOUNTED

D–15450–4

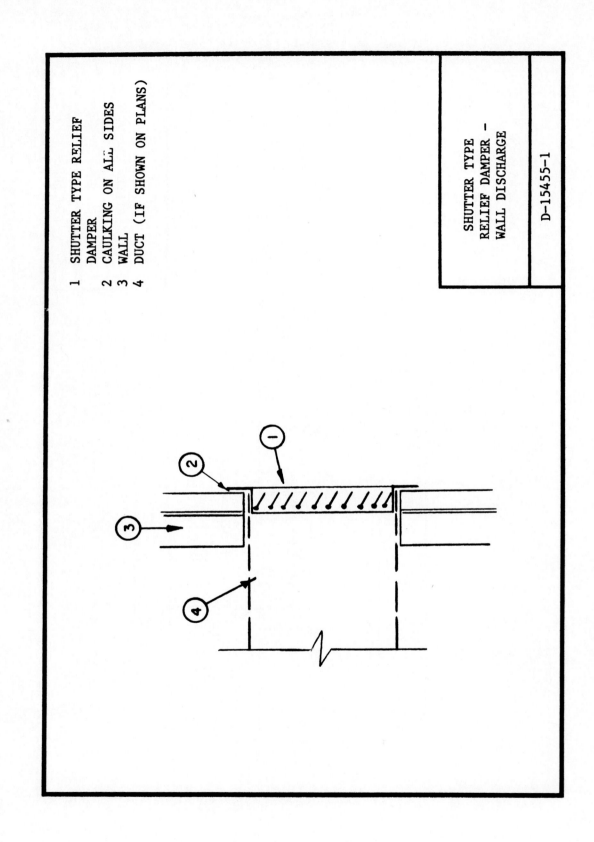

1 SHUTTER TYPE RELIEF
  DAMPER
2 CAULKING ON ALL SIDES
3 WALL
4 DUCT (IF SHOWN ON PLANS)

SHUTTER TYPE
RELIEF DAMPER –
WALL DISCHARGE

D-15455-1

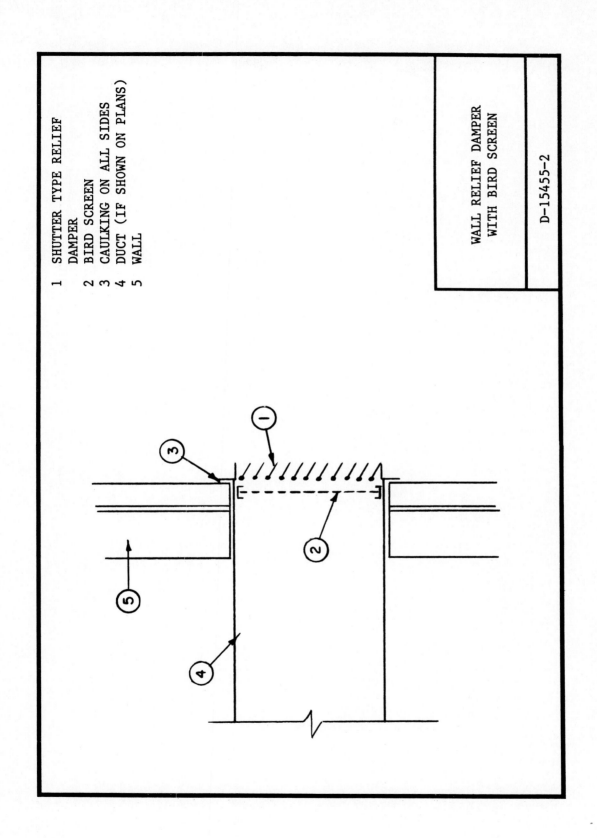

1 SHUTTER TYPE RELIEF DAMPER
2 BIRD SCREEN
3 CAULKING ON ALL SIDES
4 DUCT (IF SHOWN ON PLANS)
5 WALL

WALL RELIEF DAMPER
WITH BIRD SCREEN

D-15455-2

Ventilation Intakes and Hoods

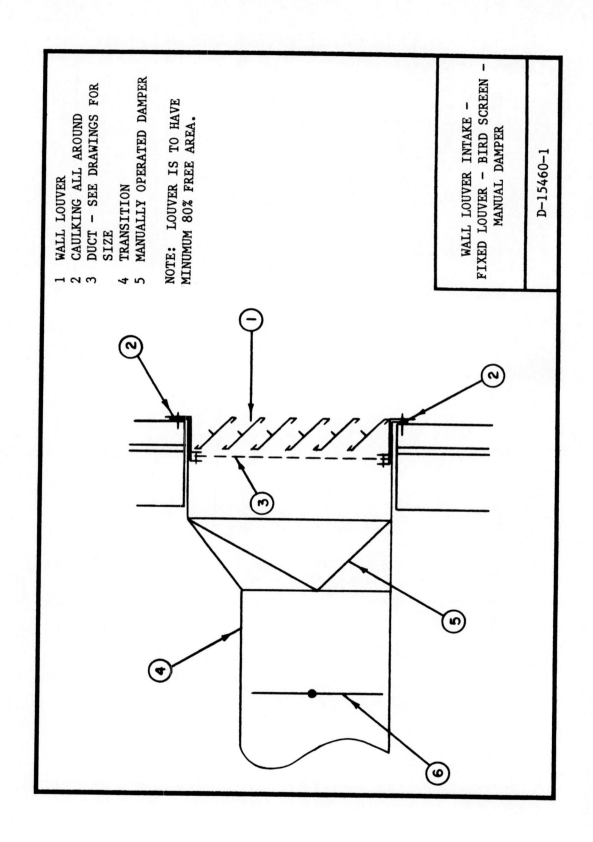

1 WALL LOUVER
2 CAULKING ALL AROUND
3 DUCT – SEE DRAWINGS FOR
  SIZE
4 TRANSITION
5 MANUALLY OPERATED DAMPER

NOTE: LOUVER IS TO HAVE
MINUMUM 80% FREE AREA.

WALL LOUVER INTAKE –
FIXED LOUVER – BIRD SCREEN –
MANUAL DAMPER

D–15460–1

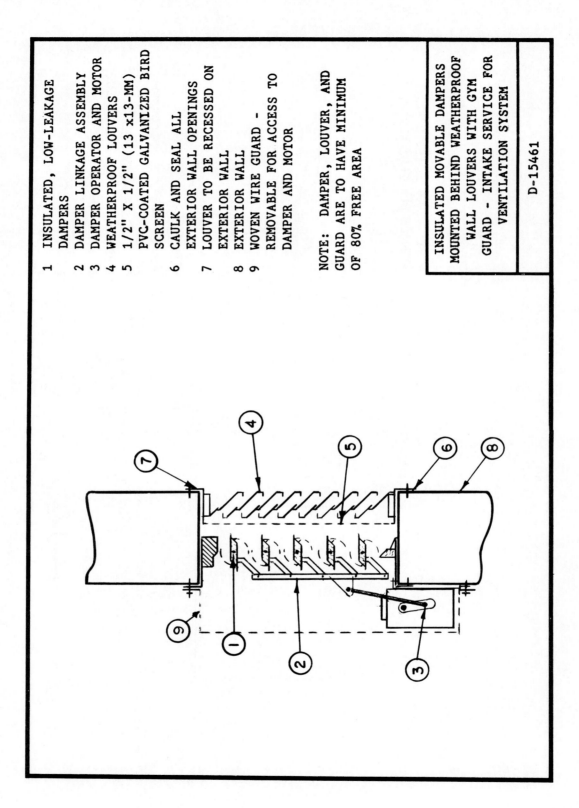

1 INSULATED, LOW-LEAKAGE
  DAMPERS
2 DAMPER LINKAGE ASSEMBLY
3 DAMPER OPERATOR AND MOTOR
4 WEATHERPROOF LOUVERS
5 1/2" X 1/2" (13 x13-MM)
  PVC-COATED GALVANIZED BIRD
  SCREEN
6 CAULK AND SEAL ALL
  EXTERIOR WALL OPENINGS
7 LOUVER TO BE RECESSED ON
  EXTERIOR WALL
8 EXTERIOR WALL
9 WOVEN WIRE GUARD -
  REMOVABLE FOR ACCESS TO
  DAMPER AND MOTOR

NOTE: DAMPER, LOUVER, AND
GUARD ARE TO HAVE MINIMUM
OF 80% FREE AREA

INSULATED MOVABLE DAMPERS
MOUNTED BEHIND WEATHERPROOF
WALL LOUVERS WITH GYM
GUARD - INTAKE SERVICE FOR
VENTILATION SYSTEM

D-15461

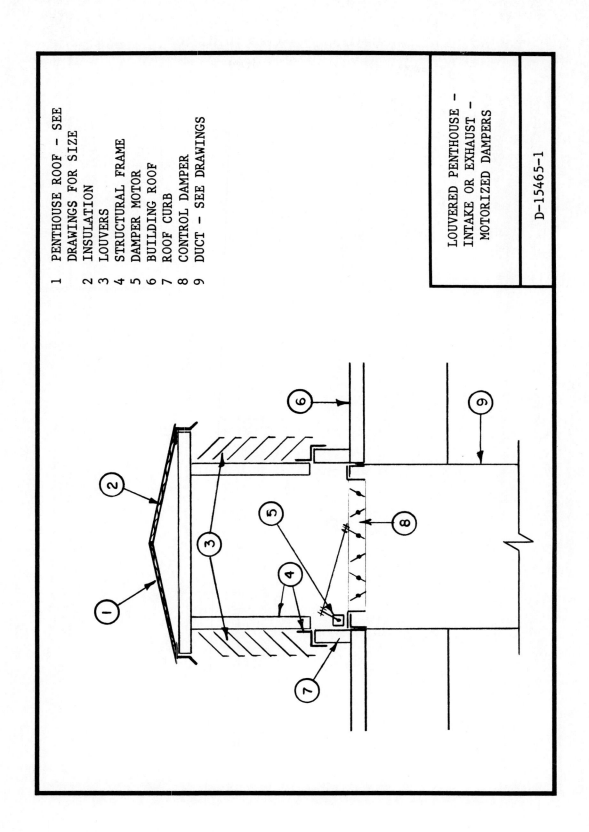

1 PENTHOUSE ROOF – SEE DRAWINGS FOR SIZE
2 INSULATION
3 LOUVERS
4 STRUCTURAL FRAME
5 DAMPER MOTOR
6 BUILDING ROOF
7 ROOF CURB
8 CONTROL DAMPER
9 DUCT – SEE DRAWINGS

LOUVERED PENTHOUSE –
INTAKE OR EXHAUST –
MOTORIZED DAMPERS

D–15465–1

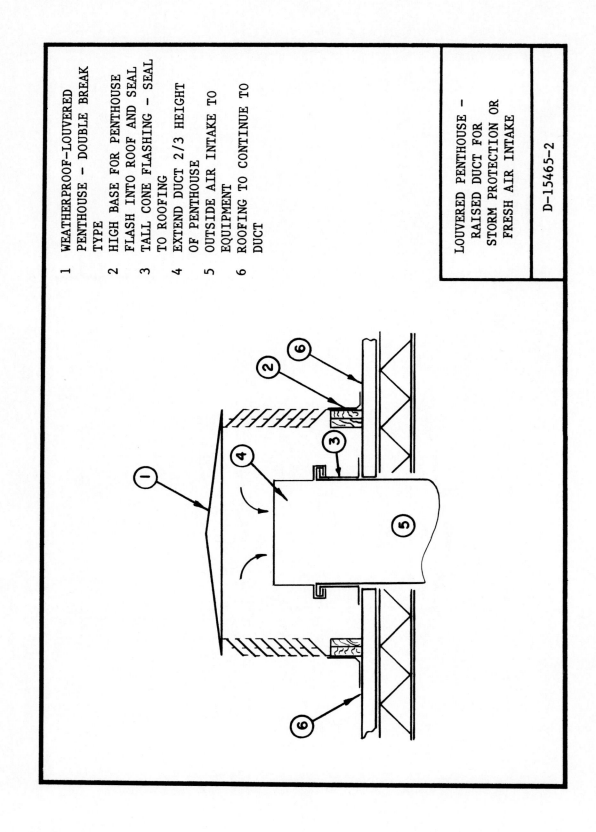

1 WEATHERPROOF-LOUVERED PENTHOUSE – DOUBLE BREAK TYPE
2 HIGH BASE FOR PENTHOUSE FLASH INTO ROOF AND SEAL TO ROOFING
3 TALL CONE FLASHING – SEAL TO ROOFING
4 EXTEND DUCT 2/3 HEIGHT OF PENTHOUSE
5 OUTSIDE AIR INTAKE TO EQUIPMENT
6 ROOFING TO CONTINUE TO DUCT

LOUVERED PENTHOUSE – RAISED DUCT FOR STORM PROTECTION OR FRESH AIR INTAKE

D–15465–2

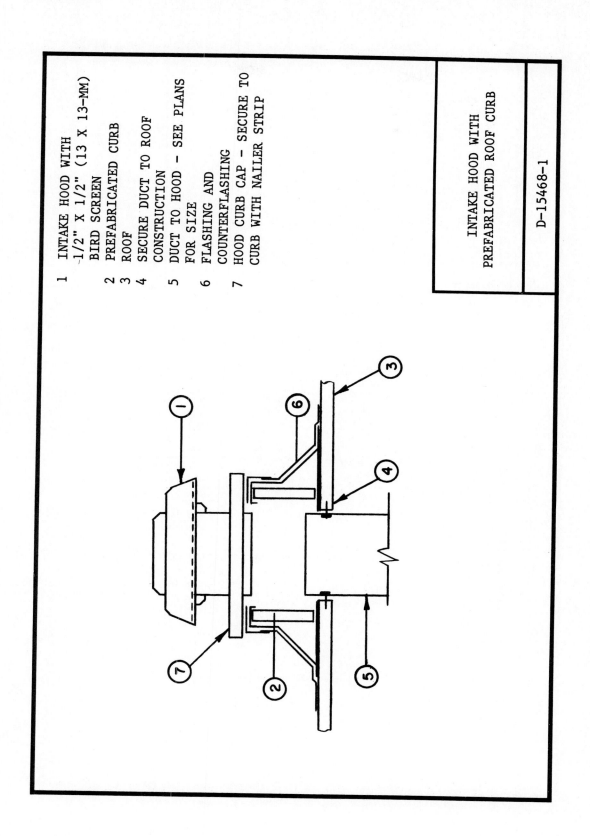

1 INTAKE HOOD WITH
-1/2" X 1/2" (13 X 13—MM)
BIRD SCREEN
2 PREFABRICATED CURB
3 ROOF
4 SECURE DUCT TO ROOF
CONSTRUCTION
5 DUCT TO HOOD – SEE PLANS
FOR SIZE
6 FLASHING AND
COUNTERFLASHING
7 HOOD CURB CAP – SECURE TO
CURB WITH NAILER STRIP

INTAKE HOOD WITH
PREFABRICATED ROOF CURB

D-15468-1

1 HEAVY-GAUGE SHEET-METAL
  DUCT WITH PITTSBURGH LOCK
  SEAM
2 12" (300-MM) MINIMUM
3 1 1/2" (38-MM) MINIMUM
4 1 1/2" (38-MM) STANDING,
  SEAM RIVETED OR BOLTED ON
  12" (300-MM) CENTERS
5 FLASHING WITH WELDED
  CORNER SEAMS
6 ROOF CURB
7 1 1/2" X 1 1/2" X 1/4"
  (38 X 38 X 6-MM) ANGLE,
  ALL AROUND BOLTED WITH
  1/4" (6-MM) BOLTS TO DUCT

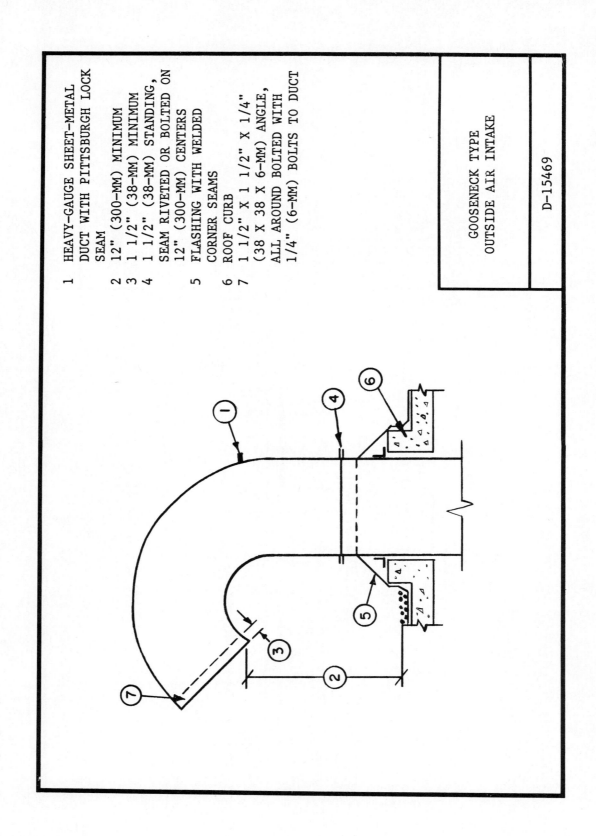

GOOSENECK TYPE
OUTSIDE AIR INTAKE

D-15469

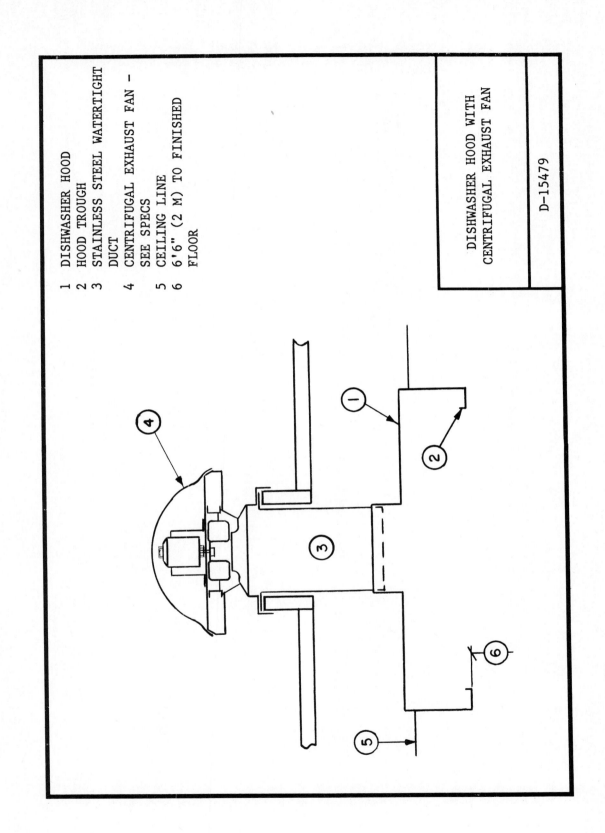

1 DISHWASHER HOOD
2 HOOD TROUGH
3 STAINLESS STEEL WATERTIGHT
   DUCT
4 CENTRIFUGAL EXHAUST FAN –
   SEE SPECS
5 CEILING LINE
6 6'6" (2 M) TO FINISHED
   FLOOR

DISHWASHER HOOD WITH
CENTRIFUGAL EXHAUST FAN

D–15479

CHAPTER **6**

Ventilation Systems and Equipment

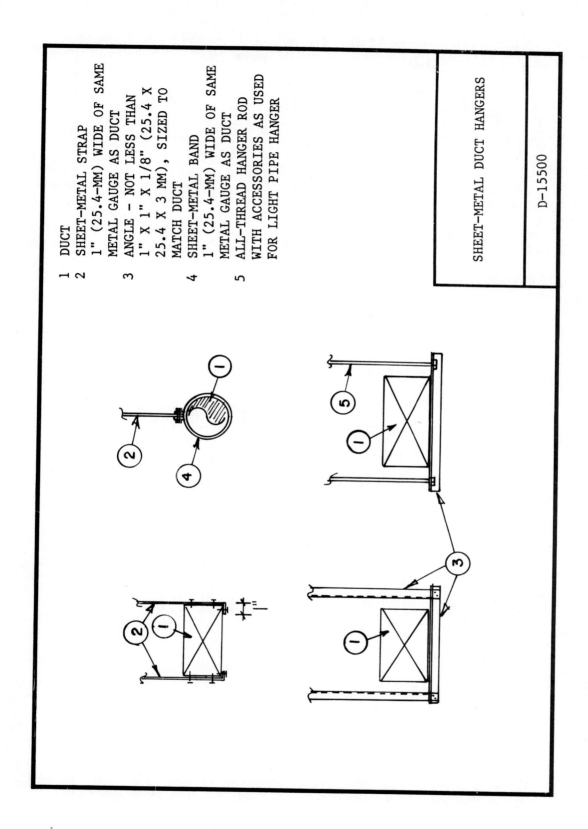

1 DUCT
2 SHEET-METAL STRAP
   1" (25.4-MM) WIDE OF SAME
   METAL GAUGE AS DUCT
3 ANGLE – NOT LESS THAN
   1" X 1" X 1/8" (25.4 X
   25.4 X 3 MM), SIZED TO
   MATCH DUCT
4 SHEET-METAL BAND
   1" (25.4-MM) WIDE OF SAME
   METAL GAUGE AS DUCT
5 ALL-THREAD HANGER ROD
   WITH ACCESSORIES AS USED
   FOR LIGHT PIPE HANGER

SHEET-METAL DUCT HANGERS

D-15500

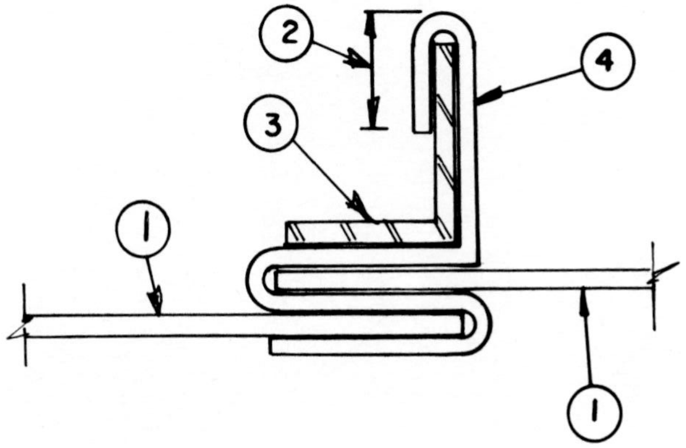

1 DUCTWORK OR EQUIPMENT
   DUCT CONNECTION
2 3/4" (18-MM) MINIMUM
3 1 1/2" X 1 1/2" X 1/8"
   (36 X 36 X 3-MM) ANGLE
4 ANGLE "S" SLIP OF SAME
   GAUGE AND MATERIAL AS
   DUCTWORK

REINFORCED ANGLE
"S" SLIP CONNECTOR

D-15500-1

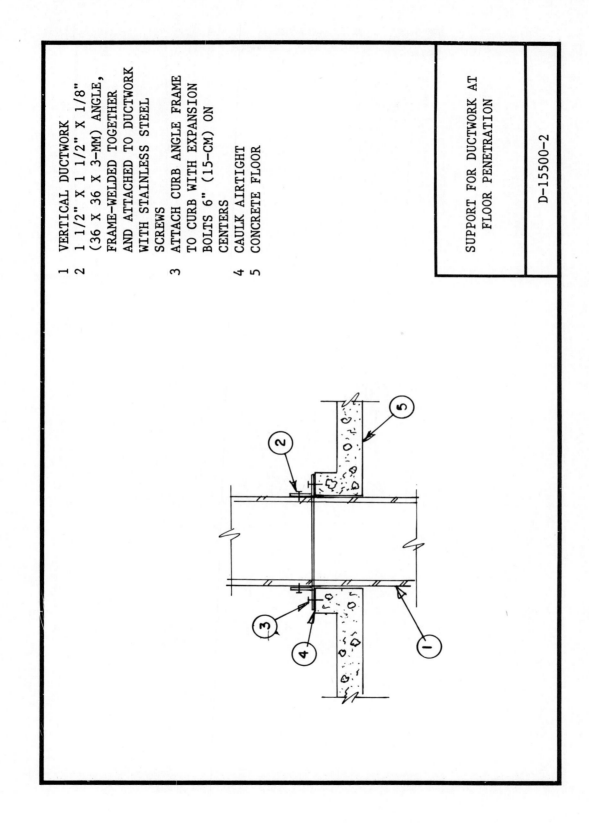

1 VERTICAL DUCTWORK
2 1 1/2" X 1 1/2" X 1/8" (36 X 36 X 3-MM) ANGLE, FRAME-WELDED TOGETHER AND ATTACHED TO DUCTWORK WITH STAINLESS STEEL SCREWS
3 ATTACH CURB ANGLE FRAME TO CURB WITH EXPANSION BOLTS 6" (15-CM) ON CENTERS
4 CAULK AIRTIGHT
5 CONCRETE FLOOR

SUPPORT FOR DUCTWORK AT FLOOR PENETRATION

D-15500-2

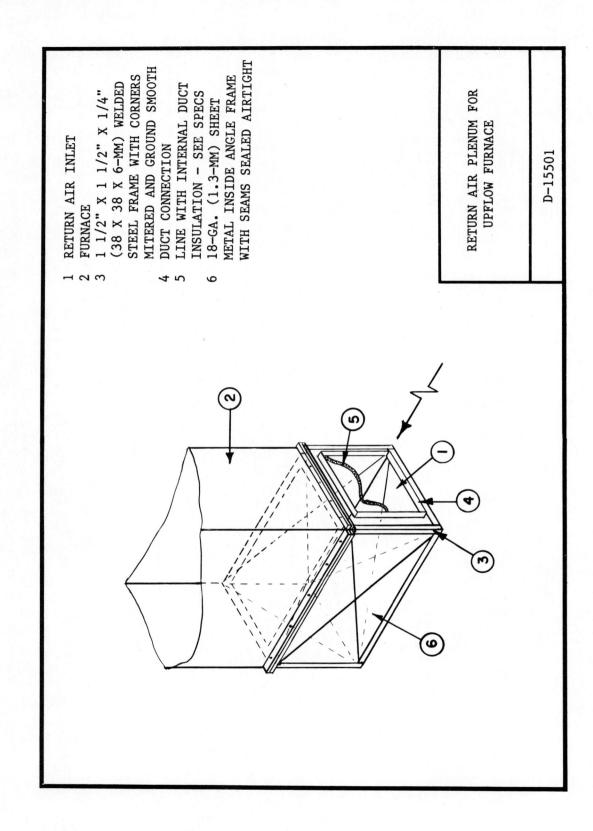

1 RETURN AIR INLET
2 FURNACE
3 1 1/2" X 1 1/2" X 1/4"
   (38 X 38 X 6-MM) WELDED
   STEEL FRAME WITH CORNERS
   MITERED AND GROUND SMOOTH
4 DUCT CONNECTION
5 LINE WITH INTERNAL DUCT
   INSULATION – SEE SPECS
6 18-GA. (1.3-MM) SHEET
   METAL INSIDE ANGLE FRAME
   WITH SEAMS SEALED AIRTIGHT

RETURN AIR PLENUM FOR
UPFLOW FURNACE

D–15501

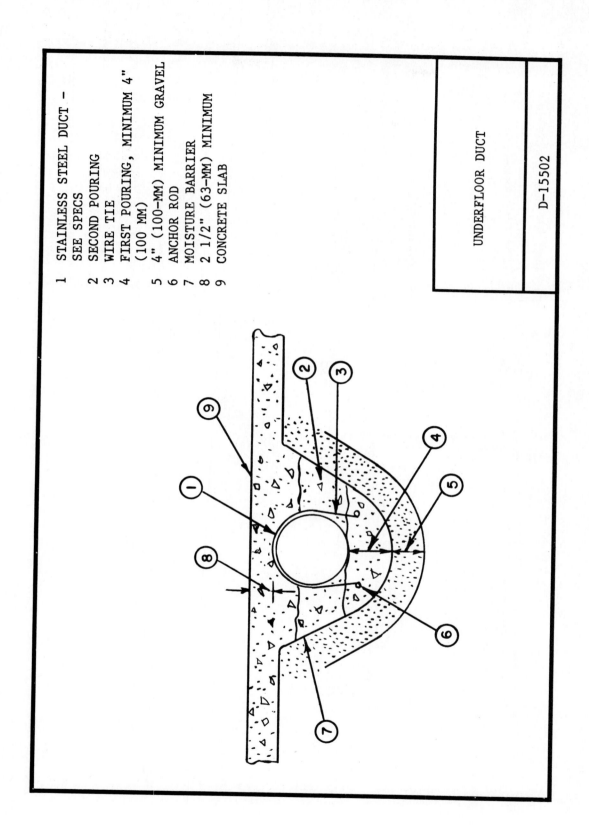

1 STAINLESS STEEL DUCT –
  SEE SPECS
2 SECOND POURING
3 WIRE TIE
4 FIRST POURING, MINIMUM 4"
  (100 MM)
5 4" (100-MM) MINIMUM GRAVEL
6 ANCHOR ROD
7 MOISTURE BARRIER
8 2 1/2" (63-MM) MINIMUM
9 CONCRETE SLAB

UNDERFLOOR DUCT

D–15502

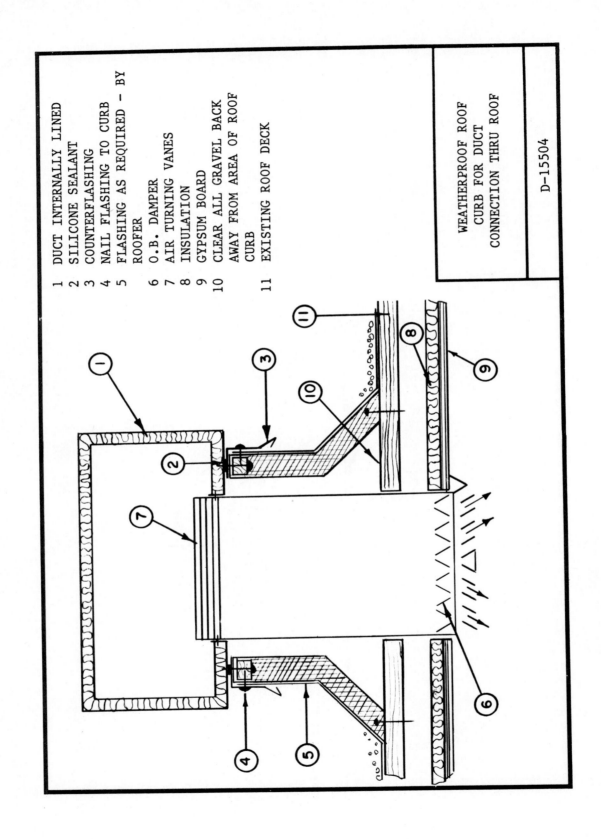

1 DUCT INTERNALLY LINED
2 SILICONE SEALANT
3 COUNTERFLASHING
4 NAIL FLASHING TO CURB
5 FLASHING AS REQUIRED – BY ROOFER
6 O.B. DAMPER
7 AIR TURNING VANES
8 INSULATION
9 GYPSUM BOARD
10 CLEAR ALL GRAVEL BACK AWAY FROM AREA OF ROOF CURB
11 EXISTING ROOF DECK

WEATHERPROOF ROOF
CURB FOR DUCT
CONNECTION THRU ROOF

D–15504

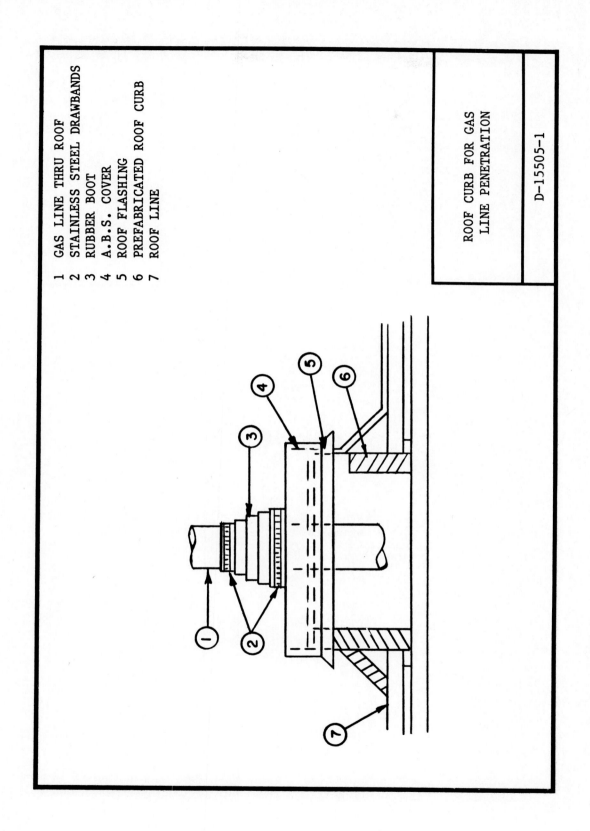

1 GAS LINE THRU ROOF
2 STAINLESS STEEL DRAWBANDS
3 RUBBER BOOT
4 A.B.S. COVER
5 ROOF FLASHING
6 PREFABRICATED ROOF CURB
7 ROOF LINE

ROOF CURB FOR GAS
LINE PENETRATION

D-15505-1

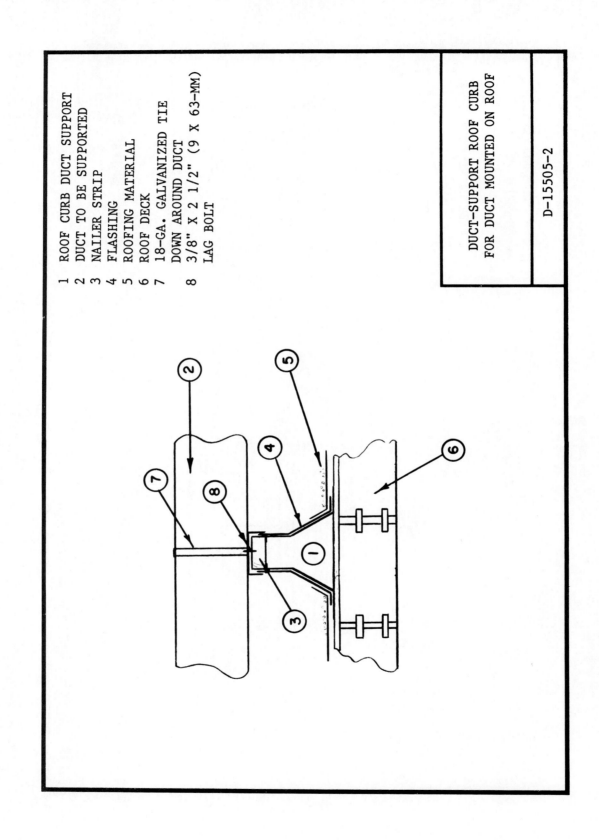

1 ROOF CURB DUCT SUPPORT
2 DUCT TO BE SUPPORTED
3 NAILER STRIP
4 FLASHING
5 ROOFING MATERIAL
6 ROOF DECK
7 18-GA. GALVANIZED TIE
  DOWN AROUND DUCT
8 3/8" X 2 1/2" (9 X 63-MM)
  LAG BOLT

DUCT-SUPPORT ROOF CURB
FOR DUCT MOUNTED ON ROOF

D-15505-2

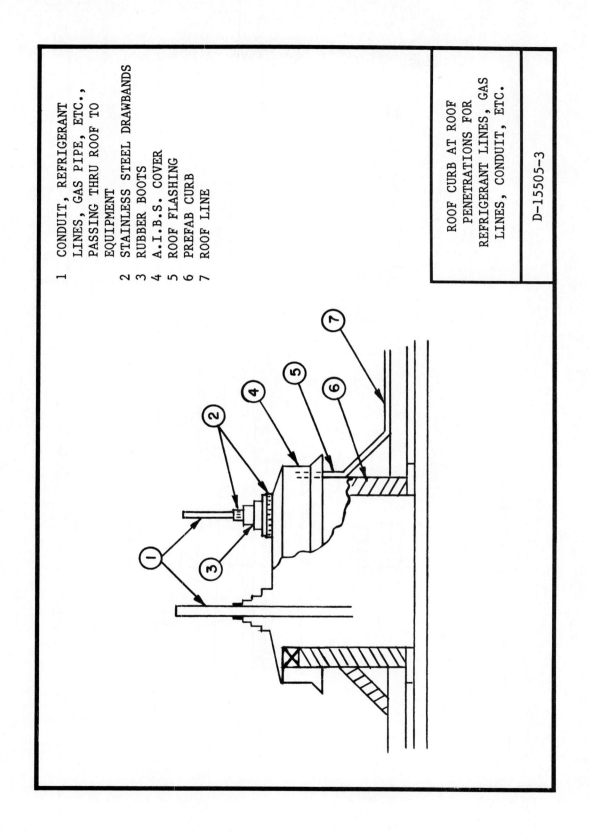

1 CONDUIT, REFRIGERANT LINES, GAS PIPE, ETC., PASSING THRU ROOF TO EQUIPMENT
2 STAINLESS STEEL DRAWBANDS
3 RUBBER BOOTS
4 A.I.B.S. COVER
5 ROOF FLASHING
6 PREFAB CURB
7 ROOF LINE

ROOF CURB AT ROOF PENETRATIONS FOR REFRIGERANT LINES, GAS LINES, CONDUIT, ETC.

D–15505–3

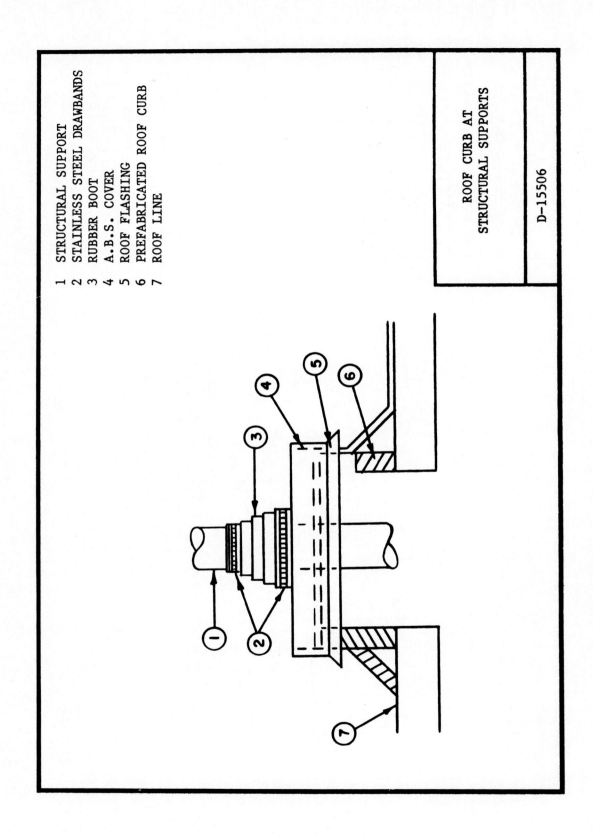

1 STRUCTURAL SUPPORT
2 STAINLESS STEEL DRAWBANDS
3 RUBBER BOOT
4 A.B.S. COVER
5 ROOF FLASHING
6 PREFABRICATED ROOF CURB
7 ROOF LINE

ROOF CURB AT
STRUCTURAL SUPPORTS

D-15506

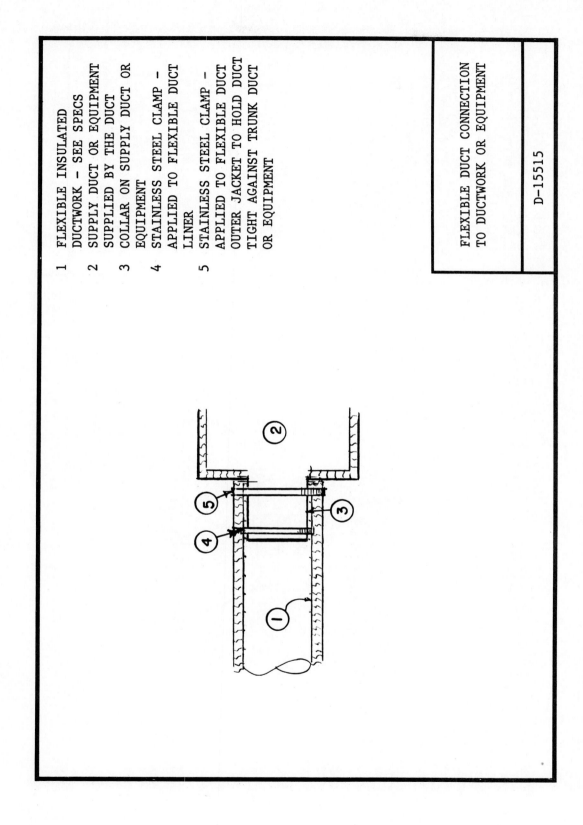

1 FLEXIBLE INSULATED
DUCTWORK – SEE SPECS

2 SUPPLY DUCT OR EQUIPMENT
SUPPLIED BY THE DUCT

3 COLLAR ON SUPPLY DUCT OR
EQUIPMENT

4 STAINLESS STEEL CLAMP –
APPLIED TO FLEXIBLE DUCT
LINER

5 STAINLESS STEEL CLAMP –
APPLIED TO FLEXIBLE DUCT
OUTER JACKET TO HOLD DUCT
TIGHT AGAINST TRUNK DUCT
OR EQUIPMENT

FLEXIBLE DUCT CONNECTION
TO DUCTWORK OR EQUIPMENT

D–15515

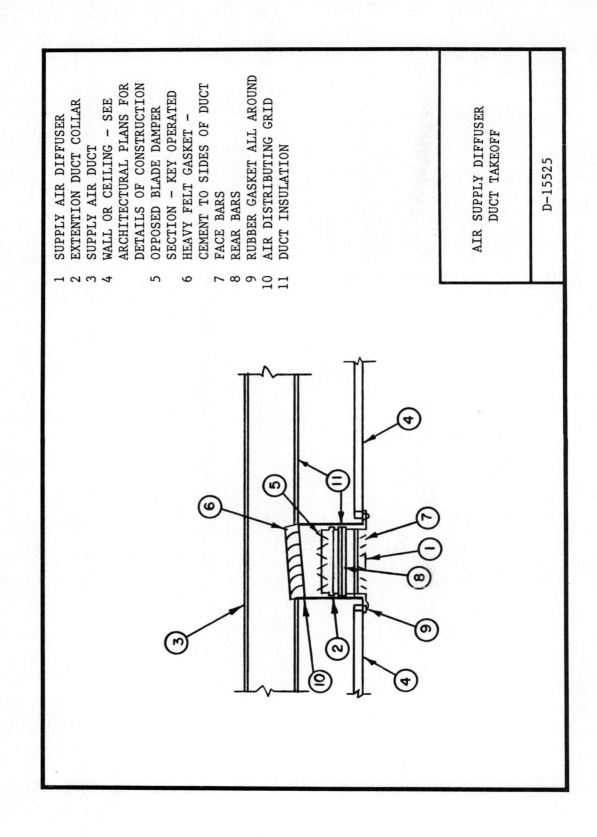

1 SUPPLY AIR DIFFUSER
2 EXTENTION DUCT COLLAR
3 SUPPLY AIR DUCT
4 WALL OR CEILING – SEE
   ARCHITECTURAL PLANS FOR
   DETAILS OF CONSTRUCTION
5 OPPOSED BLADE DAMPER
   SECTION – KEY OPERATED
6 HEAVY FELT GASKET –
   CEMENT TO SIDES OF DUCT
7 FACE BARS
8 REAR BARS
9 RUBBER GASKET ALL AROUND
10 AIR DISTRIBUTING GRID
11 DUCT INSULATION

AIR SUPPLY DIFFUSER
DUCT TAKEOFF

D–15525

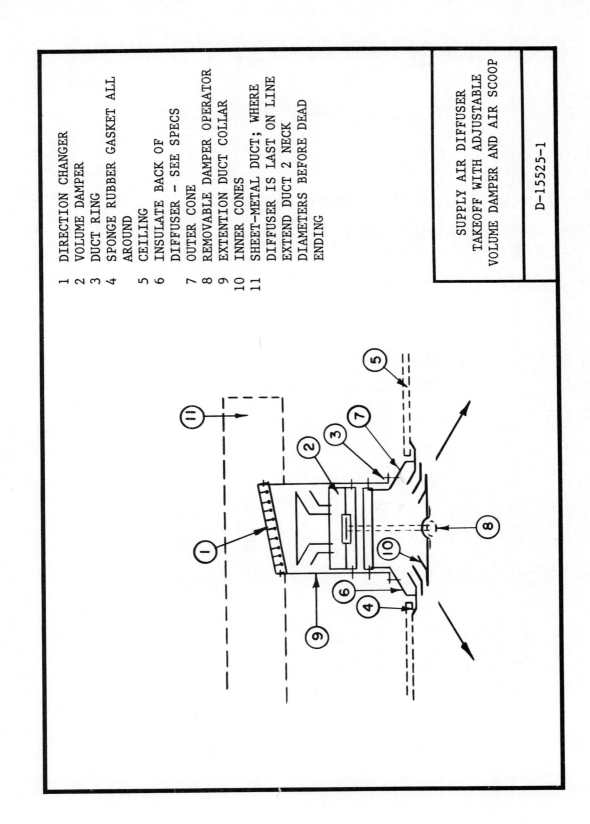

1 DIRECTION CHANGER
2 VOLUME DAMPER
3 DUCT RING
4 SPONGE RUBBER GASKET ALL
  AROUND
5 CEILING
6 INSULATE BACK OF
  DIFFUSER – SEE SPECS
7 OUTER CONE
8 REMOVABLE DAMPER OPERATOR
9 EXTENTION DUCT COLLAR
10 INNER CONES
11 SHEET-METAL DUCT; WHERE
   DIFFUSER IS LAST ON LINE
   EXTEND DUCT 2 NECK
   DIAMETERS BEFORE DEAD
   ENDING

SUPPLY AIR DIFFUSER
TAKEOFF WITH ADJUSTABLE
VOLUME DAMPER AND AIR SCOOP

D-15525-1

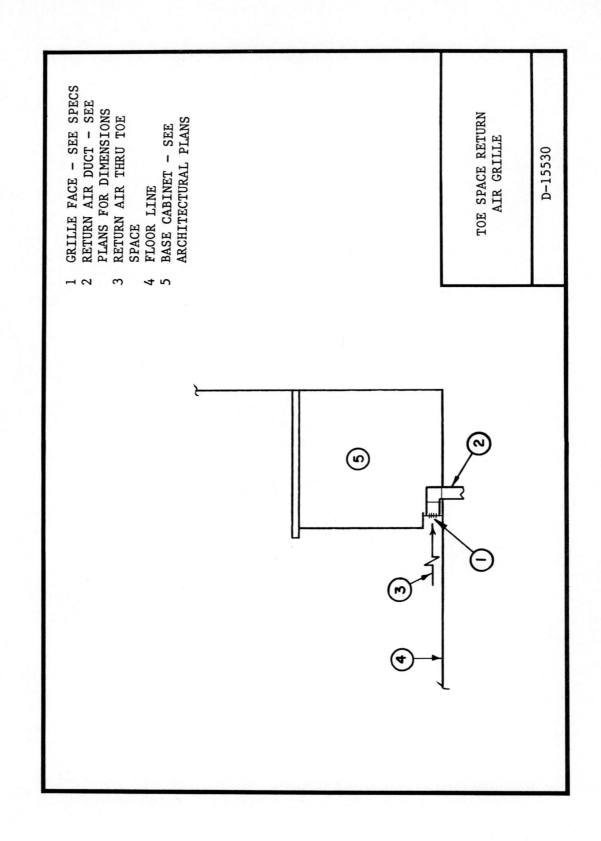

1 GRILLE FACE – SEE SPECS
2 RETURN AIR DUCT – SEE PLANS FOR DIMENSIONS
3 RETURN AIR THRU TOE SPACE
4 FLOOR LINE
5 BASE CABINET – SEE ARCHITECTURAL PLANS

TOE SPACE RETURN
AIR GRILLE

D–15530

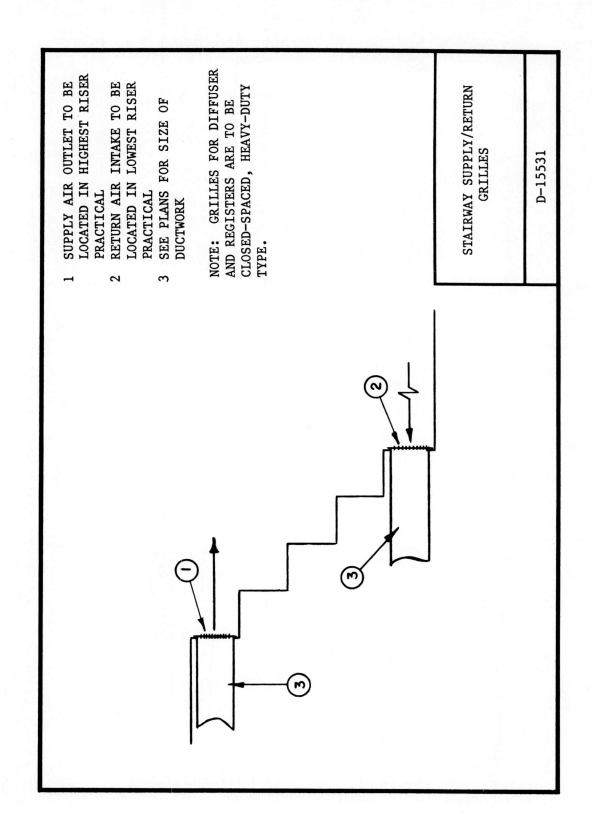

1 SUPPLY AIR OUTLET TO BE LOCATED IN HIGHEST RISER PRACTICAL

2 RETURN AIR INTAKE TO BE LOCATED IN LOWEST RISER PRACTICAL

3 SEE PLANS FOR SIZE OF DUCTWORK

NOTE: GRILLES FOR DIFFUSER AND REGISTERS ARE TO BE CLOSED-SPACED, HEAVY-DUTY TYPE.

STAIRWAY SUPPLY/RETURN GRILLES

D-15531

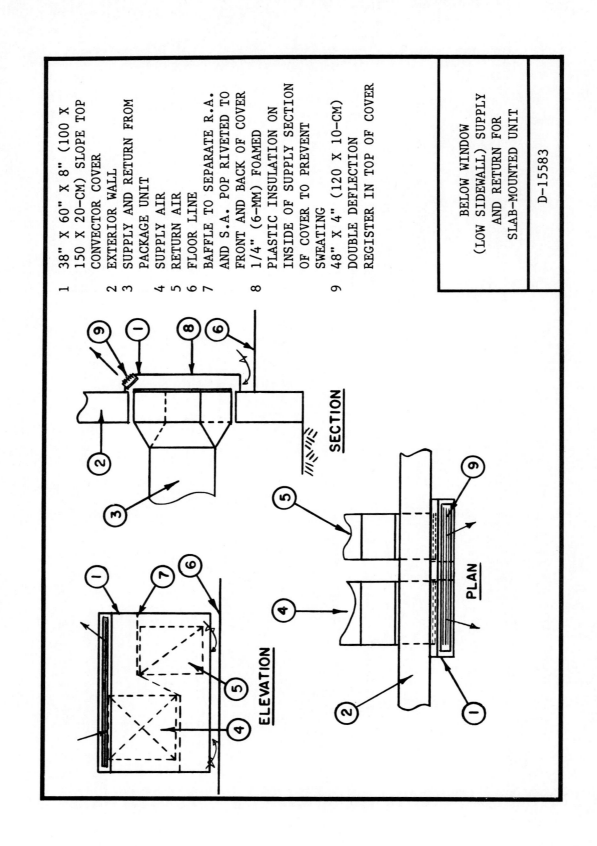

1. 38" X 60" X 8" (100 X 150 X 20-CM) SLOPE TOP CONVECTOR COVER
2. EXTERIOR WALL
3. SUPPLY AND RETURN FROM PACKAGE UNIT
4. SUPPLY AIR
5. RETURN AIR
6. FLOOR LINE
7. BAFFLE TO SEPARATE R.A. AND S.A. POP RIVETED TO FRONT AND BACK OF COVER
8. 1/4" (6-MM) FOAMED PLASTIC INSULATION ON INSIDE OF SUPPLY SECTION OF COVER TO PREVENT SWEATING
9. 48" X 4" (120 X 10-CM) DOUBLE DEFLECTION REGISTER IN TOP OF COVER

SECTION

ELEVATION

PLAN

BELOW WINDOW
(LOW SIDEWALL) SUPPLY
AND RETURN FOR
SLAB-MOUNTED UNIT

D-15583

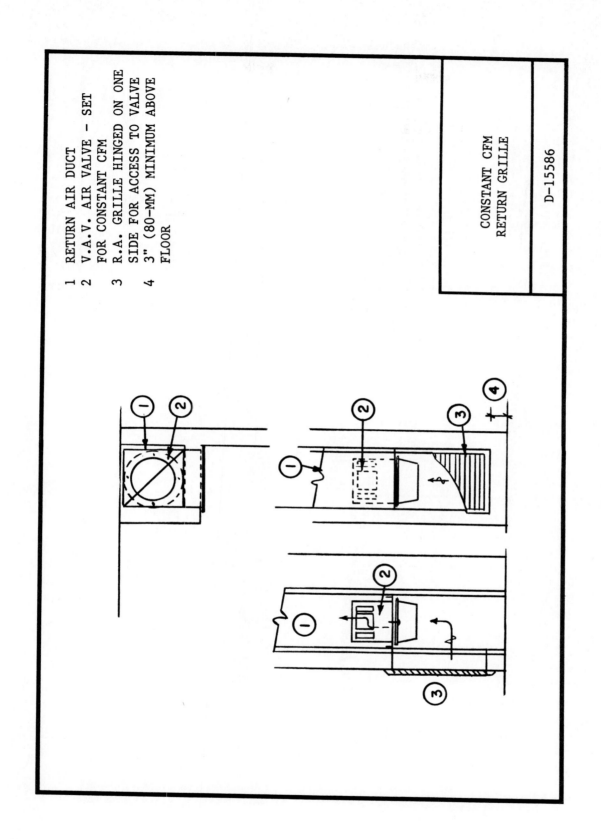

1 RETURN AIR DUCT
2 V.A.V. AIR VALVE – SET
   FOR CONSTANT CFM
3 R.A. GRILLE HINGED ON ONE
   SIDE FOR ACCESS TO VALVE
4 3" (80-MM) MINIMUM ABOVE
   FLOOR

CONSTANT CFM
RETURN GRILLE

D-15586

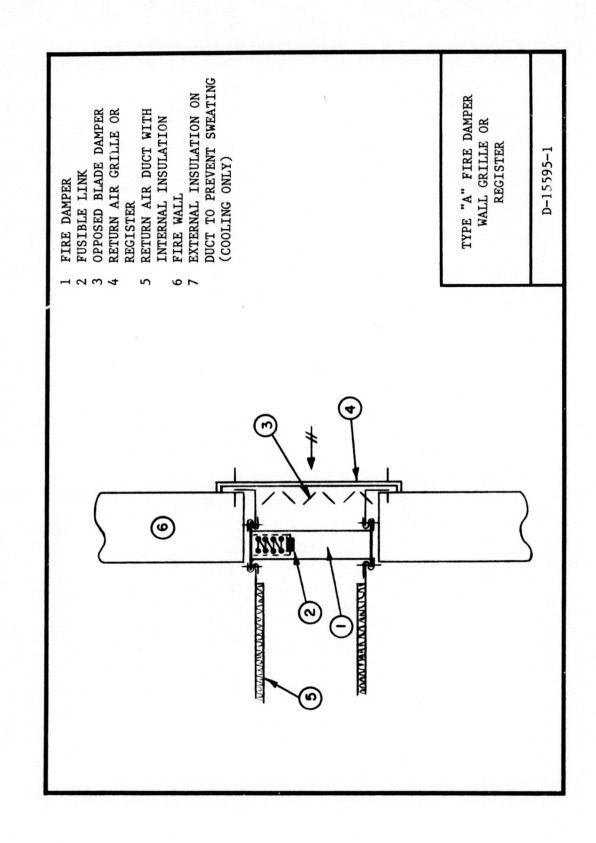

1 FIRE DAMPER
2 FUSIBLE LINK
3 OPPOSED BLADE DAMPER
4 RETURN AIR GRILLE OR
  REGISTER
5 RETURN AIR DUCT WITH
  INTERNAL INSULATION
6 FIRE WALL
7 EXTERNAL INSULATION ON
  DUCT TO PREVENT SWEATING
  (COOLING ONLY)

TYPE "A" FIRE DAMPER
WALL GRILLE OR
REGISTER

D-15595-1

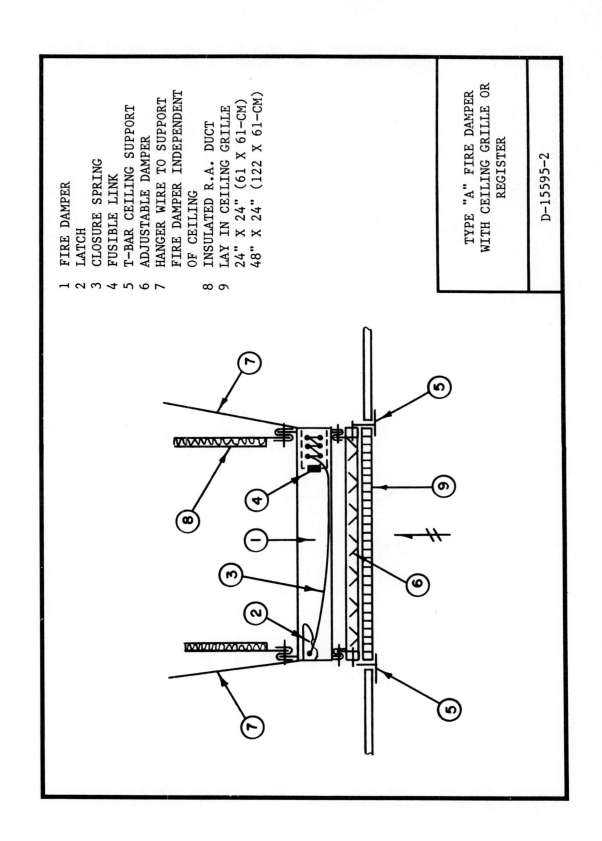

1 FIRE DAMPER
2 LATCH
3 CLOSURE SPRING
4 FUSIBLE LINK
5 T-BAR CEILING SUPPORT
6 ADJUSTABLE DAMPER
7 HANGER WIRE TO SUPPORT
  FIRE DAMPER INDEPENDENT
  OF CEILING
8 INSULATED R.A. DUCT
9 LAY IN CEILING GRILLE
  24" X 24" (61 X 61-CM)
  48" X 24" (122 X 61-CM)

TYPE "A" FIRE DAMPER
WITH CEILING GRILLE OR
REGISTER

D-15595-2

6-21

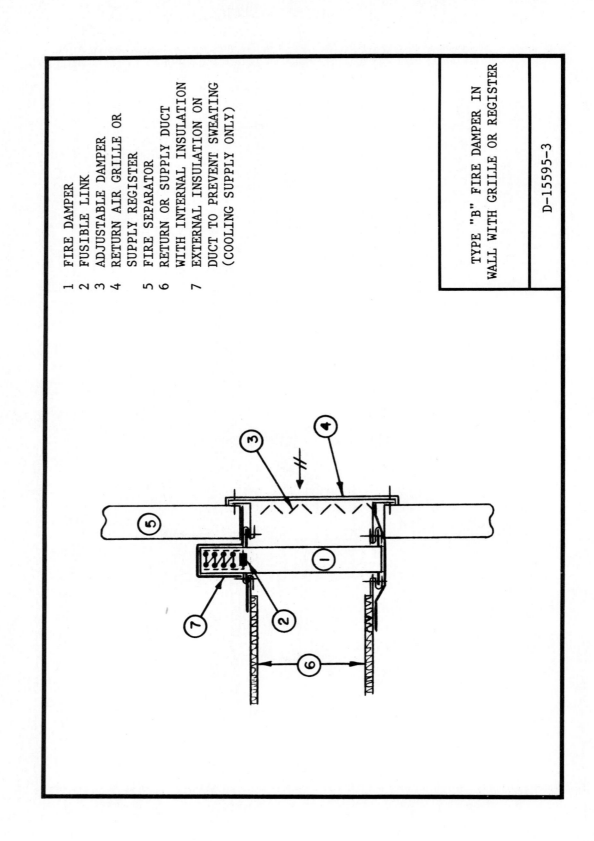

1 FIRE DAMPER
2 FUSIBLE LINK
3 ADJUSTABLE DAMPER
4 RETURN AIR GRILLE OR
  SUPPLY REGISTER
5 FIRE SEPARATOR
6 RETURN OR SUPPLY DUCT
  WITH INTERNAL INSULATION
7 EXTERNAL INSULATION ON
  DUCT TO PREVENT SWEATING
  (COOLING SUPPLY ONLY)

TYPE "B" FIRE DAMPER IN
WALL WITH GRILLE OR REGISTER

D-15595-3

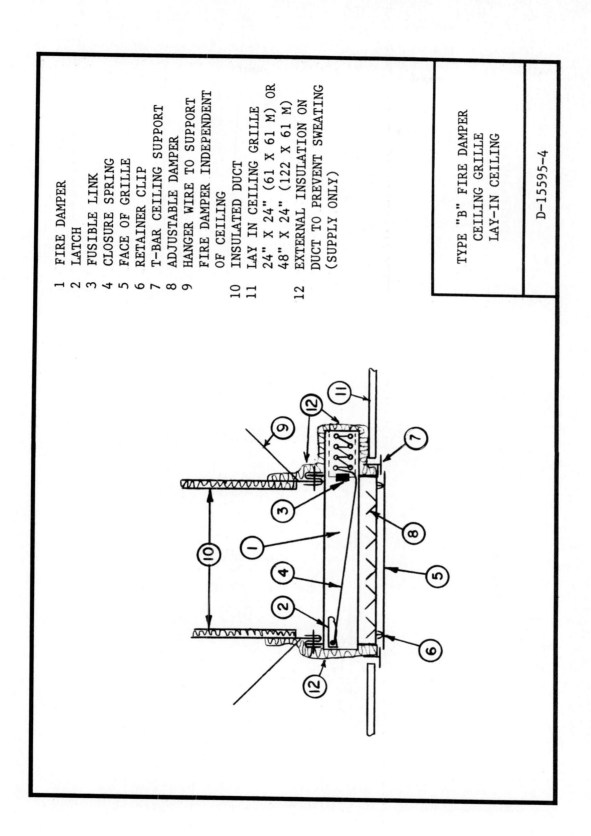

1 FIRE DAMPER
2 LATCH
3 FUSIBLE LINK
4 CLOSURE SPRING
5 FACE OF GRILLE
6 RETAINER CLIP
7 T-BAR CEILING SUPPORT
8 ADJUSTABLE DAMPER
9 HANGER WIRE TO SUPPORT
   FIRE DAMPER INDEPENDENT
   OF CEILING
10 INSULATED DUCT
11 LAY IN CEILING GRILLE
    24" X 24" (61 X 61 M) OR
    48" X 24" (122 X 61 M)
12 EXTERNAL INSULATION ON
    DUCT TO PREVENT SWEATING
    (SUPPLY ONLY)

TYPE "B" FIRE DAMPER
CEILING GRILLE
LAY-IN CEILING

D-15595-4

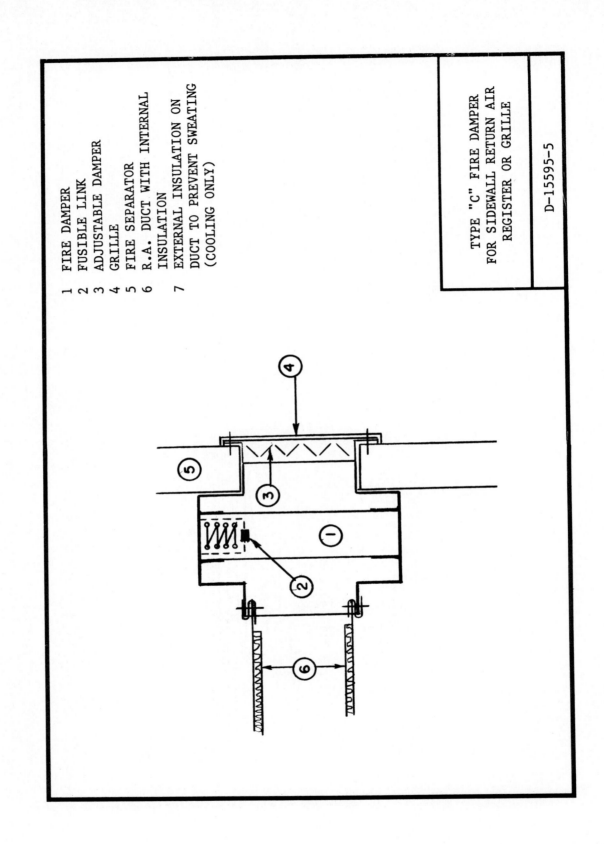

1 FIRE DAMPER
2 FUSIBLE LINK
3 ADJUSTABLE DAMPER
4 GRILLE
5 FIRE SEPARATOR
6 R.A. DUCT WITH INTERNAL
   INSULATION
7 EXTERNAL INSULATION ON
   DUCT TO PREVENT SWEATING
   (COOLING ONLY)

TYPE "C" FIRE DAMPER
FOR SIDEWALL RETURN AIR
REGISTER OR GRILLE

D-15595-5

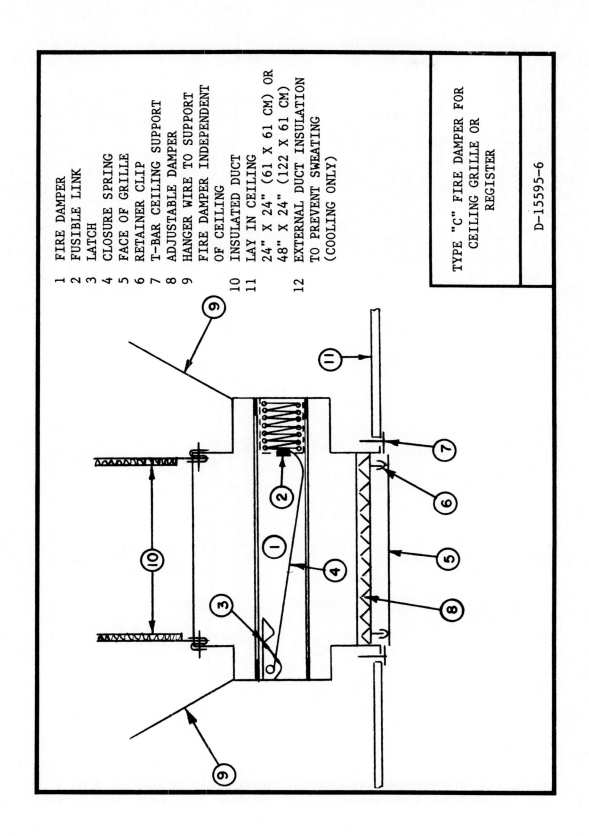

1   FIRE DAMPER
2   FUSIBLE LINK
3   LATCH
4   CLOSURE SPRING
5   FACE OF GRILLE
6   RETAINER CLIP
7   T-BAR CEILING SUPPORT
8   ADJUSTABLE DAMPER
9   HANGER WIRE TO SUPPORT
    FIRE DAMPER INDEPENDENT
    OF CEILING
10 INSULATED DUCT
11 LAY IN CEILING
    24" X 24" (61 X 61 CM) OR
    48" X 24" (122 X 61 CM)
12 EXTERNAL DUCT INSULATION
    TO PREVENT SWEATING
    (COOLING ONLY)

TYPE "C" FIRE DAMPER FOR
CEILING GRILLE OR
REGISTER

D-1595-6

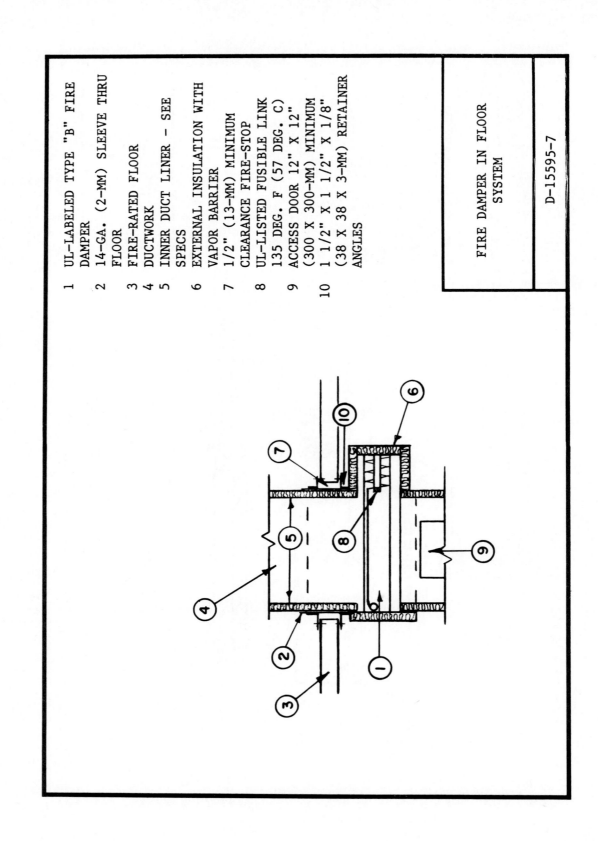

1 UL-LABELED TYPE "B" FIRE DAMPER
2 14-GA. (2-MM) SLEEVE THRU FLOOR
3 FIRE-RATED FLOOR
4 DUCTWORK
5 INNER DUCT LINER – SEE SPECS
6 EXTERNAL INSULATION WITH VAPOR BARRIER
7 1/2" (13-MM) MINIMUM CLEARANCE FIRE-STOP
8 UL-LISTED FUSIBLE LINK 135 DEG. F (57 DEG. C)
9 ACCESS DOOR 12" X 12" (300 X 300-MM) MINIMUM
10 1 1/2" X 1 1/2" X 1/8" (38 X 38 X 3-MM) RETAINER ANGLES

FIRE DAMPER IN FLOOR SYSTEM

D-15595-7

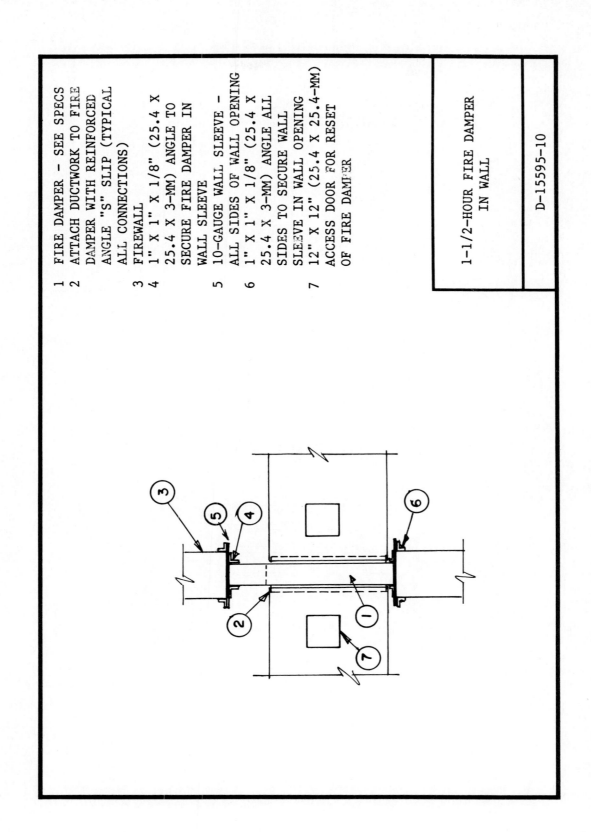

1 FIRE DAMPER – SEE SPECS
2 ATTACH DUCTWORK TO FIRE DAMPER WITH REINFORCED ANGLE "S" SLIP (TYPICAL ALL CONNECTIONS)
3 FIREWALL
4 1" X 1" X 1/8" (25.4 X 25.4 X 3–MM) ANGLE TO SECURE FIRE DAMPER IN WALL SLEEVE
5 10–GAUGE WALL SLEEVE – ALL SIDES OF WALL OPENING
6 1" X 1" X 1/8" (25.4 X 25.4 X 3–MM) ANGLE ALL SIDES TO SECURE WALL SLEEVE IN WALL OPENING
7 12" X 12" (25.4 X 25.4–MM) ACCESS DOOR FOR RESET OF FIRE DAMPER

1-1/2-HOUR FIRE DAMPER IN WALL

D–15595–10

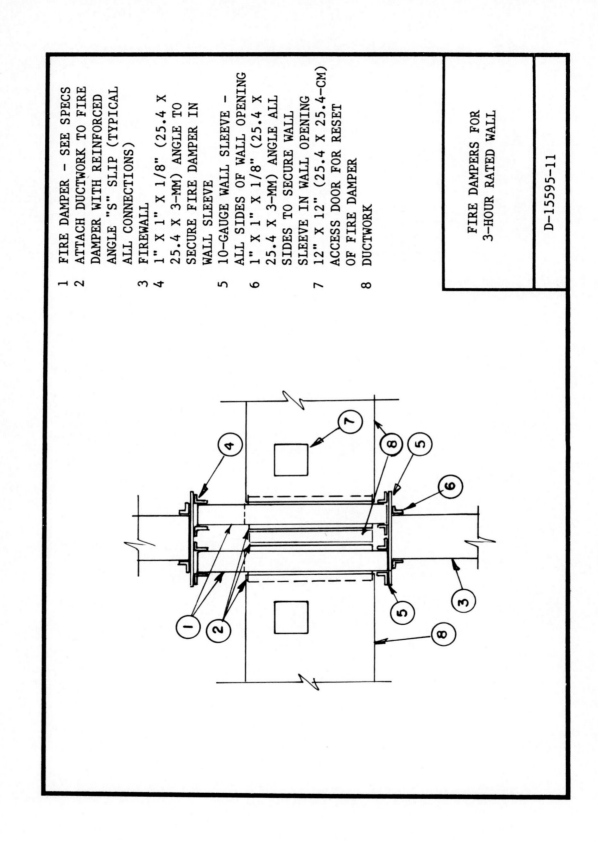

1 FIRE DAMPER - SEE SPECS
2 ATTACH DUCTWORK TO FIRE
   DAMPER WITH REINFORCED
   ANGLE "S" SLIP (TYPICAL
   ALL CONNECTIONS)
3 FIREWALL
4 1" X 1" X 1/8" (25.4 X
   25.4 X 3-MM) ANGLE TO
   SECURE FIRE DAMPER IN
   WALL SLEEVE
5 10-GAUGE WALL SLEEVE -
   ALL SIDES OF WALL OPENING
6 1" X 1" X 1/8" (25.4 X
   25.4 X 3-MM) ANGLE ALL
   SIDES TO SECURE WALL
   SLEEVE IN WALL OPENING
7 12" X 12" (25.4 X 25.4-CM)
   ACCESS DOOR FOR RESET
   OF FIRE DAMPER
8 DUCTWORK

FIRE DAMPERS FOR
3-HOUR RATED WALL

D-15595-11

Heating Sources

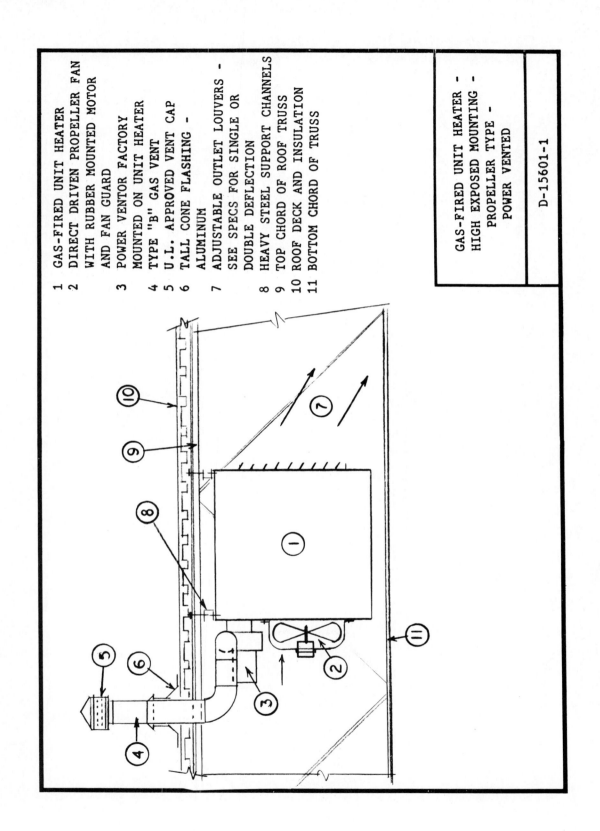

1 GAS-FIRED UNIT HEATER
2 DIRECT DRIVEN PROPELLER FAN
  WITH RUBBER MOUNTED MOTOR
  AND FAN GUARD
3 POWER VENTOR FACTORY
  MOUNTED ON UNIT HEATER
4 TYPE "B" GAS VENT
5 U.L. APPROVED VENT CAP
6 TALL CONE FLASHING -
  ALUMINUM
7 ADJUSTABLE OUTLET LOUVERS -
  SEE SPECS FOR SINGLE OR
  DOUBLE DEFLECTION
8 HEAVY STEEL SUPPORT CHANNELS
9 TOP CHORD OF ROOF TRUSS
10 ROOF DECK AND INSULATION
11 BOTTOM CHORD OF TRUSS

GAS-FIRED UNIT HEATER -
HIGH EXPOSED MOUNTING -
PROPELLER TYPE -
POWER VENTED

D-15601-1

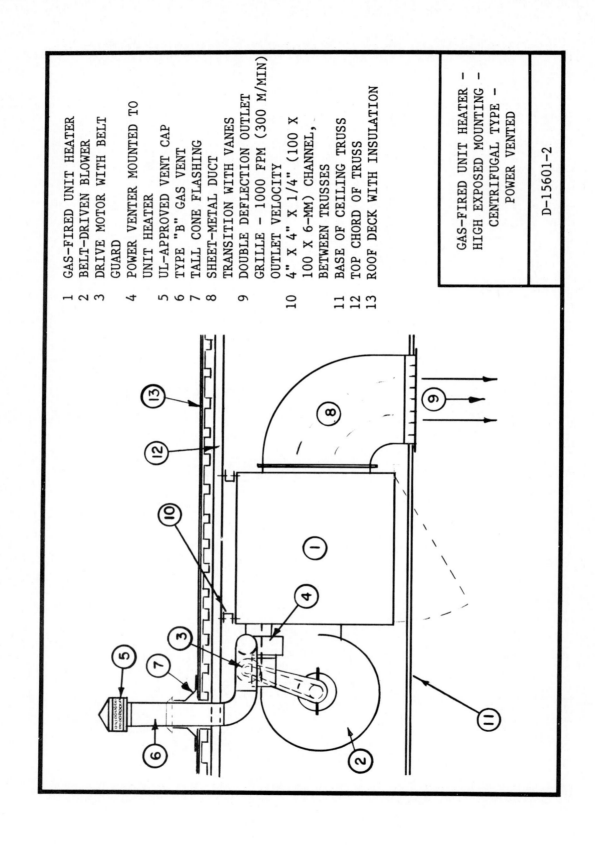

1 GAS-FIRED UNIT HEATER
2 BELT-DRIVEN BLOWER
3 DRIVE MOTOR WITH BELT
  GUARD
4 POWER VENTER MOUNTED TO
  UNIT HEATER
5 UL-APPROVED VENT CAP
6 TYPE "B" GAS VENT
7 TALL CONE FLASHING
8 SHEET-METAL DUCT
  TRANSITION WITH VANES
9 DOUBLE DEFLECTION OUTLET
  GRILLE – 1000 FPM (300 M/MIN)
  OUTLET VELOCITY
10 4" X 4" X 1/4" (100 X
   100 X 6-MM) CHANNEL,
   BETWEEN TRUSSES
11 BASE OF CEILING TRUSS
12 TOP CHORD OF TRUSS
13 ROOF DECK WITH INSULATION

GAS-FIRED UNIT HEATER –
HIGH EXPOSED MOUNTING –
CENTRIFUGAL TYPE –
POWER VENTED

D-15601-2

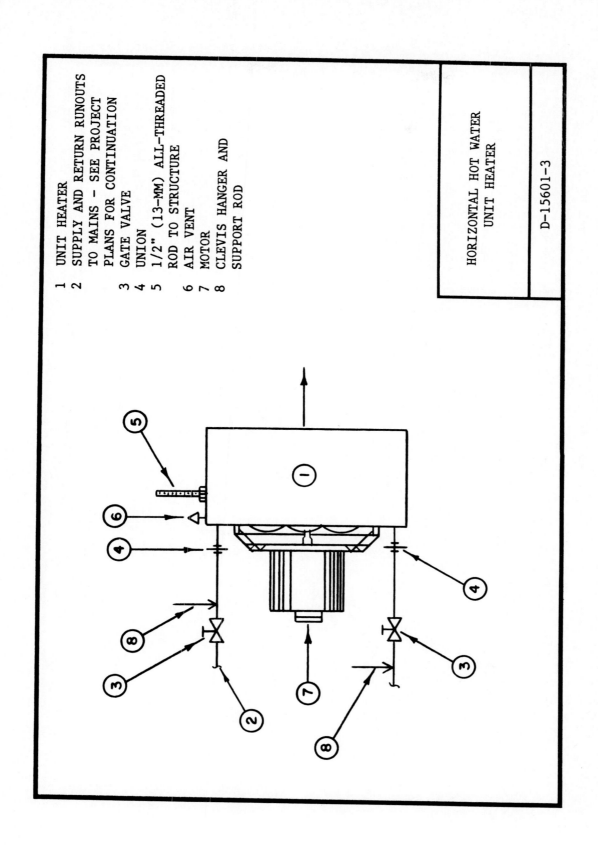

1 UNIT HEATER
2 SUPPLY AND RETURN RUNOUTS
  TO MAINS – SEE PROJECT
  PLANS FOR CONTINUATION
3 GATE VALVE
4 UNION
5 1/2" (13-MM) ALL-THREADED
  ROD TO STRUCTURE
6 AIR VENT
7 MOTOR
8 CLEVIS HANGER AND
  SUPPORT ROD

HORIZONTAL HOT WATER
UNIT HEATER

D-15601-3

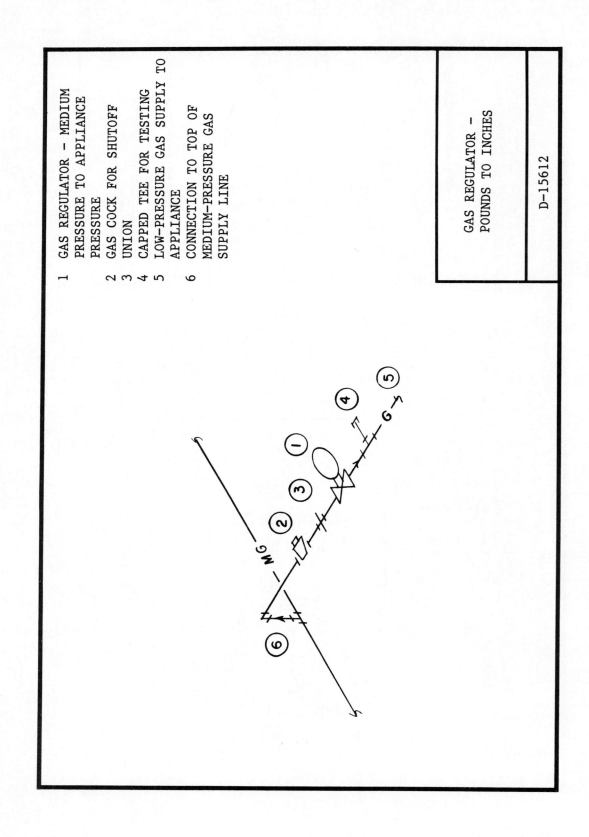

1 GAS REGULATOR - MEDIUM PRESSURE TO APPLIANCE PRESSURE
2 GAS COCK FOR SHUTOFF
3 UNION
4 CAPPED TEE FOR TESTING
5 LOW-PRESSURE GAS SUPPLY TO APPLIANCE
6 CONNECTION TO TOP OF MEDIUM-PRESSURE GAS SUPPLY LINE

GAS REGULATOR –
POUNDS TO INCHES

D–15612

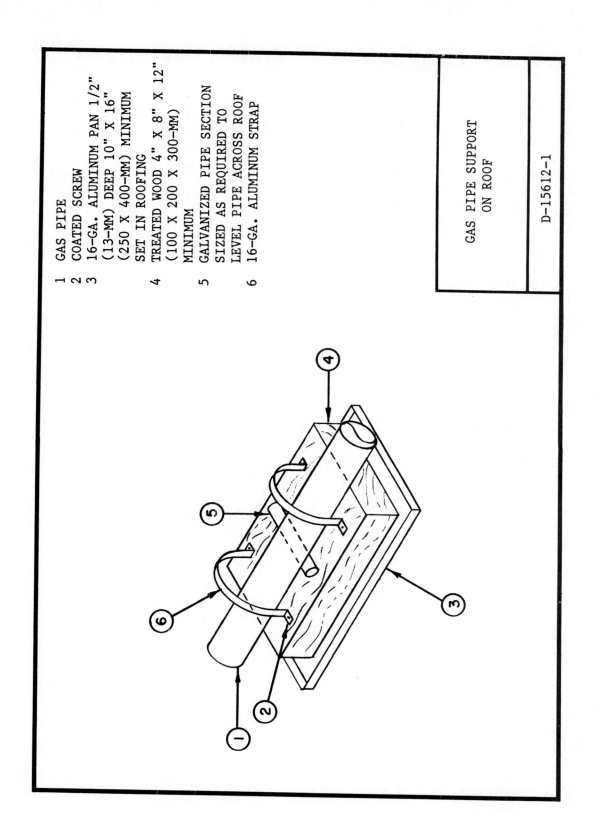

1 GAS PIPE
2 COATED SCREW
3 16-GA. ALUMINUM PAN 1/2"
  (13-MM) DEEP 10" X 16"
  (250 X 400-MM) MINIMUM
  SET IN ROOFING
4 TREATED WOOD 4" X 8" X 12"
  (100 X 200 X 300-MM)
  MINIMUM
5 GALVANIZED PIPE SECTION
  SIZED AS REQUIRED TO
  LEVEL PIPE ACROSS ROOF
6 16-GA. ALUMINUM STRAP

GAS PIPE SUPPORT
ON ROOF

D-15612-1

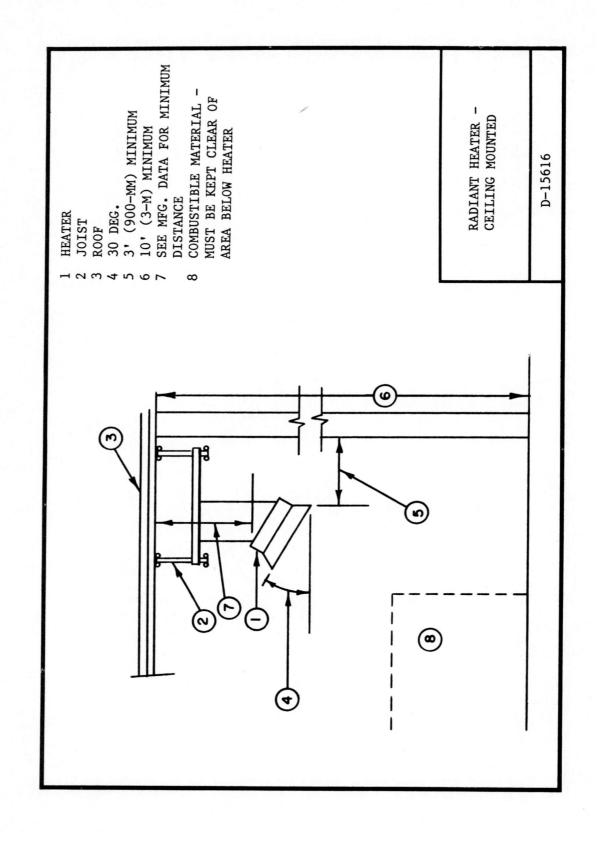

1 HEATER
2 JOIST
3 ROOF
4 30 DEG.
5 3' (900–MM) MINIMUM
6 10' (3–M) MINIMUM
7 SEE MFG. DATA FOR MINIMUM
  DISTANCE
8 COMBUSTIBLE MATERIAL –
  MUST BE KEPT CLEAR OF
  AREA BELOW HEATER

RADIANT HEATER –
CEILING MOUNTED

D–15616

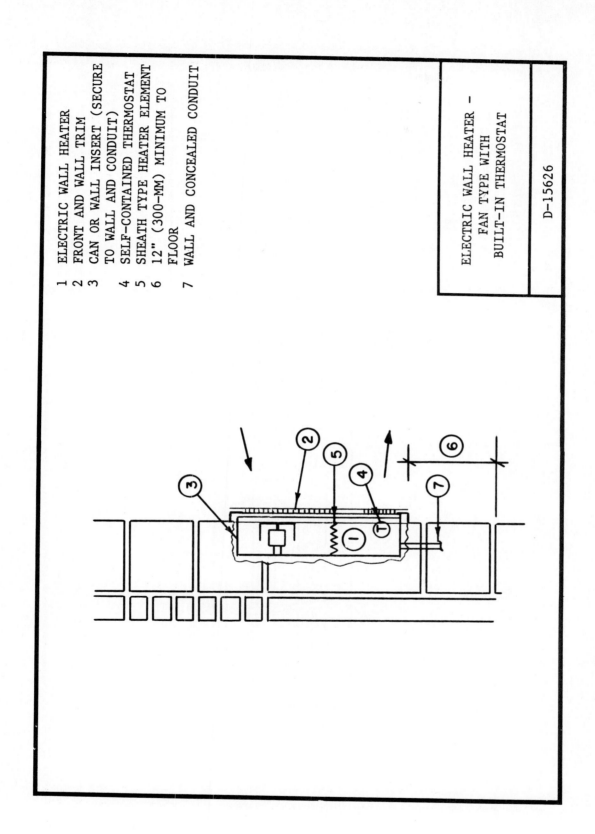

1 ELECTRIC WALL HEATER
2 FRONT AND WALL TRIM
3 CAN OR WALL INSERT (SECURE TO WALL AND CONDUIT)
4 SELF-CONTAINED THERMOSTAT
5 SHEATH TYPE HEATER ELEMENT
6 12" (300-MM) MINIMUM TO FLOOR
7 WALL AND CONCEALED CONDUIT

ELECTRIC WALL HEATER - FAN TYPE WITH BUILT-IN THERMOSTAT

D-15626

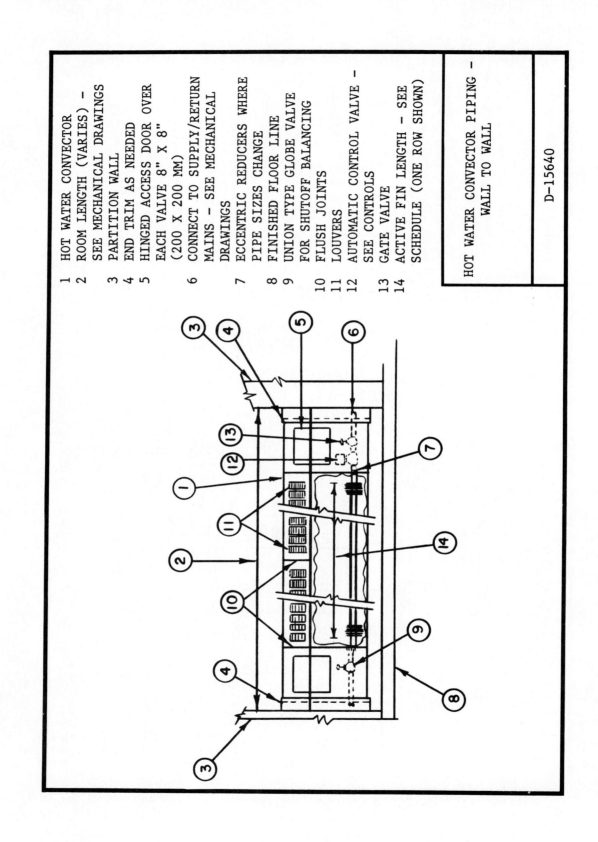

1 HOT WATER CONVECTOR
2 ROOM LENGTH (VARIES) –
SEE MECHANICAL DRAWINGS
3 PARTITION WALL
4 END TRIM AS NEEDED
5 HINGED ACCESS DOOR OVER
EACH VALVE 8" X 8"
(200 X 200 MM)
6 CONNECT TO SUPPLY/RETURN
MAINS – SEE MECHANICAL
DRAWINGS
7 ECCENTRIC REDUCERS WHERE
PIPE SIZES CHANGE
8 FINISHED FLOOR LINE
9 UNION TYPE GLOBE VALVE
FOR SHUTOFF BALANCING
10 FLUSH JOINTS
11 LOUVERS
12 AUTOMATIC CONTROL VALVE –
SEE CONTROLS
13 GATE VALVE
14 ACTIVE FIN LENGTH – SEE
SCHEDULE (ONE ROW SHOWN)

HOT WATER CONVECTOR PIPING –
WALL TO WALL

D–15640

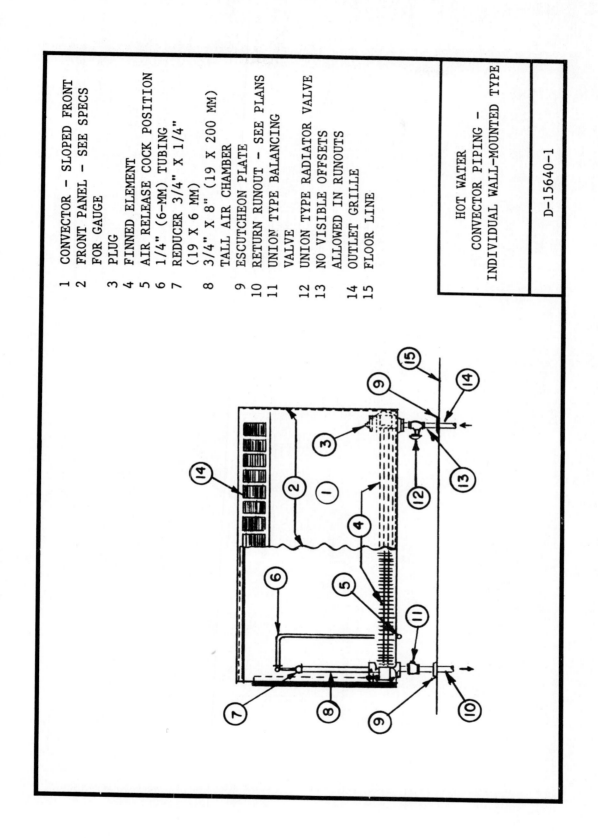

1 CONVECTOR – SLOPED FRONT
2 FRONT PANEL – SEE SPECS
   FOR GAUGE
3 PLUG
4 FINNED ELEMENT
5 AIR RELEASE COCK POSITION
6 1/4" (6-MM) TUBING
7 REDUCER 3/4" X 1/4"
   (19 X 6 MM)
8 3/4" X 8" (19 X 200 MM)
   TALL AIR CHAMBER
9 ESCUTCHEON PLATE
10 RETURN RUNOUT – SEE PLANS
11 UNION TYPE BALANCING
   VALVE
12 UNION TYPE RADIATOR VALVE
13 NO VISIBLE OFFSETS
   ALLOWED IN RUNOUTS
14 OUTLET GRILLE
15 FLOOR LINE

HOT WATER
CONVECTOR PIPING –
INDIVIDUAL WALL–MOUNTED TYPE

D–15640–1

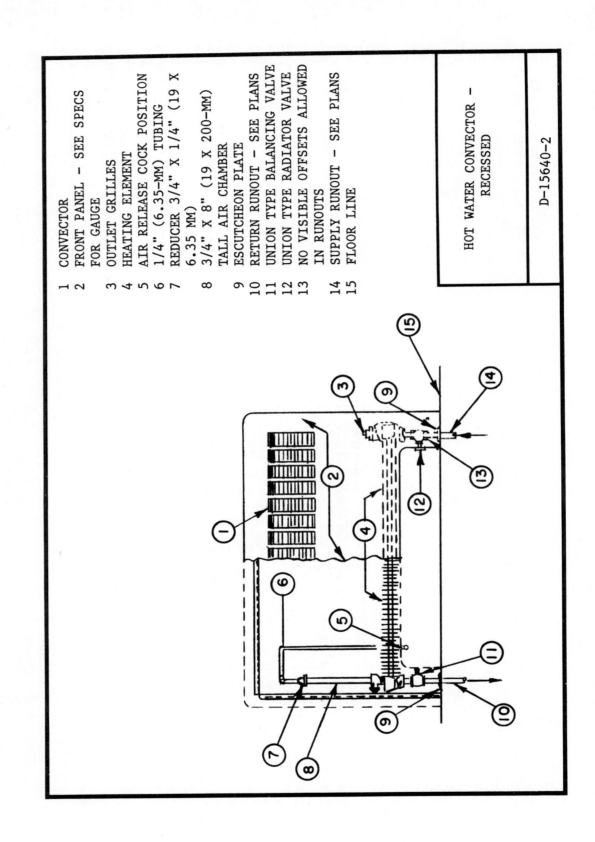

1 CONVECTOR
2 FRONT PANEL – SEE SPECS
   FOR GAUGE
3 OUTLET GRILLES
4 HEATING ELEMENT
5 AIR RELEASE COCK POSITION
6 1/4" (6.35–MM) TUBING
7 REDUCER 3/4" X 1/4" (19 X
   6.35 MM)
8 3/4" X 8" (19 X 200–MM)
   TALL AIR CHAMBER
9 ESCUTCHEON PLATE
10 RETURN RUNOUT – SEE PLANS
11 UNION TYPE BALANCING VALVE
12 UNION TYPE RADIATOR VALVE
13 NO VISIBLE OFFSETS ALLOWED
   IN RUNOUTS
14 SUPPLY RUNOUT – SEE PLANS
15 FLOOR LINE

HOT WATER CONVECTOR –
RECESSED

D–15640–2

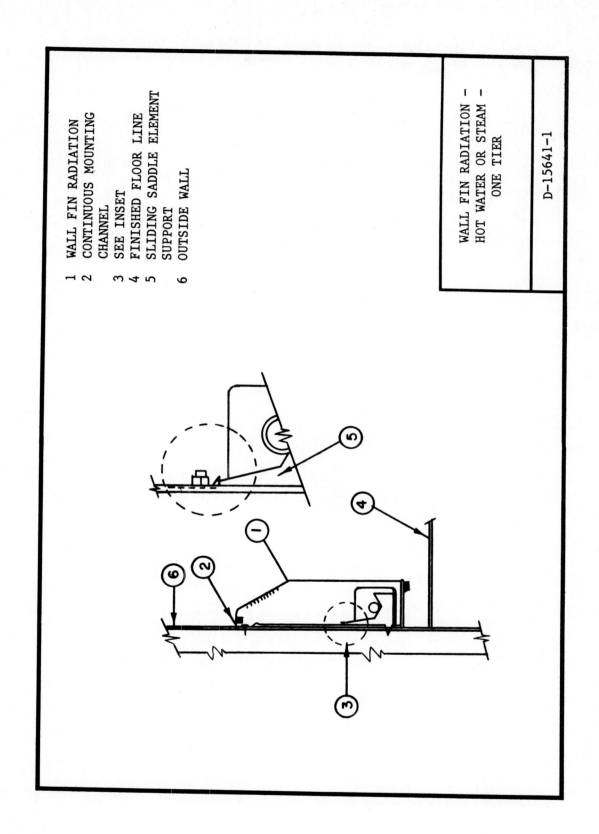

1 WALL FIN RADIATION
2 CONTINUOUS MOUNTING
  CHANNEL
3 SEE INSET
4 FINISHED FLOOR LINE
5 SLIDING SADDLE ELEMENT
  SUPPORT
6 OUTSIDE WALL

WALL FIN RADIATION –
HOT WATER OR STEAM –
ONE TIER

D–15641–1

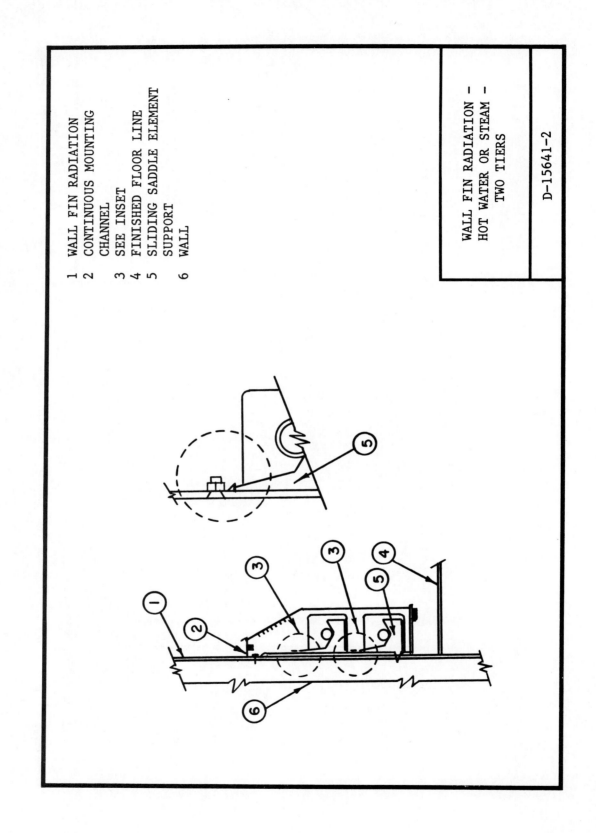

1 WALL FIN RADIATION
2 CONTINUOUS MOUNTING
   CHANNEL
3 SEE INSET
4 FINISHED FLOOR LINE
5 SLIDING SADDLE ELEMENT
   SUPPORT
6 WALL

WALL FIN RADIATION –
HOT WATER OR STEAM –
TWO TIERS

D–15641–2

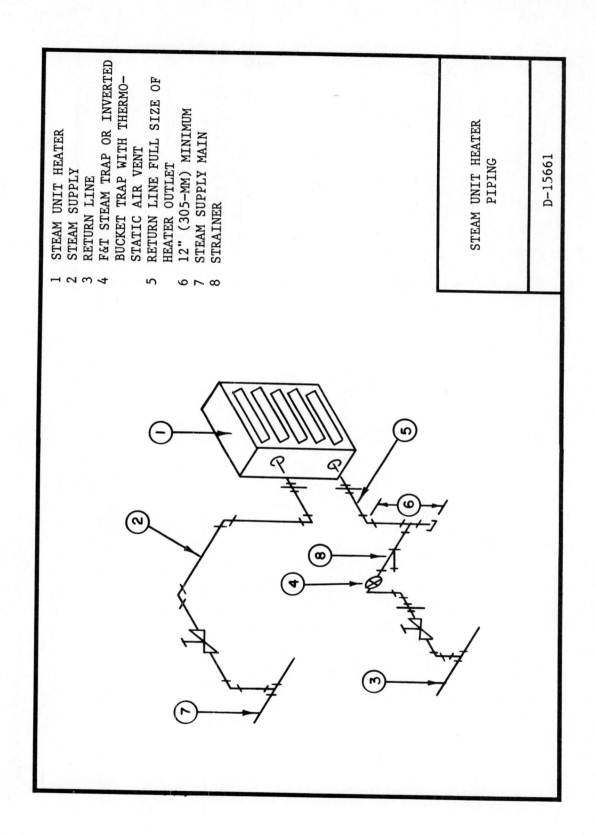

1 STEAM UNIT HEATER
2 STEAM SUPPLY
3 RETURN LINE
4 F&T STEAM TRAP OR INVERTED
  BUCKET TRAP WITH THERMO-
  STATIC AIR VENT
5 RETURN LINE FULL SIZE OF
  HEATER OUTLET
6 12" (305-MM) MINIMUM
7 STEAM SUPPLY MAIN
8 STRAINER

STEAM UNIT HEATER
PIPING

D-15661

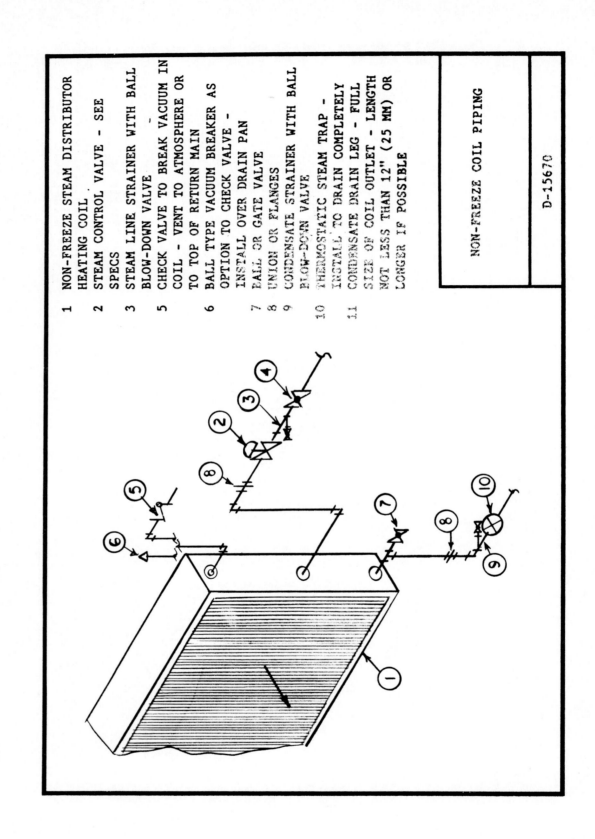

1 NON-FREEZE STEAM DISTRIBUTOR HEATING COIL

2 STEAM CONTROL VALVE - SEE SPECS

3 STEAM LINE STRAINER WITH BALL BLOW-DOWN VALVE

5 CHECK VALVE TO BREAK VACUUM IN COIL - VENT TO ATMOSPHERE OR TO TOP OF RETURN MAIN

6 BALL TYPE VACUUM BREAKER AS OPTION TO CHECK VALVE - INSTALL OVER DRAIN PAN

7 BALL OR GATE VALVE

8 UNION OR FLANGES

9 CONDENSATE STRAINER WITH BALL BLOW-DOWN VALVE

10 THERMOSTATIC STEAM TRAP - INSTALL TO DRAIN COMPLETELY

11 CONDENSATE DRAIN LEG - FULL SIZE OF COIL OUTLET - LENGTH NOT LESS THAN 12" (25 MM) OR LONGER IF POSSIBLE

NON-FREEZE COIL PIPING

D-15670

Pipe System
Auxiliary Equipment

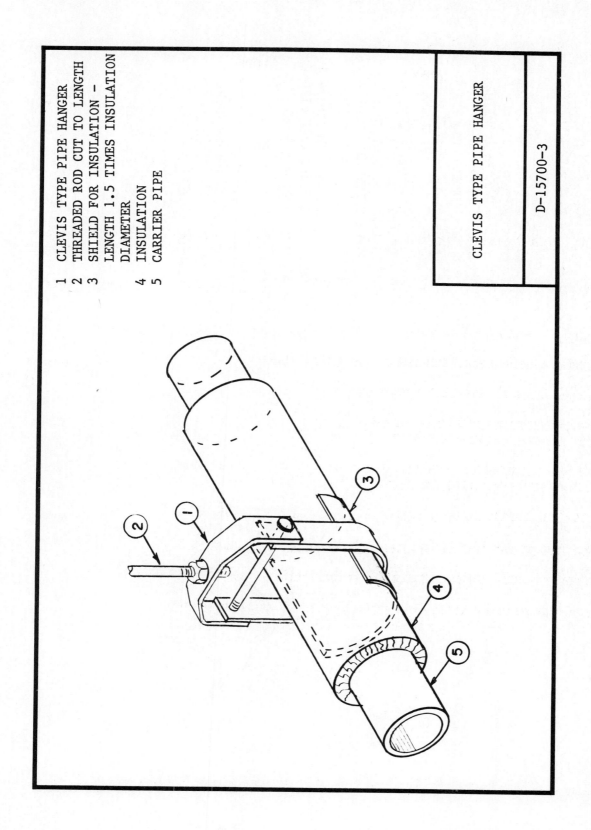

1 CLEVIS TYPE PIPE HANGER
2 THREADED ROD CUT TO LENGTH
3 SHIELD FOR INSULATION –
   LENGTH 1.5 TIMES INSULATION
   DIAMETER
4 INSULATION
5 CARRIER PIPE

CLEVIS TYPE PIPE HANGER

D–15700–3

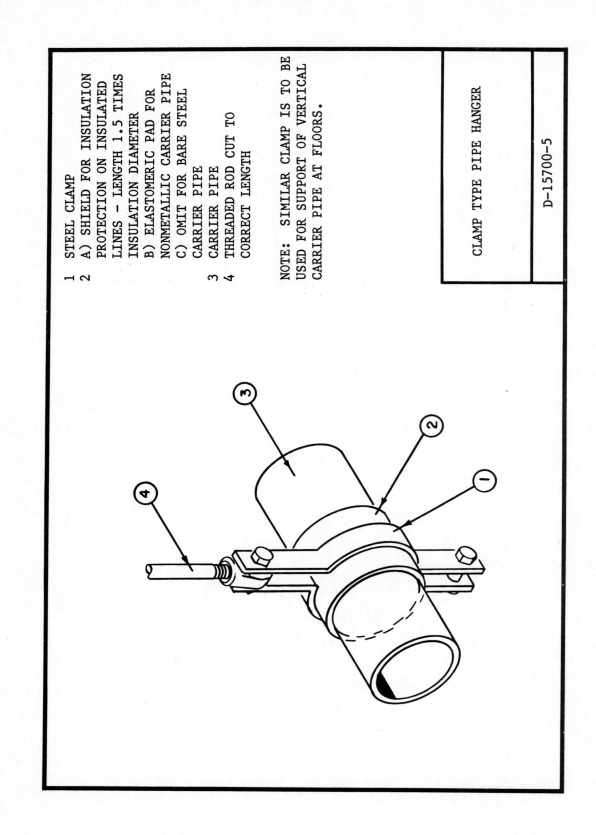

1 STEEL CLAMP
2 A) SHIELD FOR INSULATION
   PROTECTION ON INSULATED
   LINES - LENGTH 1.5 TIMES
   INSULATION DIAMETER
   B) ELASTOMERIC PAD FOR
   NONMETALLIC CARRIER PIPE
   C) OMIT FOR BARE STEEL
   CARRIER PIPE
3 CARRIER PIPE
4 THREADED ROD CUT TO
   CORRECT LENGTH

NOTE: SIMILAR CLAMP IS TO BE
USED FOR SUPPORT OF VERTICAL
CARRIER PIPE AT FLOORS.

CLAMP TYPE PIPE HANGER

D-15700-5

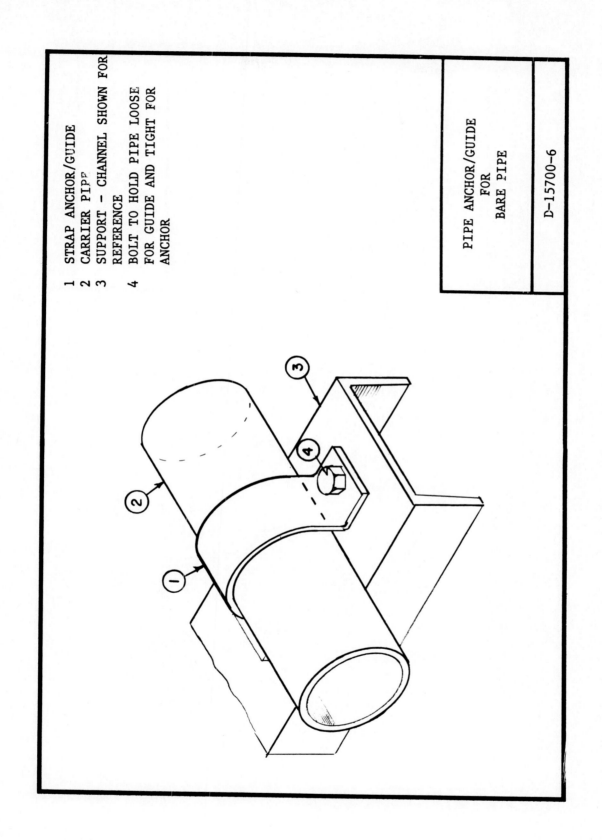

1 STRAP ANCHOR/GUIDE
2 CARRIER PIPE
3 SUPPORT - CHANNEL SHOWN FOR
   REFERENCE
4 BOLT TO HOLD PIPE LOOSE
   FOR GUIDE AND TIGHT FOR
   ANCHOR

PIPE ANCHOR/GUIDE
FOR
BARE PIPE

D-15700-6

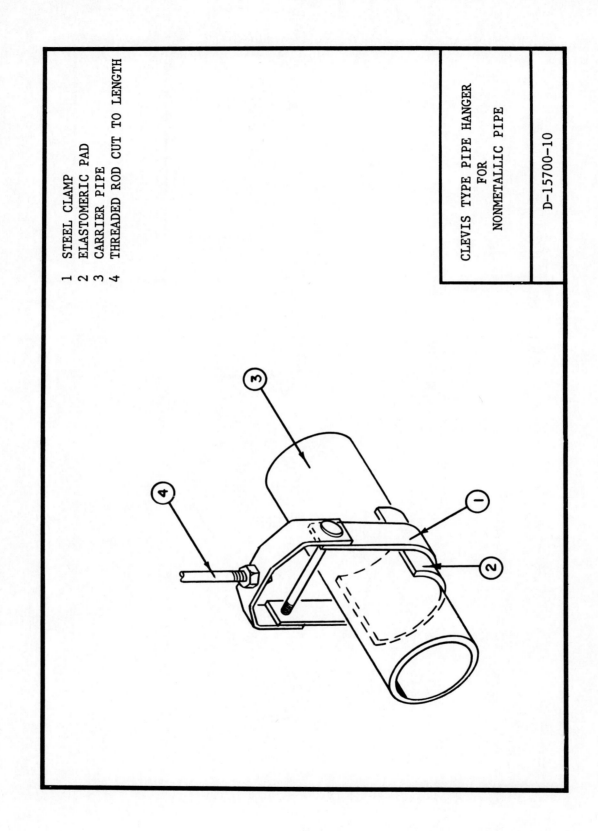

1 STEEL CLAMP
2 ELASTOMERIC PAD
3 CARRIER PIPE
4 THREADED ROD CUT TO LENGTH

CLEVIS TYPE PIPE HANGER
FOR
NONMETALLIC PIPE

D-15700-10

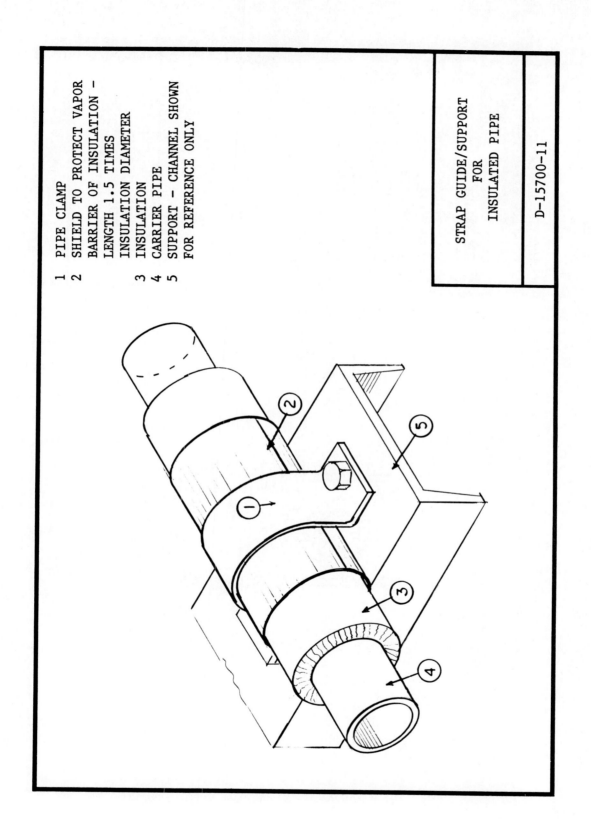

1 PIPE CLAMP
2 SHIELD TO PROTECT VAPOR
  BARRIER OF INSULATION –
  LENGTH 1.5 TIMES
  INSULATION DIAMETER
3 INSULATION
4 CARRIER PIPE
5 SUPPORT – CHANNEL SHOWN
  FOR REFERENCE ONLY

STRAP GUIDE/SUPPORT
FOR
INSULATED PIPE

D-15700-11

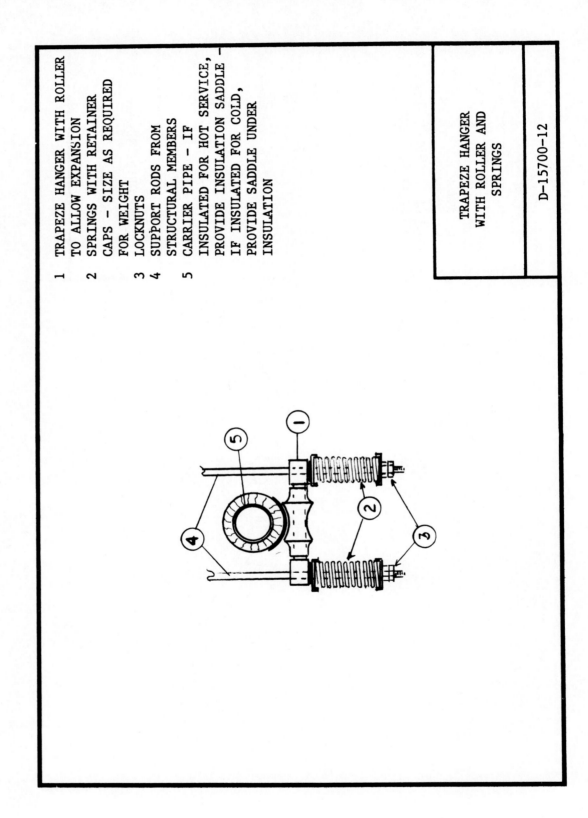

1 TRAPEZE HANGER WITH ROLLER
   TO ALLOW EXPANSION
2 SPRINGS WITH RETAINER
   CAPS – SIZE AS REQUIRED
   FOR WEIGHT
3 LOCKNUTS
4 SUPPORT RODS FROM
   STRUCTURAL MEMBERS
5 CARRIER PIPE – IF
   INSULATED FOR HOT SERVICE,
   PROVIDE INSULATION SADDLE
   IF INSULATED FOR COLD,
   PROVIDE SADDLE UNDER
   INSULATION

TRAPEZE HANGER
WITH ROLLER AND
SPRINGS

D–15700–12

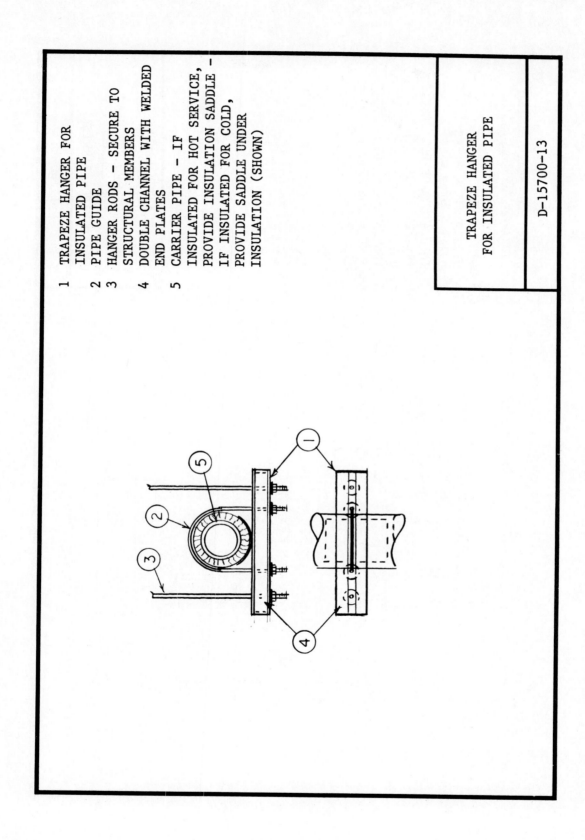

1 TRAPEZE HANGER FOR
  INSULATED PIPE
2 PIPE GUIDE
3 HANGER RODS – SECURE TO
  STRUCTURAL MEMBERS
4 DOUBLE CHANNEL WITH WELDED
  END PLATES
5 CARRIER PIPE – IF
  INSULATED FOR HOT SERVICE,
  PROVIDE INSULATION SADDLE –
  IF INSULATED FOR COLD,
  PROVIDE SADDLE UNDER
  INSULATION (SHOWN)

TRAPEZE HANGER
FOR INSULATED PIPE

D–15700–13

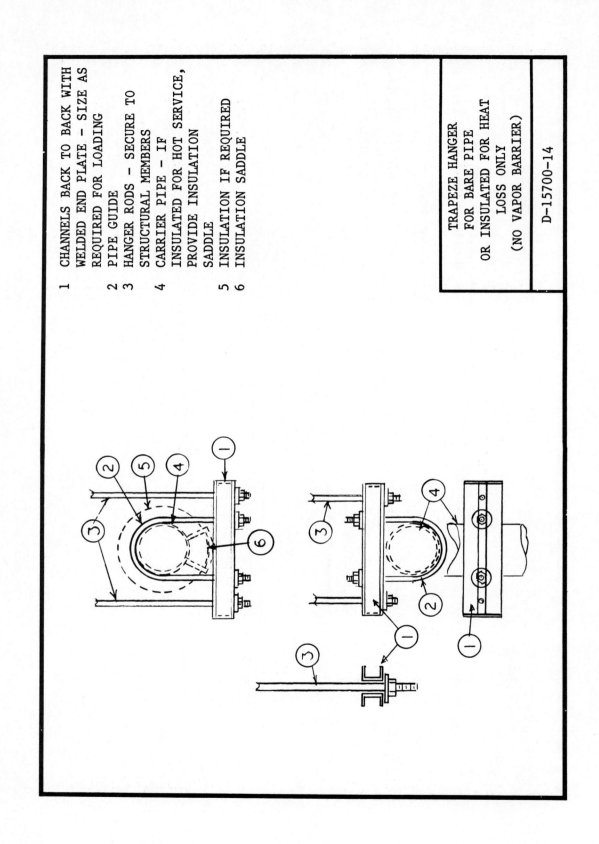

1 CHANNELS BACK TO BACK WITH WELDED END PLATE – SIZE AS REQUIRED FOR LOADING
2 PIPE GUIDE
3 HANGER RODS – SECURE TO STRUCTURAL MEMBERS
4 CARRIER PIPE – IF INSULATED FOR HOT SERVICE, PROVIDE INSULATION SADDLE
5 INSULATION IF REQUIRED
6 INSULATION SADDLE

TRAPEZE HANGER
FOR BARE PIPE
OR INSULATED FOR HEAT
LOSS ONLY
(NO VAPOR BARRIER)

D–15700–14

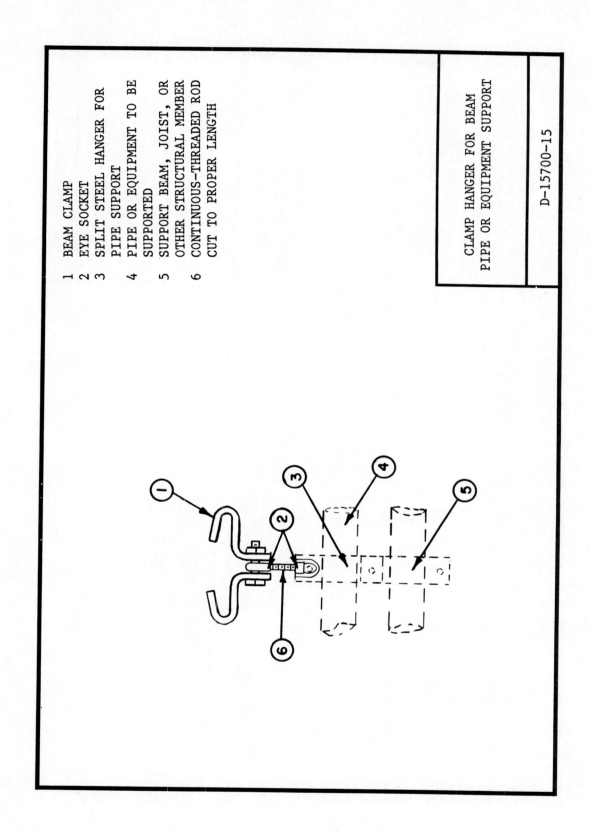

1 BEAM CLAMP
2 EYE SOCKET
3 SPLIT STEEL HANGER FOR
   PIPE SUPPORT
4 PIPE OR EQUIPMENT TO BE
   SUPPORTED
5 SUPPORT BEAM, JOIST, OR
   OTHER STRUCTURAL MEMBER
6 CONTINUOUS-THREADED ROD
   CUT TO PROPER LENGTH

CLAMP HANGER FOR BEAM
PIPE OR EQUIPMENT SUPPORT

D-15700-15

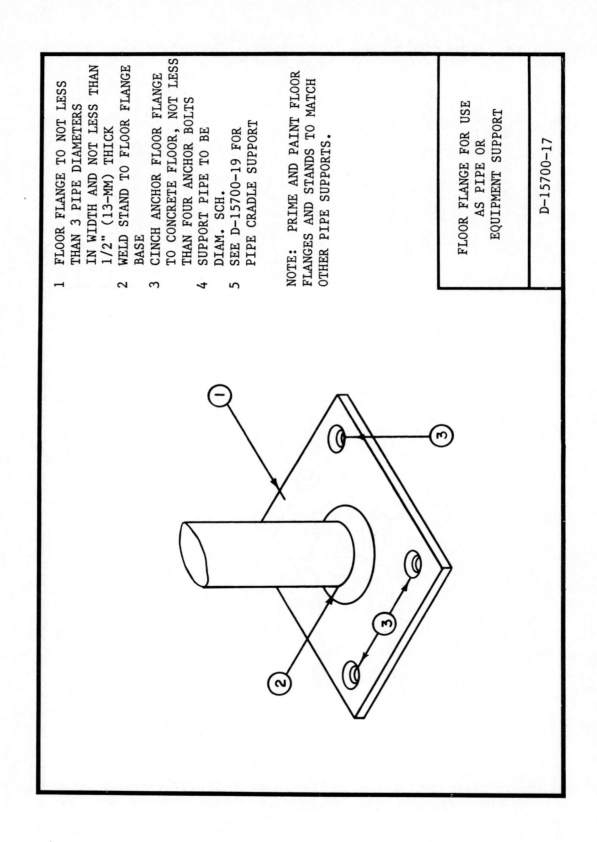

1 FLOOR FLANGE TO NOT LESS
  THAN 3 PIPE DIAMETERS
  IN WIDTH AND NOT LESS THAN
  1/2" (13-MM) THICK
2 WELD STAND TO FLOOR FLANGE
  BASE
3 CINCH ANCHOR FLOOR FLANGE
  TO CONCRETE FLOOR, NOT LESS
  THAN FOUR ANCHOR BOLTS
4 SUPPORT PIPE TO BE
  DIAM. SCH.
5 SEE D-15700-19 FOR
  PIPE CRADLE SUPPORT

NOTE: PRIME AND PAINT FLOOR
FLANGES AND STANDS TO MATCH
OTHER PIPE SUPPORTS.

FLOOR FLANGE FOR USE
AS PIPE OR
EQUIPMENT SUPPORT

D-15700-17

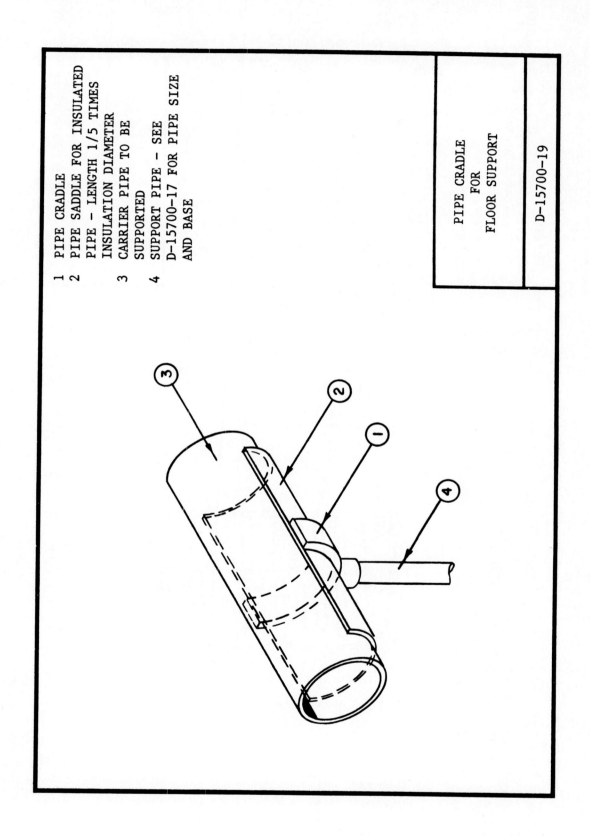

1 PIPE CRADLE
2 PIPE SADDLE FOR INSULATED
  PIPE - LENGTH 1/5 TIMES
  INSULATION DIAMETER
3 CARRIER PIPE TO BE
  SUPPORTED
4 SUPPORT PIPE - SEE
  D-15700-17 FOR PIPE SIZE
  AND BASE

PIPE CRADLE
FOR
FLOOR SUPPORT

D-15700-19

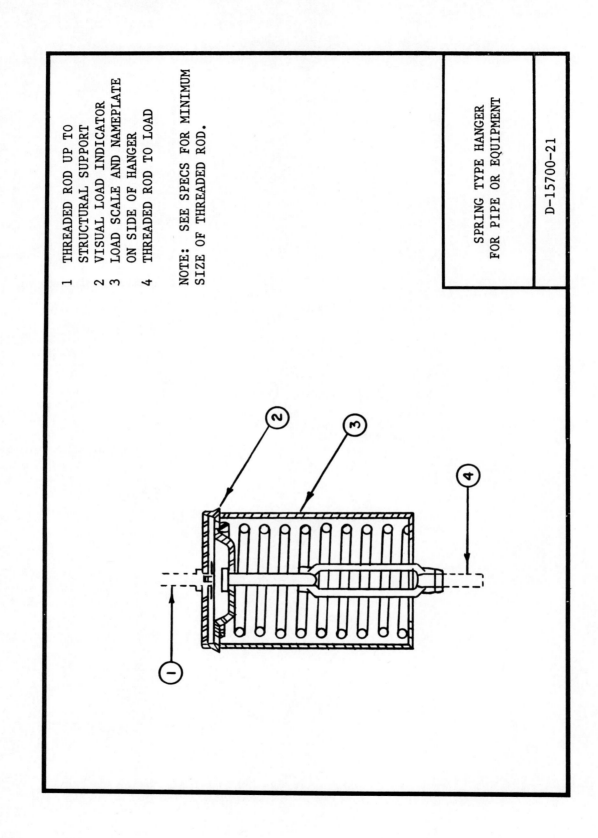

1 THREADED ROD UP TO
   STRUCTURAL SUPPORT
2 VISUAL LOAD INDICATOR
3 LOAD SCALE AND NAMEPLATE
   ON SIDE OF HANGER
4 THREADED ROD TO LOAD

NOTE: SEE SPECS FOR MINIMUM
SIZE OF THREADED ROD.

SPRING TYPE HANGER
FOR PIPE OR EQUIPMENT

D-15700-21

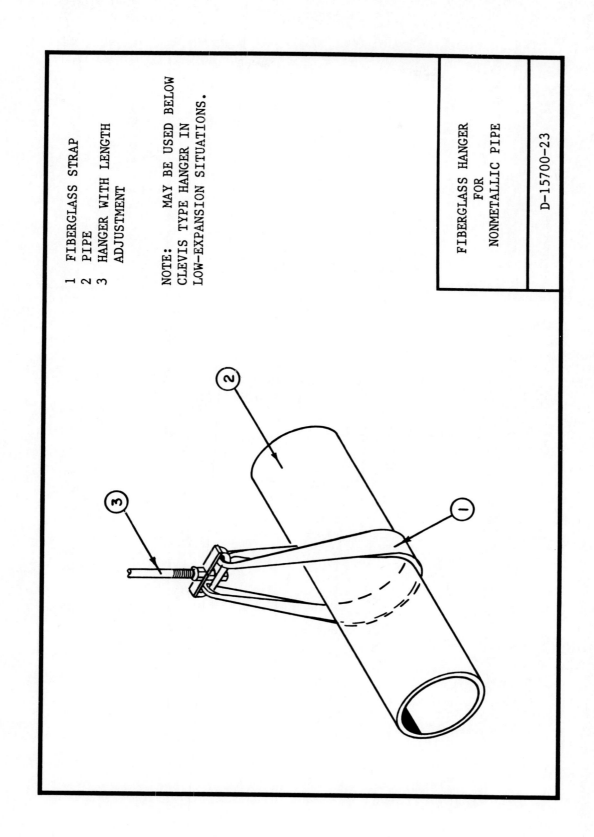

1 FIBERGLASS STRAP
2 PIPE
3 HANGER WITH LENGTH
  ADJUSTMENT

NOTE: MAY BE USED BELOW
CLEVIS TYPE HANGER IN
LOW-EXPANSION SITUATIONS.

FIBERGLASS HANGER
FOR
NONMETALLIC PIPE

D-15700-23

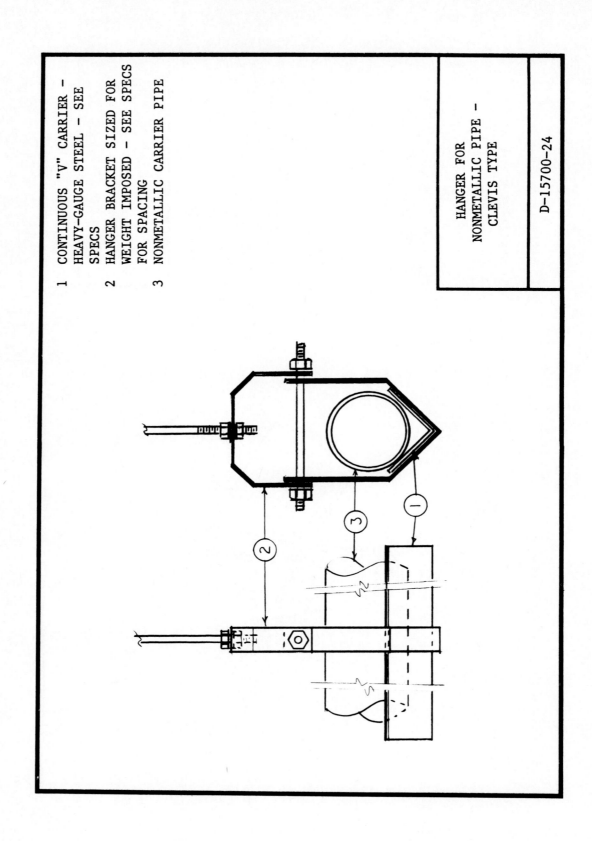

1 CONTINUOUS "V" CARRIER –
HEAVY–GAUGE STEEL – SEE
SPECS

2 HANGER BRACKET SIZED FOR
WEIGHT IMPOSED – SEE SPECS
FOR SPACING

3 NONMETALLIC CARRIER PIPE

HANGER FOR
NONMETALLIC PIPE –
CLEVIS TYPE

D–15700–24

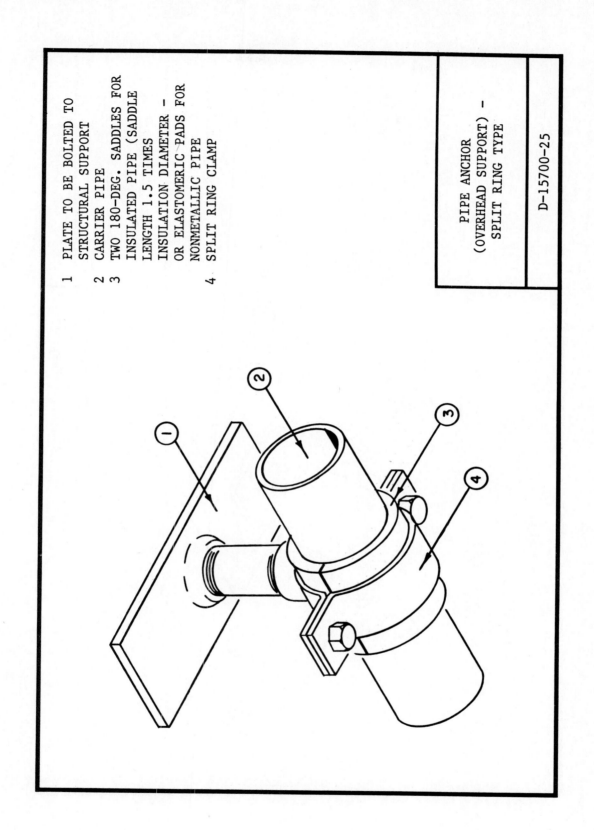

1 PLATE TO BE BOLTED TO
  STRUCTURAL SUPPORT
2 CARRIER PIPE
3 TWO 180-DEG. SADDLES FOR
  INSULATED PIPE (SADDLE
  LENGTH 1.5 TIMES
  INSULATION DIAMETER –
  OR ELASTOMERIC PADS FOR
  NONMETALLIC PIPE
4 SPLIT RING CLAMP

PIPE ANCHOR
(OVERHEAD SUPPORT) –
SPLIT RING TYPE

D–15700–25

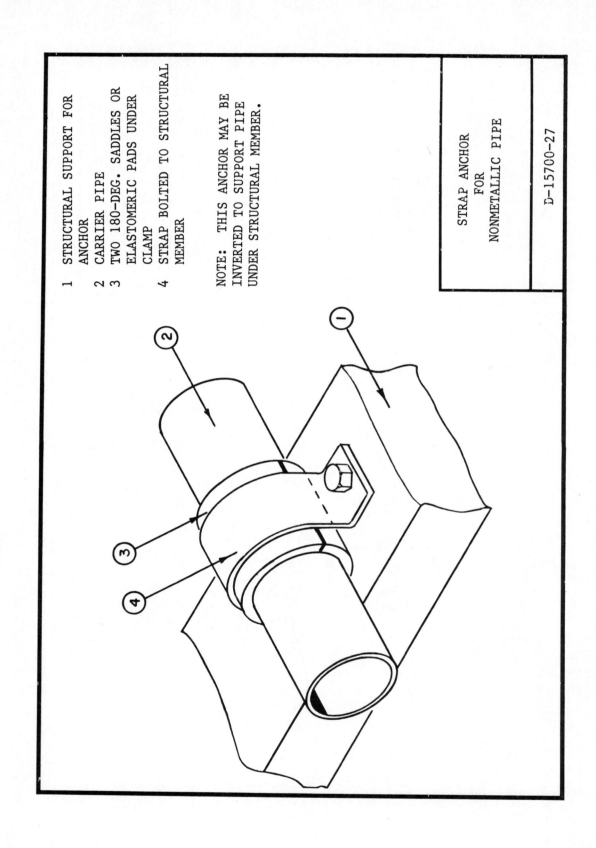

1 STRUCTURAL SUPPORT FOR ANCHOR
2 CARRIER PIPE
3 TWO 180-DEG. SADDLES OR ELASTOMERIC PADS UNDER CLAMP
4 STRAP BOLTED TO STRUCTURAL MEMBER

NOTE: THIS ANCHOR MAY BE INVERTED TO SUPPORT PIPE UNDER STRUCTURAL MEMBER.

STRAP ANCHOR
FOR
NONMETALLIC PIPE

D-15700-27

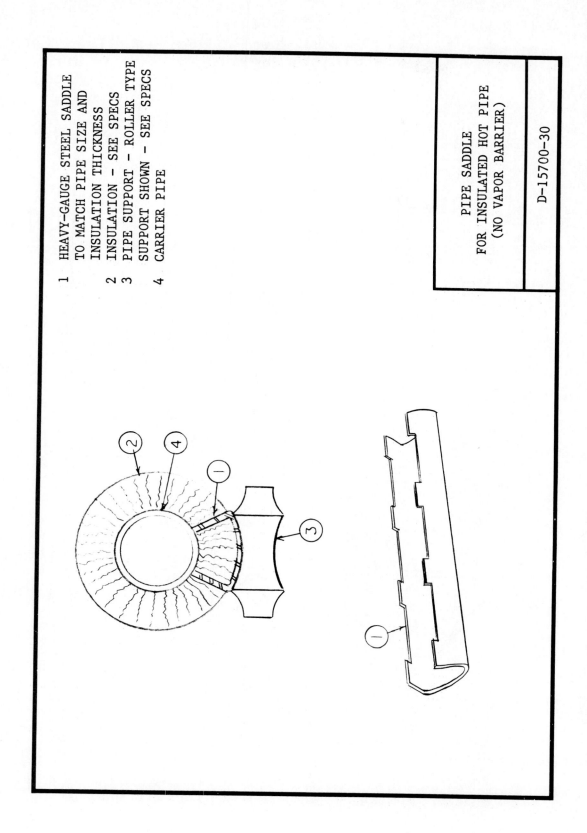

1 HEAVY-GAUGE STEEL SADDLE
  TO MATCH PIPE SIZE AND
  INSULATION THICKNESS
2 INSULATION – SEE SPECS
3 PIPE SUPPORT – ROLLER TYPE
  SUPPORT SHOWN – SEE SPECS
4 CARRIER PIPE

PIPE SADDLE
FOR INSULATED HOT PIPE
(NO VAPOR BARRIER)

D–15700–30

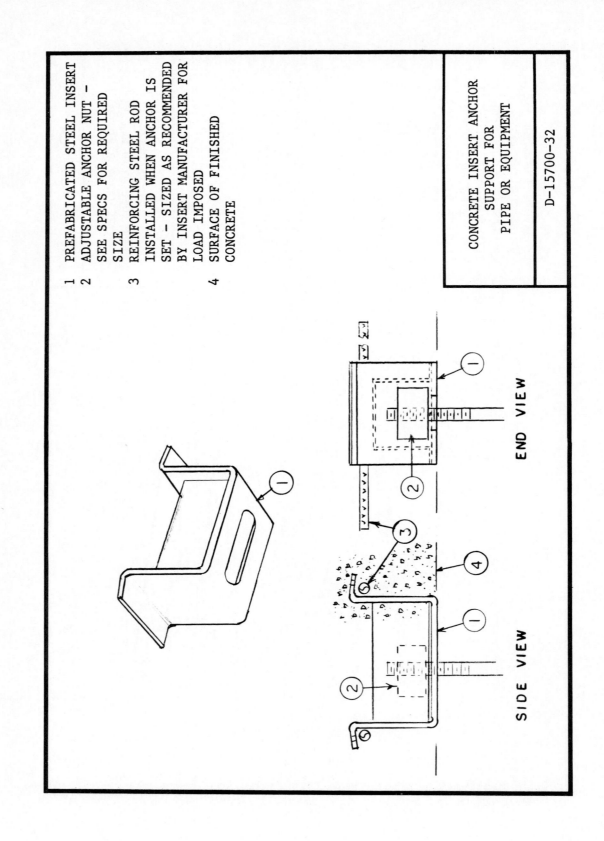

1 PREFABRICATED STEEL INSERT
2 ADJUSTABLE ANCHOR NUT –
  SEE SPECS FOR REQUIRED
  SIZE
3 REINFORCING STEEL ROD
  INSTALLED WHEN ANCHOR IS
  SET – SIZED AS RECOMMENDED
  BY INSERT MANUFACTURER FOR
  LOAD IMPOSED
4 SURFACE OF FINISHED
  CONCRETE

END VIEW

SIDE VIEW

CONCRETE INSERT ANCHOR
SUPPORT FOR
PIPE OR EQUIPMENT

D–15700–32

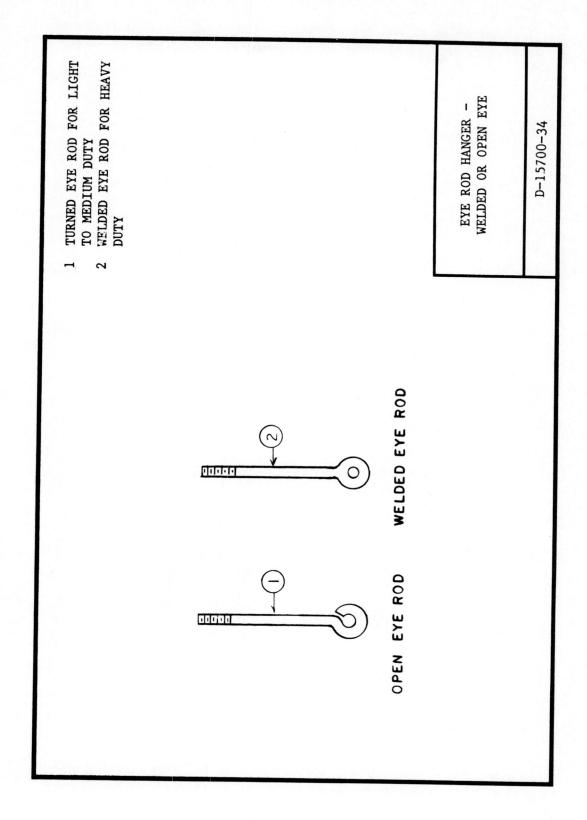

1. TURNED EYE ROD FOR LIGHT TO MEDIUM DUTY
2. WELDED EYE ROD FOR HEAVY DUTY

OPEN EYE ROD

WELDED EYE ROD

EYE ROD HANGER – WELDED OR OPEN EYE

D-15700-34

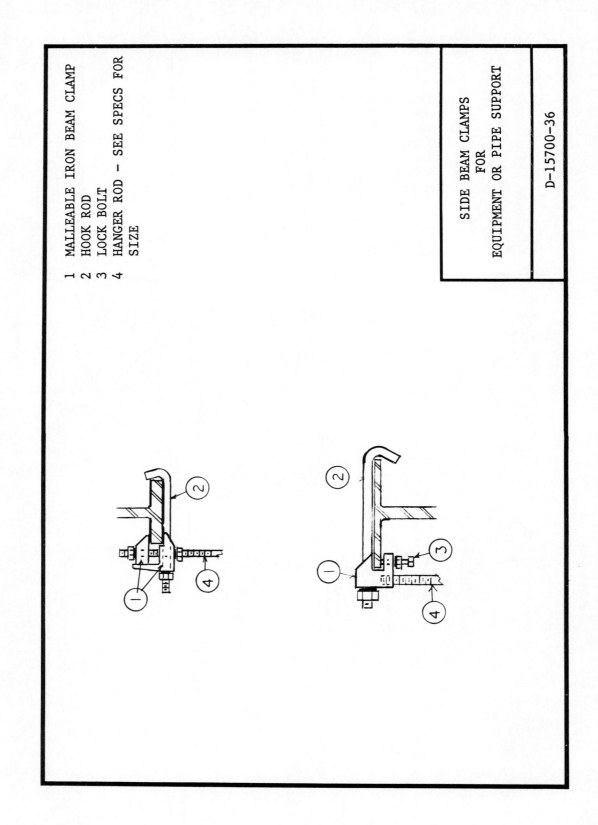

1 MALLEABLE IRON BEAM CLAMP
2 HOOK ROD
3 LOCK BOLT
4 HANGER ROD – SEE SPECS FOR
  SIZE

SIDE BEAM CLAMPS
FOR
EQUIPMENT OR PIPE SUPPORT

D–15700–36

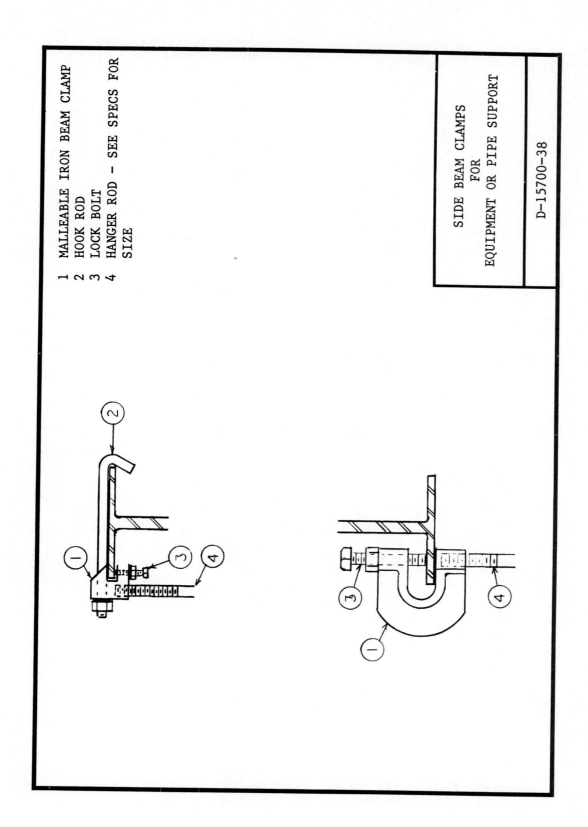

1 MALLEABLE IRON BEAM CLAMP
2 HOOK ROD
3 LOCK BOLT
4 HANGER ROD — SEE SPECS FOR
    SIZE

SIDE BEAM CLAMPS
FOR
EQUIPMENT OR PIPE SUPPORT

D—15700—38

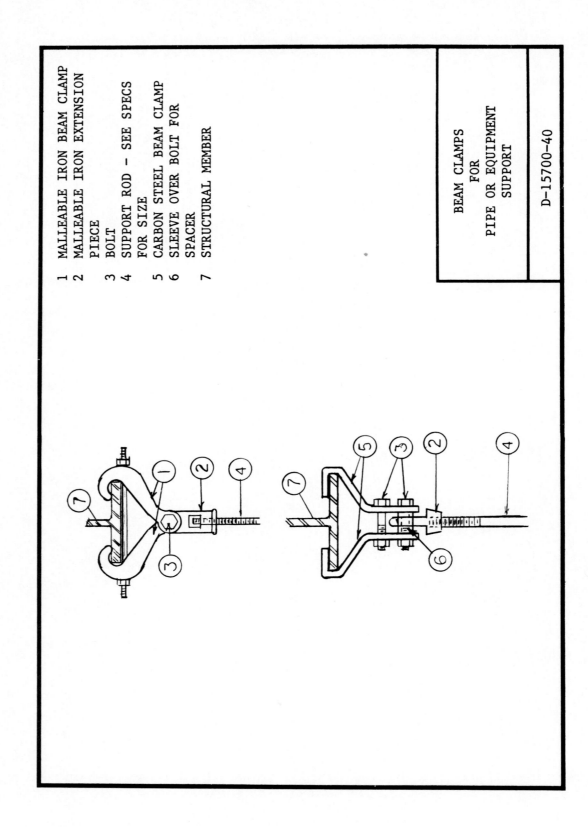

1 MALLEABLE IRON BEAM CLAMP
2 MALLEABLE IRON EXTENSION
   PIECE
3 BOLT
4 SUPPORT ROD – SEE SPECS
   FOR SIZE
5 CARBON STEEL BEAM CLAMP
6 SLEEVE OVER BOLT FOR
   SPACER
7 STRUCTURAL MEMBER

BEAM CLAMPS
FOR
PIPE OR EQUIPMENT
SUPPORT

D–15700–40

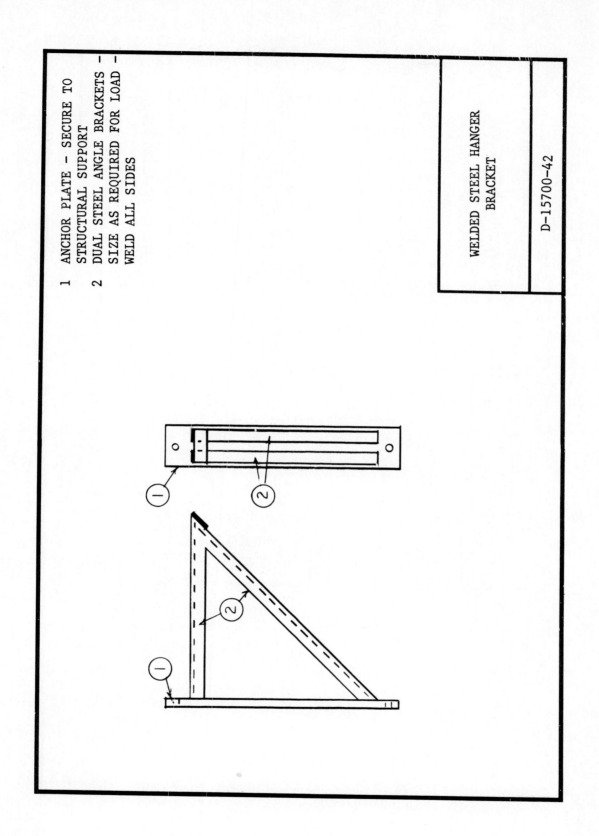

1 ANCHOR PLATE – SECURE TO
  STRUCTURAL SUPPORT
2 DUAL STEEL ANGLE BRACKETS –
  SIZE AS REQUIRED FOR LOAD –
  WELD ALL SIDES

WELDED STEEL HANGER
BRACKET

D–15700–42

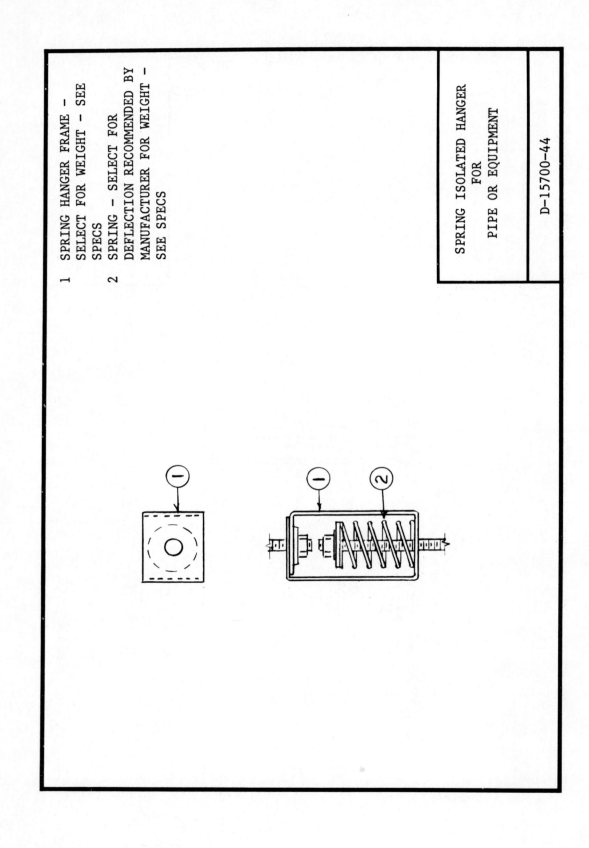

1 SPRING HANGER FRAME –
  SELECT FOR WEIGHT – SEE
  SPECS
2 SPRING – SELECT FOR
  DEFLECTION RECOMMENDED BY
  MANUFACTURER FOR WEIGHT –
  SEE SPECS

SPRING ISOLATED HANGER
FOR
PIPE OR EQUIPMENT

D–15700–44

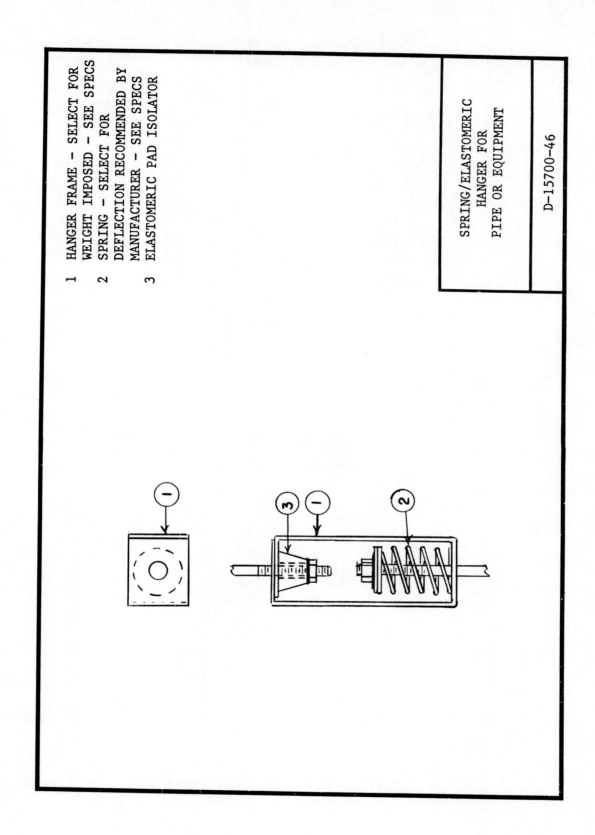

1 HANGER FRAME – SELECT FOR
   WEIGHT IMPOSED – SEE SPECS
2 SPRING – SELECT FOR
   DEFLECTION RECOMMENDED BY
   MANUFACTURER – SEE SPECS
3 ELASTOMERIC PAD ISOLATOR

SPRING/ELASTOMERIC
HANGER FOR
PIPE OR EQUIPMENT

D–15700–46

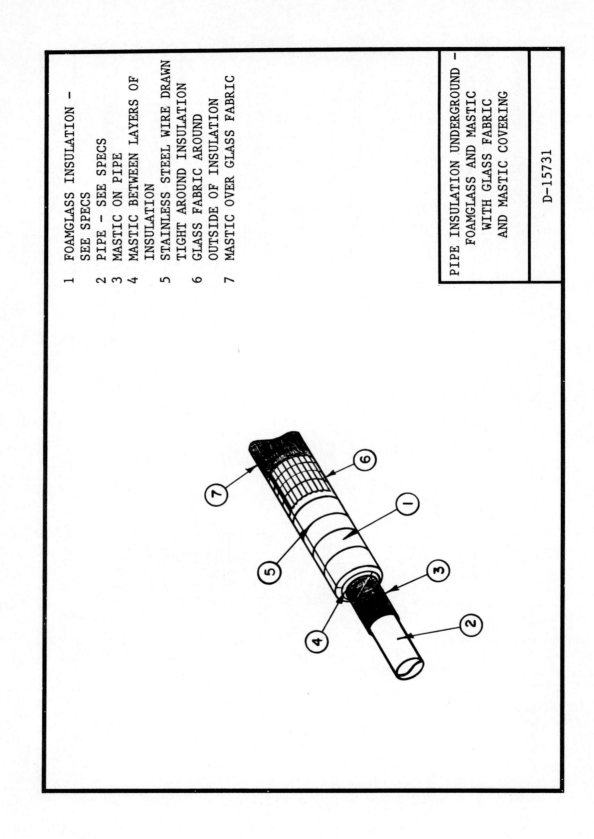

1. FOAMGLASS INSULATION – SEE SPECS
2. PIPE – SEE SPECS
3. MASTIC ON PIPE
4. MASTIC BETWEEN LAYERS OF INSULATION
5. STAINLESS STEEL WIRE DRAWN TIGHT AROUND INSULATION
6. GLASS FABRIC AROUND OUTSIDE OF INSULATION
7. MASTIC OVER GLASS FABRIC

PIPE INSULATION UNDERGROUND – FOAMGLASS AND MASTIC WITH GLASS FABRIC AND MASTIC COVERING

D-15731

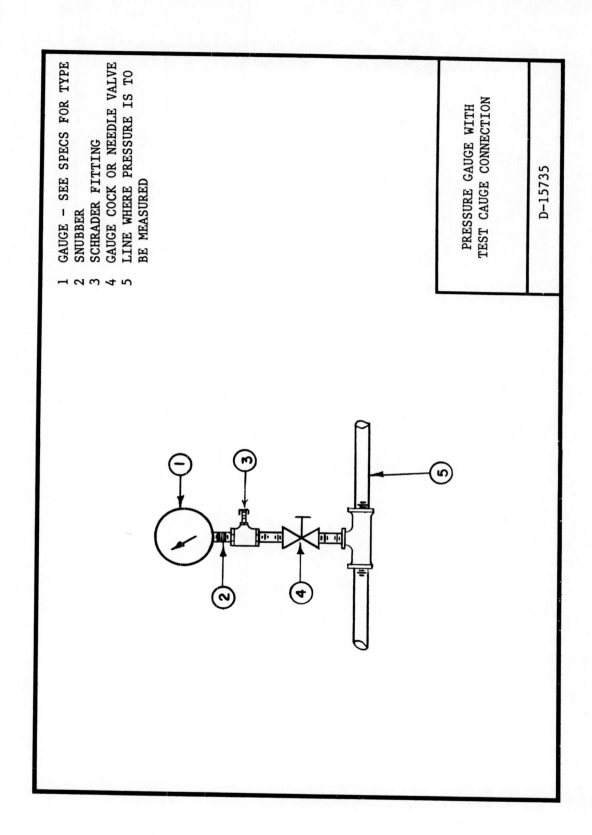

1 GAUGE – SEE SPECS FOR TYPE
2 SNUBBER
3 SCHRADER FITTING
4 GAUGE COCK OR NEEDLE VALVE
5 LINE WHERE PRESSURE IS TO
  BE MEASURED

PRESSURE GAUGE WITH
TEST GAUGE CONNECTION

D–15735

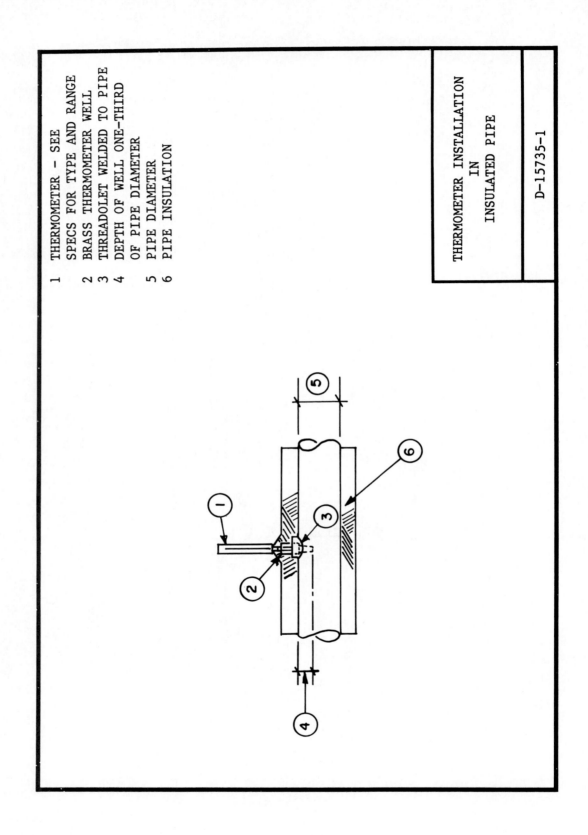

1 THERMOMETER – SEE
  SPECS FOR TYPE AND RANGE
2 BRASS THERMOMETER WELL
3 THREADOLET WELDED TO PIPE
4 DEPTH OF WELL ONE-THIRD
  OF PIPE DIAMETER
5 PIPE DIAMETER
6 PIPE INSULATION

THERMOMETER INSTALLATION
IN
INSULATED PIPE

D-15735-1

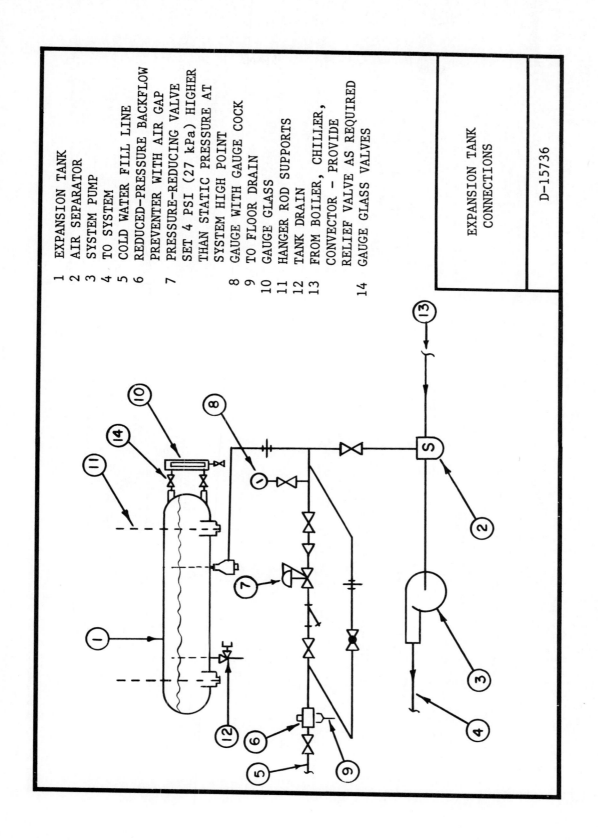

1 EXPANSION TANK
2 AIR SEPARATOR
3 SYSTEM PUMP
4 TO SYSTEM
5 COLD WATER FILL LINE
6 REDUCED-PRESSURE BACKFLOW
  PREVENTER WITH AIR GAP
7 PRESSURE-REDUCING VALVE
  SET 4 PSI (27 kPa) HIGHER
  THAN STATIC PRESSURE AT
  SYSTEM HIGH POINT
8 GAUGE WITH GAUGE COCK
9 TO FLOOR DRAIN
10 GAUGE GLASS
11 HANGER ROD SUPPORTS
12 TANK DRAIN
13 FROM BOILER, CHILLER,
   CONVECTOR - PROVIDE
   RELIEF VALVE AS REQUIRED
14 GAUGE GLASS VALVES

EXPANSION TANK
CONNECTIONS

D-15736

1. SEPARATOR BODY – SCH 80 PIPE
2. PIPE CAP EACH END – SCH 80
3. INLET STEAM PIPE – SCH 80
4. OUTLET PIPE – SCH 80
5. IMPACT AREA – BUILD UP WITH ABRASIVE RESISTANT WELD – 1/2" (13-MM) THICK
6. 1" (25.4-MM) CONDENSATE DISCHARGE
7. ONE INLET PIPE DIAMETER
8. 1" (25.4-MM) DRAIN TO FLOOR
9. FOR OPEN DRAIN, PROVIDE 45 DEG. ELL AWAY FROM OPERATOR
10. BALL VALVE – FULL DIAMETER
11. UNION OR FLANGE
12. F&T STEAM TRAP 300% MAXIMUM
13. FOUR HANGER EYES WITH RODS
14. REDUCING ELL – WELDED TO STEAM OUTLET

NOTE: ALL WELDS IN SEPARATOR BODY TO BE FULL THICKNESS OF PARENT METAL.

STEAM SEPARATOR – LOW– AND MEDIUM-PRESSURE STEAM (REMOVES MOISTURE AND TRASH) SHOP FABRICATED

D–15739

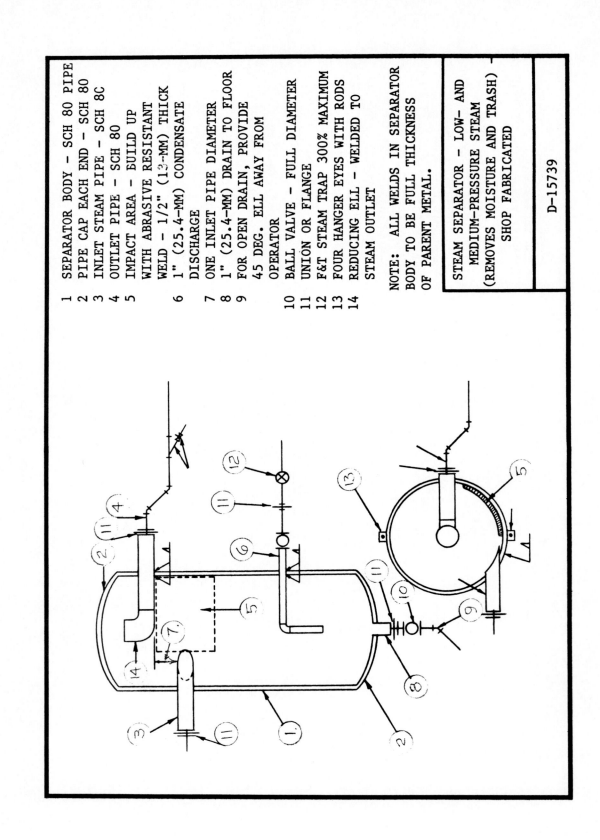

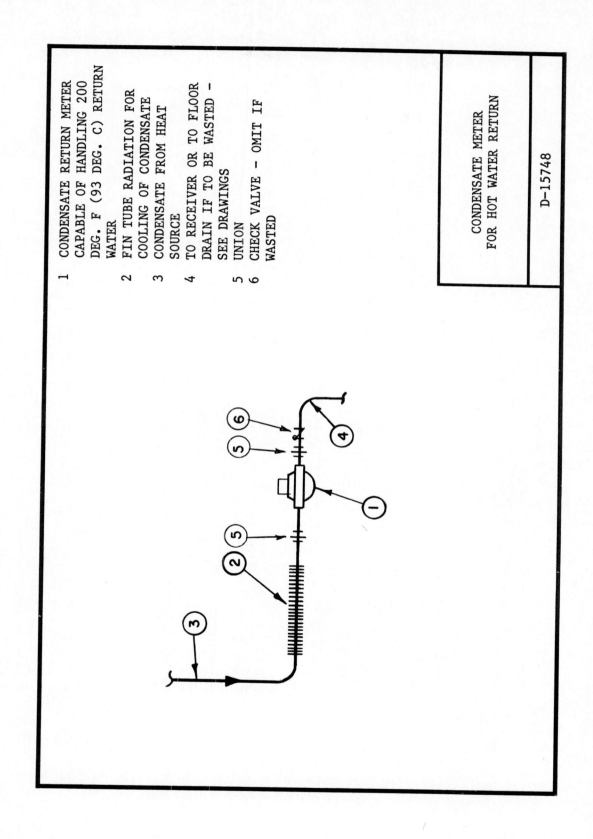

1 CONDENSATE RETURN METER CAPABLE OF HANDLING 200 DEG. F (93 DEG. C) RETURN WATER
2 FIN TUBE RADIATION FOR COOLING OF CONDENSATE
3 CONDENSATE FROM HEAT SOURCE
4 TO RECEIVER OR TO FLOOR DRAIN IF TO BE WASTED – SEE DRAWINGS
5 UNION
6 CHECK VALVE – OMIT IF WASTED

CONDENSATE METER
FOR HOT WATER RETURN

D-15748

CHAPTER 9

Pumps, Boilers, and Auxiliary Equipment

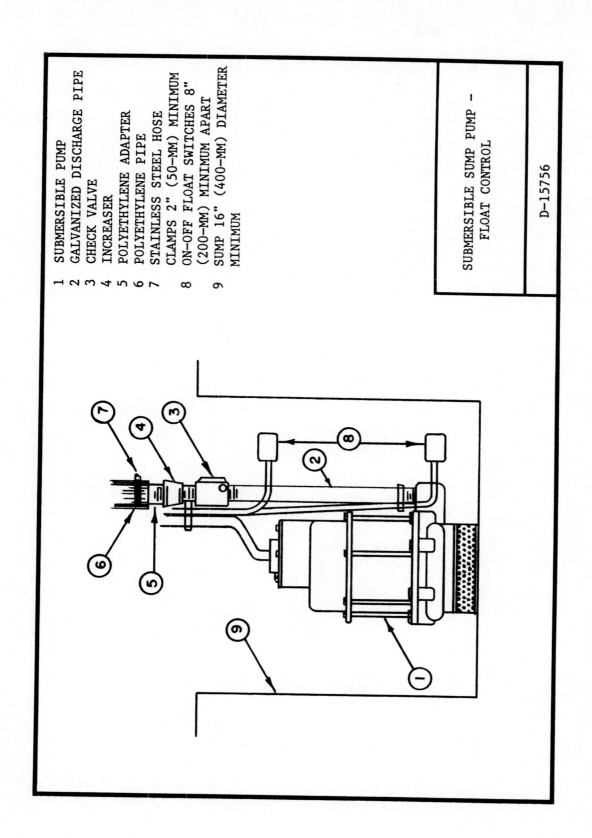

1 SUBMERSIBLE PUMP
2 GALVANIZED DISCHARGE PIPE
3 CHECK VALVE
4 INCREASER
5 POLYETHYLENE ADAPTER
6 POLYETHYLENE PIPE
7 STAINLESS STEEL HOSE
  CLAMPS 2" (50-MM) MINIMUM
8 ON-OFF FLOAT SWITCHES 8"
  (200-MM) MINIMUM APART
9 SUMP 16" (400-MM) DIAMETER
  MINIMUM

SUBMERSIBLE SUMP PUMP –
FLOAT CONTROL

D-15756

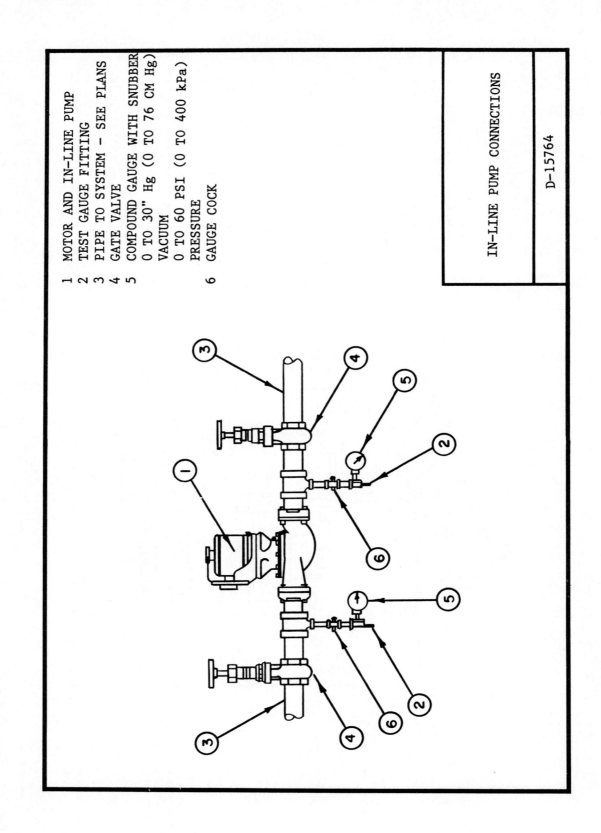

1 MOTOR AND IN-LINE PUMP
2 TEST GAUGE FITTING
3 PIPE TO SYSTEM – SEE PLANS
4 GATE VALVE
5 COMPOUND GAUGE WITH SNUBBER
  0 TO 30" Hg (0 TO 76 CM Hg)
  VACUUM
  0 TO 60 PSI (0 TO 400 kPa)
  PRESSURE
6 GAUGE COCK

IN-LINE PUMP CONNECTIONS

D–15764

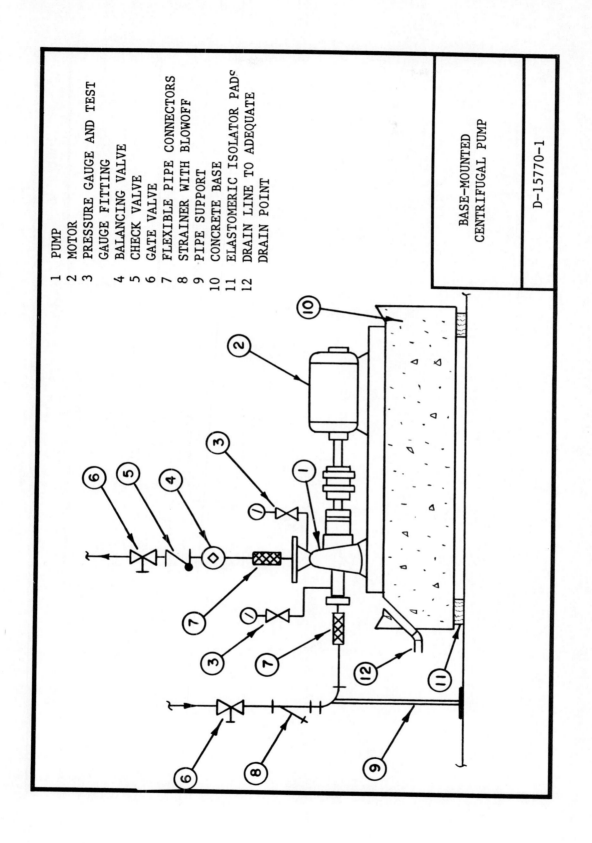

1 PUMP
2 MOTOR
3 PRESSURE GAUGE AND TEST
   GAUGE FITTING
4 BALANCING VALVE
5 CHECK VALVE
6 GATE VALVE
7 FLEXIBLE PIPE CONNECTORS
8 STRAINER WITH BLOWOFF
9 PIPE SUPPORT
10 CONCRETE BASE
11 ELASTOMERIC ISOLATOR PADS
12 DRAIN LINE TO ADEQUATE
   DRAIN POINT

BASE-MOUNTED
CENTRIFUGAL PUMP

D-15770-1

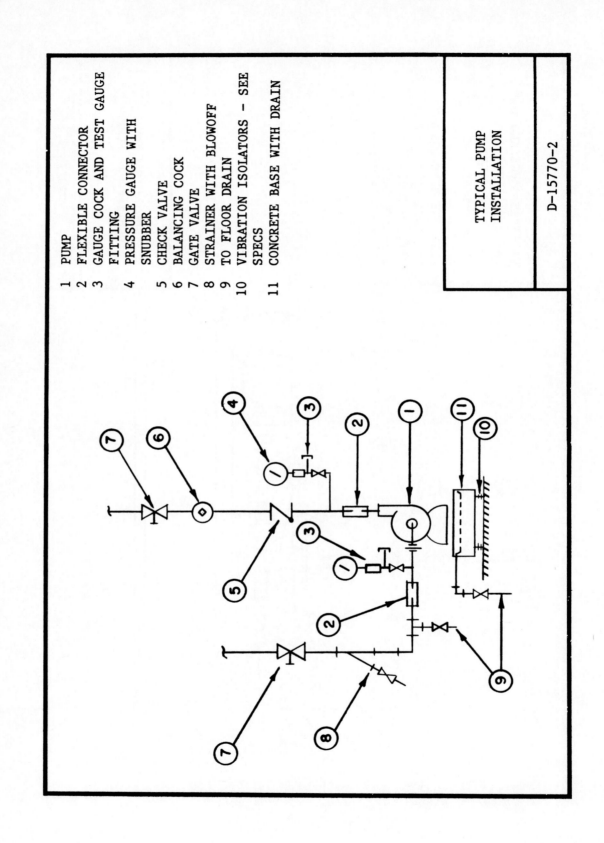

1 PUMP
2 FLEXIBLE CONNECTOR
3 GAUGE COCK AND TEST GAUGE
   FITTING
4 PRESSURE GAUGE WITH
   SNUBBER
5 CHECK VALVE
6 BALANCING COCK
7 GATE VALVE
8 STRAINER WITH BLOWOFF
9 TO FLOOR DRAIN
10 VIBRATION ISOLATORS – SEE
   SPECS
11 CONCRETE BASE WITH DRAIN

TYPICAL PUMP
INSTALLATION

D–15770–2

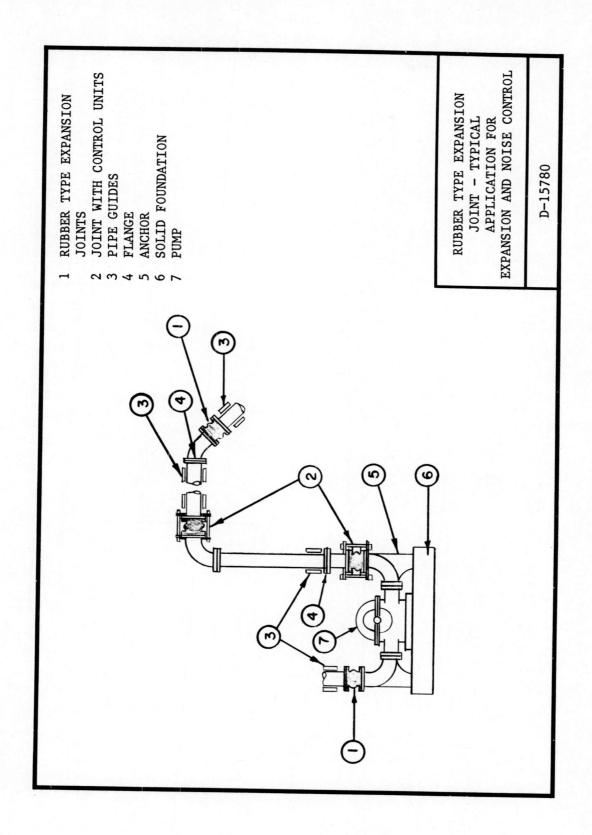

RUBBER TYPE EXPANSION JOINTS
1 JOINTS
2 JOINT WITH CONTROL UNITS
3 PIPE GUIDES
4 FLANGE
5 ANCHOR
6 SOLID FOUNDATION
7 PUMP

RUBBER TYPE EXPANSION JOINT – TYPICAL APPLICATION FOR EXPANSION AND NOISE CONTROL

D–15780

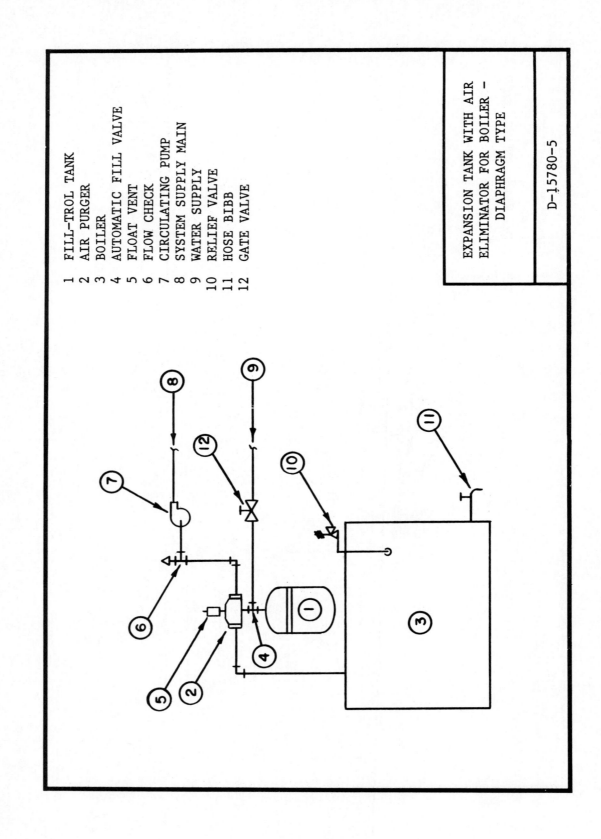

1 FILL-TROL TANK
2 AIR PURGER
3 BOILER
4 AUTOMATIC FILL VALVE
5 FLOAT VENT
6 FLOW CHECK
7 CIRCULATING PUMP
8 SYSTEM SUPPLY MAIN
9 WATER SUPPLY
10 RELIEF VALVE
11 HOSE BIBB
12 GATE VALVE

EXPANSION TANK WITH AIR
ELIMINATOR FOR BOILER –
DIAPHRAGM TYPE

D-15780-5

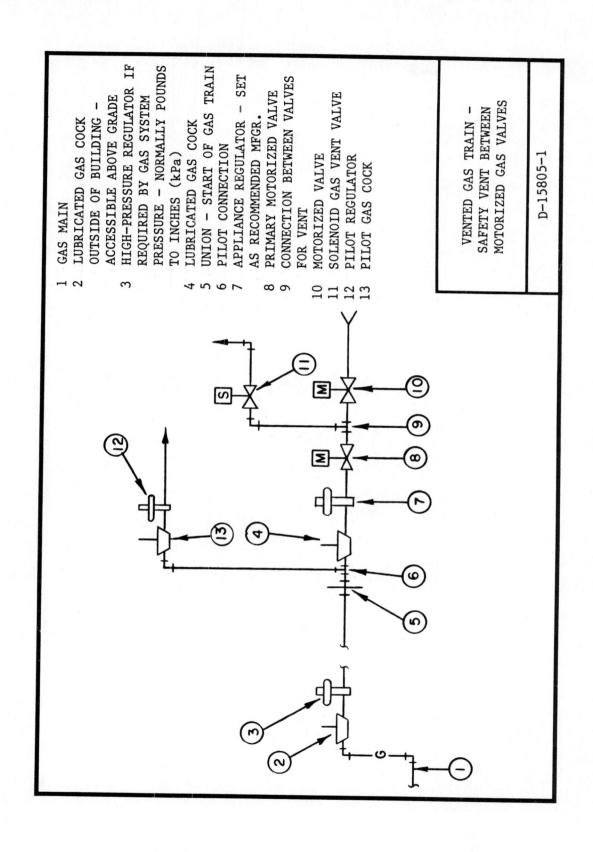

1 GAS MAIN
2 LUBRICATED GAS COCK OUTSIDE OF BUILDING – ACCESSIBLE ABOVE GRADE
3 HIGH-PRESSURE REGULATOR IF REQUIRED BY GAS SYSTEM PRESSURE – NORMALLY POUNDS TO INCHES (kPa)
4 LUBRICATED GAS COCK
5 UNION – START OF GAS TRAIN
6 PILOT CONNECTION
7 APPLIANCE REGULATOR – SET AS RECOMMENDED MFGR.
8 PRIMARY MOTORIZED VALVE
9 CONNECTION BETWEEN VALVES FOR VENT
10 MOTORIZED VALVE
11 SOLENOID GAS VENT VALVE
12 PILOT REGULATOR
13 PILOT GAS COCK

VENTED GAS TRAIN – SAFETY VENT BETWEEN MOTORIZED GAS VALVES

D-15805-1

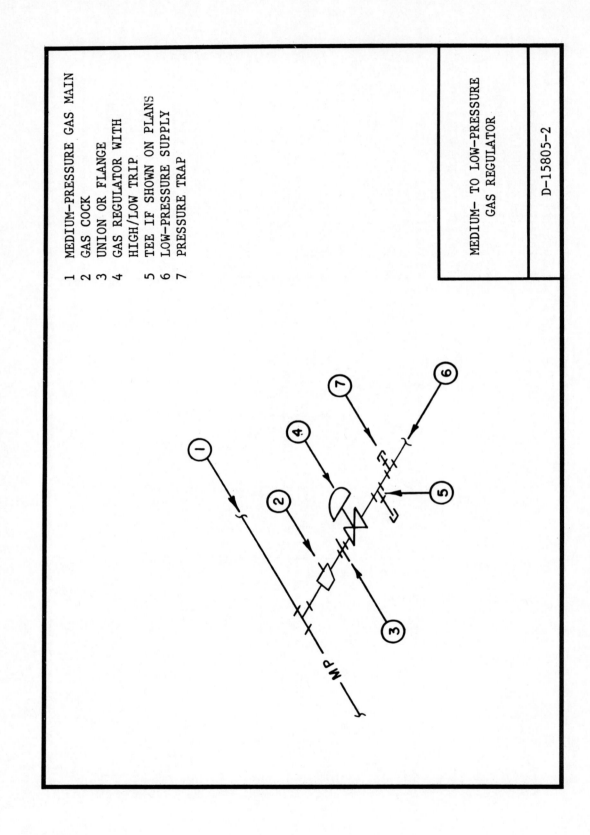

1 MEDIUM-PRESSURE GAS MAIN
2 GAS COCK
3 UNION OR FLANGE
4 GAS REGULATOR WITH
   HIGH/LOW TRIP
5 TEE IF SHOWN ON PLANS
6 LOW-PRESSURE SUPPLY
7 PRESSURE TRAP

MEDIUM- TO LOW-PRESSURE
GAS REGULATOR

D-15805-2

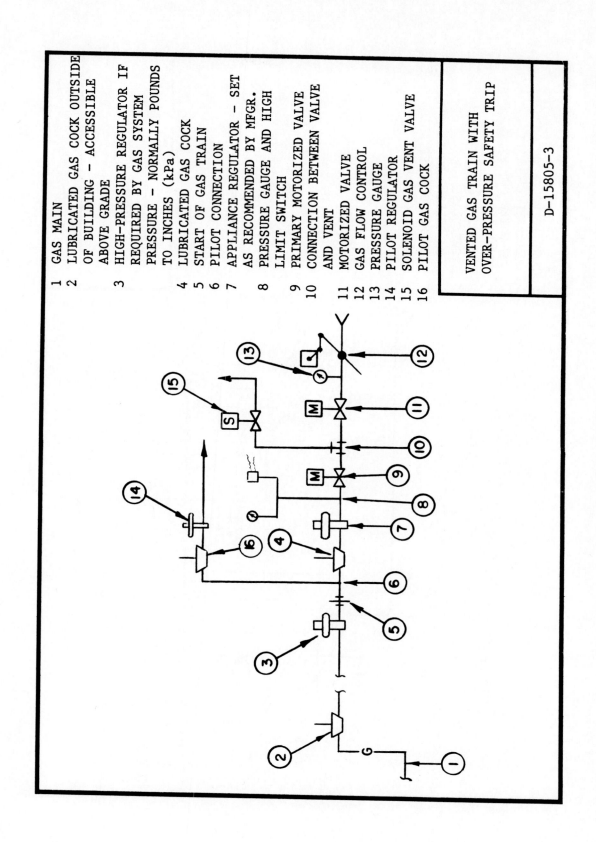

1 GAS MAIN
2 LUBRICATED GAS COCK OUTSIDE OF BUILDING – ACCESSIBLE ABOVE GRADE
3 HIGH-PRESSURE REGULATOR IF REQUIRED BY GAS SYSTEM PRESSURE – NORMALLY POUNDS TO INCHES (kPa)
4 LUBRICATED GAS COCK
5 START OF GAS TRAIN
6 PILOT CONNECTION
7 APPLIANCE REGULATOR – SET AS RECOMMENDED BY MFGR.
8 PRESSURE GAUGE AND HIGH LIMIT SWITCH
9 PRIMARY MOTORIZED VALVE
10 CONNECTION BETWEEN VALVE AND VENT
11 MOTORIZED VALVE
12 GAS FLOW CONTROL
13 PRESSURE GAUGE
14 PILOT REGULATOR
15 SOLENOID GAS VENT VALVE
16 PILOT GAS COCK

VENTED GAS TRAIN WITH
OVER-PRESSURE SAFETY TRIP

D-15805-3

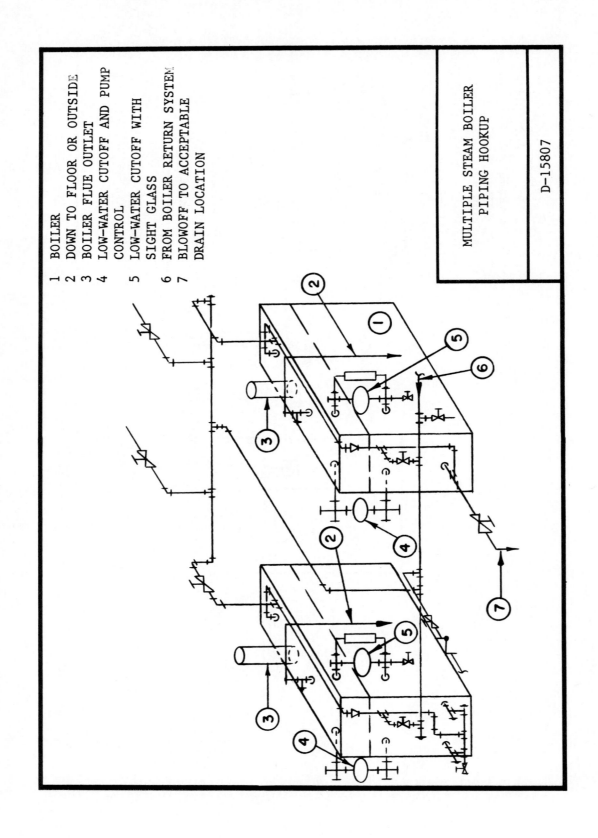

1 BOILER
2 DOWN TO FLOOR OR OUTSIDE
3 BOILER FLUE OUTLET
4 LOW-WATER CUTOFF AND PUMP
   CONTROL
5 LOW-WATER CUTOFF WITH
   SIGHT GLASS
6 FROM BOILER RETURN SYSTEM
7 BLOWOFF TO ACCEPTABLE
   DRAIN LOCATION

MULTIPLE STEAM BOILER
PIPING HOOKUP

D-15807

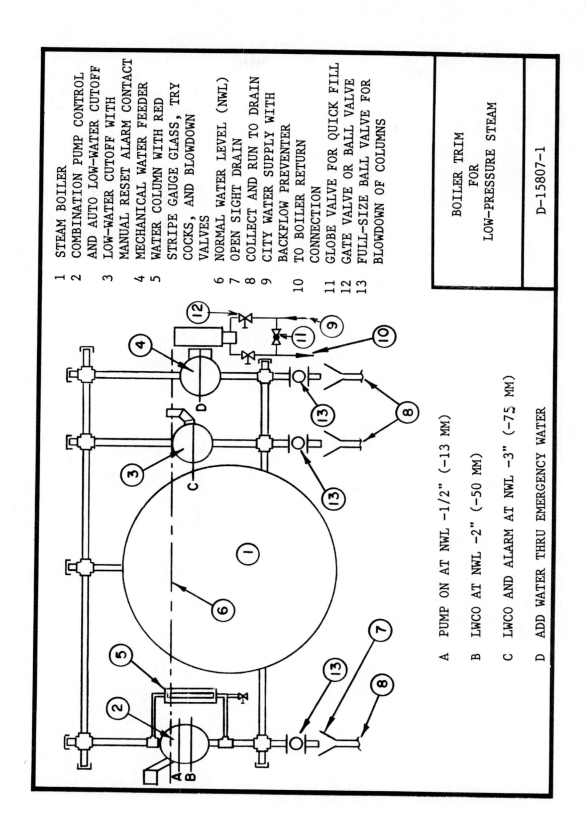

1 STEAM BOILER
2 COMBINATION PUMP CONTROL AND AUTO LOW-WATER CUTOFF
3 LOW-WATER CUTOFF WITH MANUAL RESET ALARM CONTACT
4 MECHANICAL WATER FEEDER
5 WATER COLUMN WITH RED STRIPE GAUGE GLASS, TRY COCKS, AND BLOWDOWN VALVES
6 NORMAL WATER LEVEL (NWL)
7 OPEN SIGHT DRAIN
8 COLLECT AND RUN TO DRAIN
9 CITY WATER SUPPLY WITH BACKFLOW PREVENTER
10 TO BOILER RETURN CONNECTION
11 GLOBE VALVE FOR QUICK FILL
12 GATE VALVE OR BALL VALVE
13 FULL-SIZE BALL VALVE FOR BLOWDOWN OF COLUMNS

A PUMP ON AT NWL –1/2" (–13 MM)

B LWCO AT NWL –2" (–50 MM)

C LWCO AND ALARM AT NWL –3" (–75 MM)

D ADD WATER THRU EMERGENCY WATER

BOILER TRIM
FOR
LOW-PRESSURE STEAM

D-15807-1

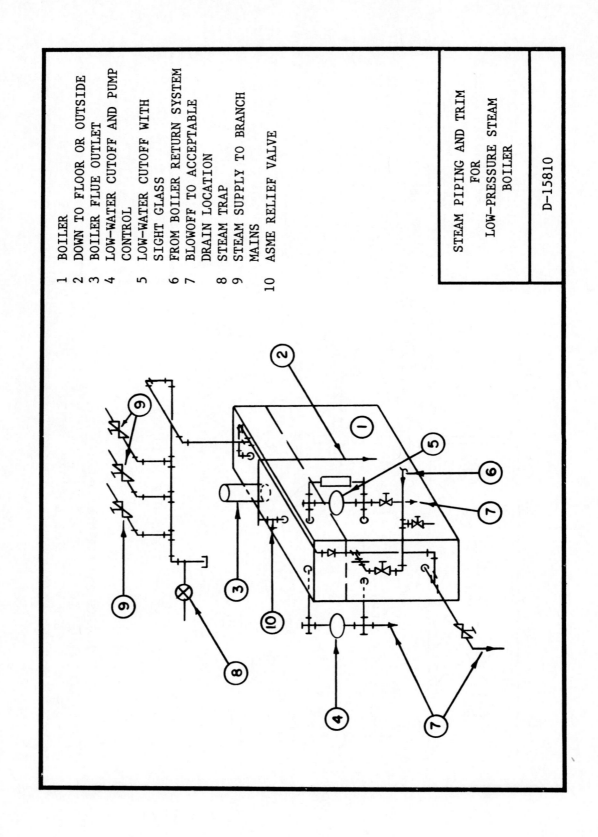

1 BOILER
2 DOWN TO FLOOR OR OUTSIDE
3 BOILER FLUE OUTLET
4 LOW-WATER CUTOFF AND PUMP
   CONTROL
5 LOW-WATER CUTOFF WITH
   SIGHT GLASS
6 FROM BOILER RETURN SYSTEM
7 BLOWOFF TO ACCEPTABLE
   DRAIN LOCATION
8 STEAM TRAP
9 STEAM SUPPLY TO BRANCH
   MAINS
10 ASME RELIEF VALVE

STEAM PIPING AND TRIM
FOR
LOW-PRESSURE STEAM
BOILER

D-15810

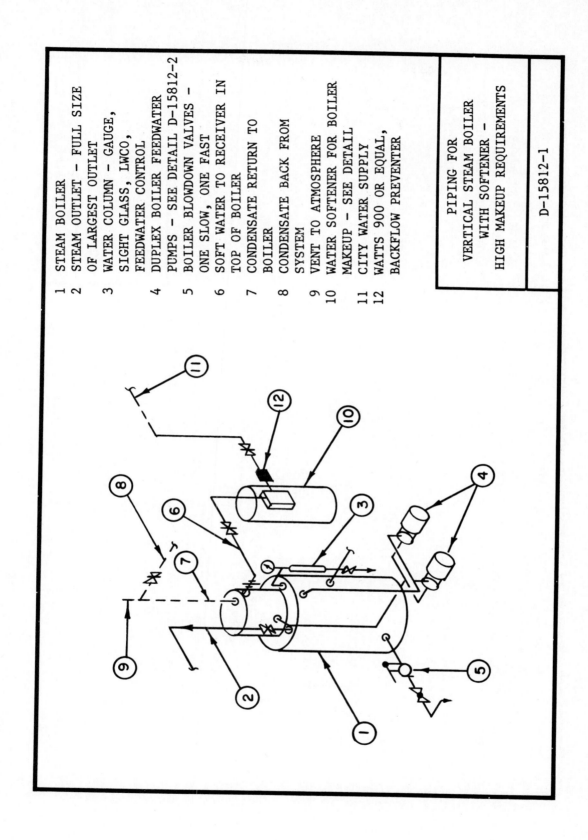

1. STEAM BOILER
2. STEAM OUTLET – FULL SIZE OF LARGEST OUTLET
3. WATER COLUMN – GAUGE, SIGHT GLASS, LWCO, FEEDWATER CONTROL
4. DUPLEX BOILER FEEDWATER PUMPS – SEE DETAIL D–15812–2
5. BOILER BLOWDOWN VALVES – ONE SLOW, ONE FAST
6. SOFT WATER TO RECEIVER IN TOP OF BOILER
7. CONDENSATE RETURN TO BOILER
8. CONDENSATE BACK FROM SYSTEM
9. VENT TO ATMOSPHERE
10. WATER SOFTENER FOR BOILER MAKEUP – SEE DETAIL
11. CITY WATER SUPPLY
12. WATTS 900 OR EQUAL, BACKFLOW PREVENTER

PIPING FOR
VERTICAL STEAM BOILER
WITH SOFTENER –
HIGH MAKEUP REQUIREMENTS

D–15812–1

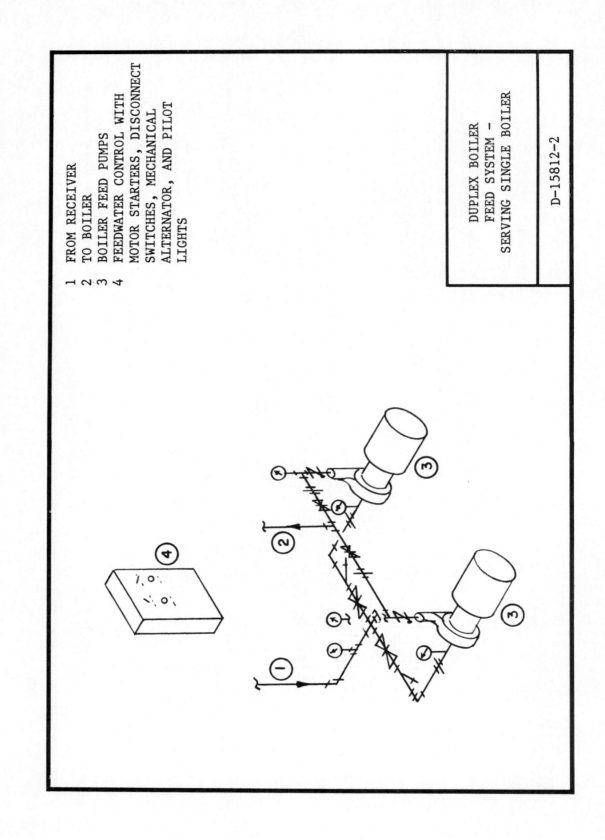

1 FROM RECEIVER
2 TO BOILER
3 BOILER FEED PUMPS
4 FEEDWATER CONTROL WITH
  MOTOR STARTERS, DISCONNECT
  SWITCHES, MECHANICAL
  ALTERNATOR, AND PILOT
  LIGHTS

DUPLEX BOILER
FEED SYSTEM –
SERVING SINGLE BOILER

D–15812–2

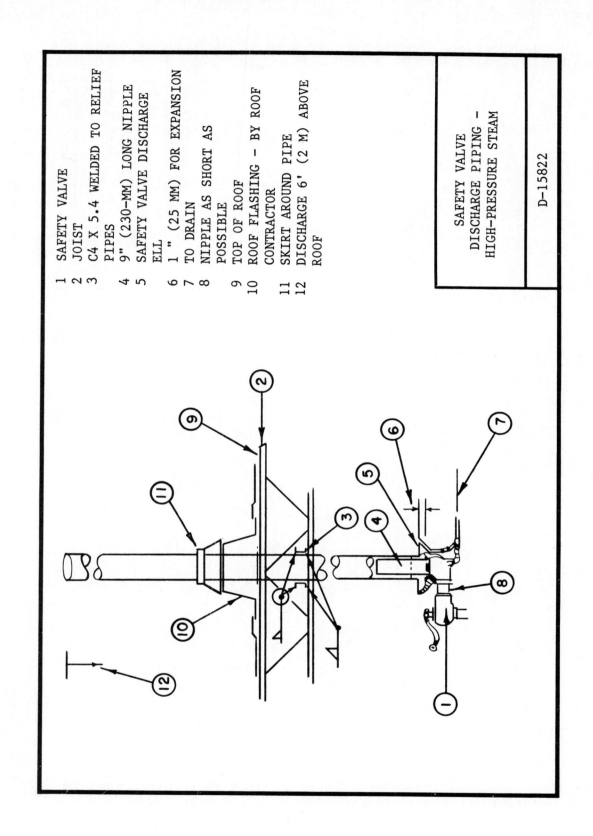

1 SAFETY VALVE
2 JOIST
3 C4 X 5.4 WELDED TO RELIEF PIPES
4 9" (230-MM) LONG NIPPLE
5 SAFETY VALVE DISCHARGE ELL
6 1 " (25 MM) FOR EXPANSION
7 TO DRAIN
8 NIPPLE AS SHORT AS POSSIBLE
9 TOP OF ROOF
10 ROOF FLASHING - BY ROOF CONTRACTOR
11 SKIRT AROUND PIPE
12 DISCHARGE 6' (2 M) ABOVE ROOF

SAFETY VALVE
DISCHARGE PIPING -
HIGH-PRESSURE STEAM

D-15822

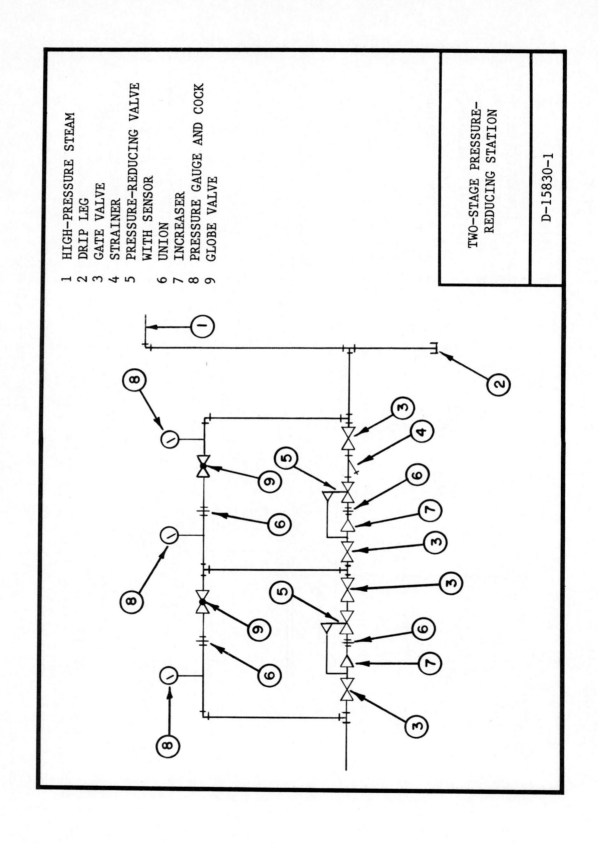

1 HIGH-PRESSURE STEAM
2 DRIP LEG
3 GATE VALVE
4 STRAINER
5 PRESSURE-REDUCING VALVE
  WITH SENSOR
6 UNION
7 INCREASER
8 PRESSURE GAUGE AND COCK
9 GLOBE VALVE

TWO-STAGE PRESSURE-
REDUCING STATION

D-15830-1

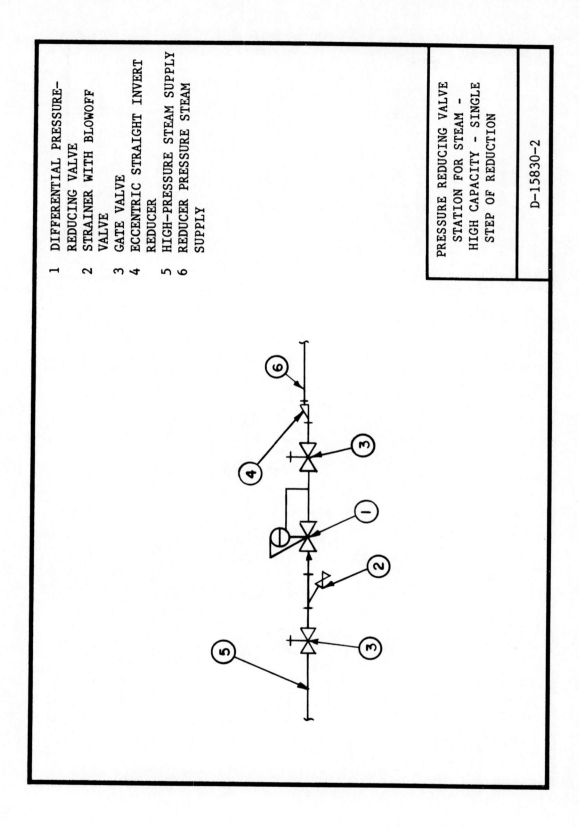

1 DIFFERENTIAL PRESSURE-
   REDUCING VALVE
2 STRAINER WITH BLOWOFF
   VALVE
3 GATE VALVE
4 ECCENTRIC STRAIGHT INVERT
   REDUCER
5 HIGH-PRESSURE STEAM SUPPLY
6 REDUCER PRESSURE STEAM
   SUPPLY

PRESSURE REDUCING VALVE
STATION FOR STEAM -
HIGH CAPACITY - SINGLE
STEP OF REDUCTION

D-15830-2

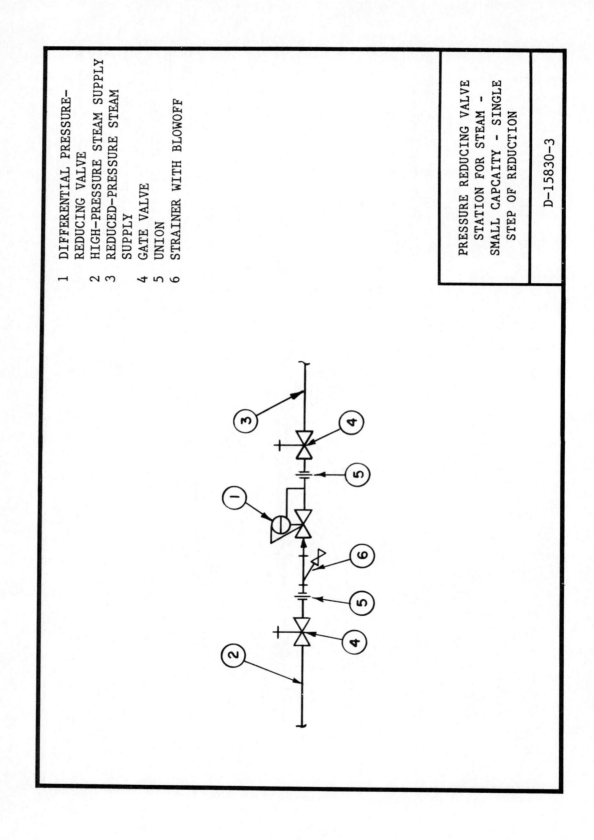

1 DIFFERENTIAL PRESSURE-
  REDUCING VALVE
2 HIGH-PRESSURE STEAM SUPPLY
3 REDUCED-PRESSURE STEAM
  SUPPLY
4 GATE VALVE
5 UNION
6 STRAINER WITH BLOWOFF

PRESSURE REDUCING VALVE
STATION FOR STEAM -
SMALL CAPCAITY - SINGLE
STEP OF REDUCTION

D-15830-3

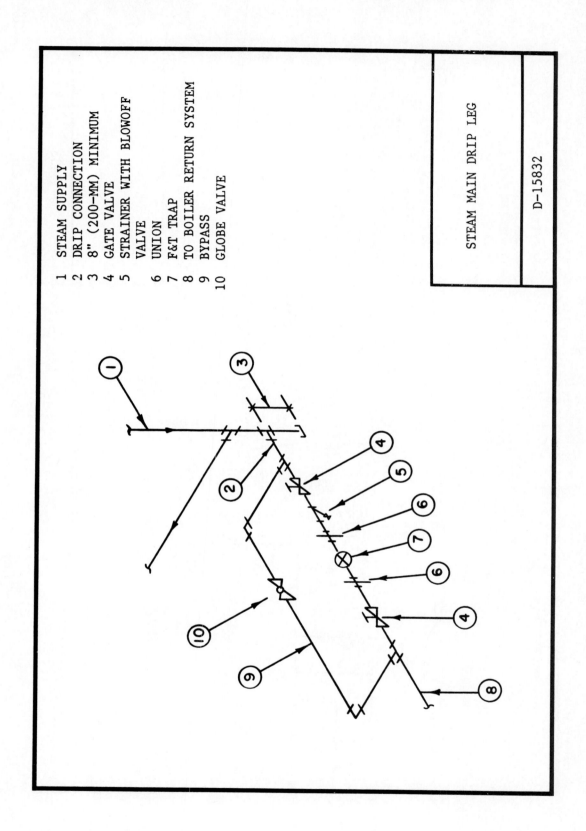

1 STEAM SUPPLY
2 DRIP CONNECTION
3 8" (200-MM) MINIMUM
4 GATE VALVE
5 STRAINER WITH BLOWOFF
   VALVE
6 UNION
7 F&T TRAP
8 TO BOILER RETURN SYSTEM
9 BYPASS
10 GLOBE VALVE

STEAM MAIN DRIP LEG

D-15832

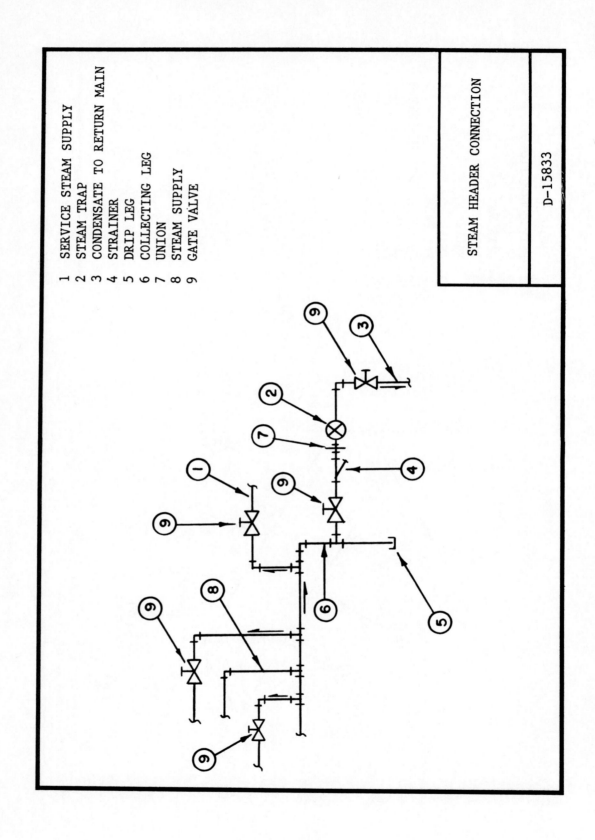

1 SERVICE STEAM SUPPLY
2 STEAM TRAP
3 CONDENSATE TO RETURN MAIN
4 STRAINER
5 DRIP LEG
6 COLLECTING LEG
7 UNION
8 STEAM SUPPLY
9 GATE VALVE

STEAM HEADER CONNECTION

D–15833

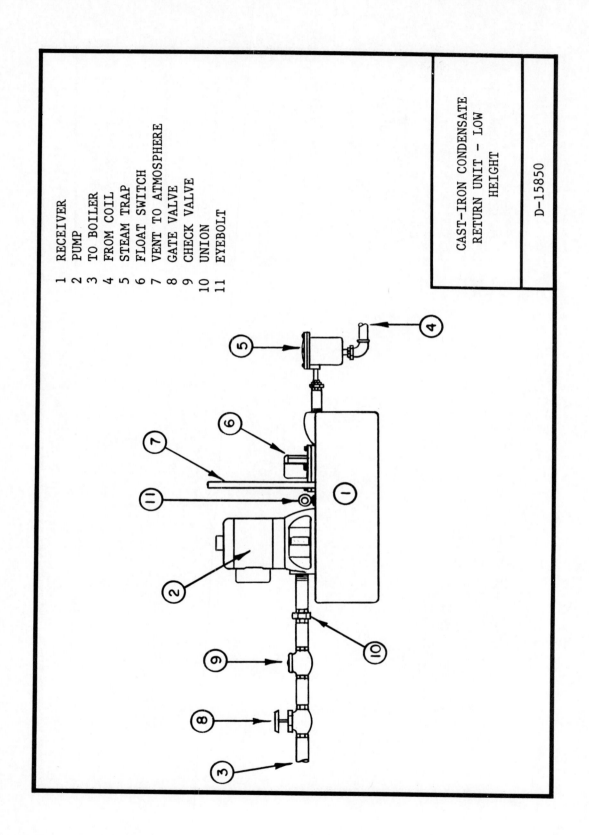

1 RECEIVER
2 PUMP
3 TO BOILER
4 FROM COIL
5 STEAM TRAP
6 FLOAT SWITCH
7 VENT TO ATMOSPHERE
8 GATE VALVE
9 CHECK VALVE
10 UNION
11 EYEBOLT

CAST-IRON CONDENSATE
RETURN UNIT – LOW
HEIGHT

D-15850

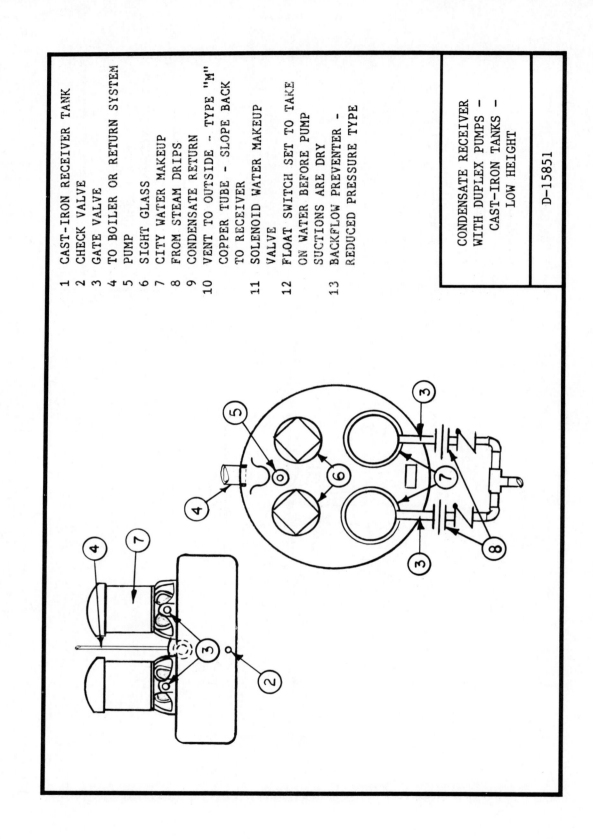

1 CAST-IRON RECEIVER TANK
2 CHECK VALVE
3 GATE VALVE
4 TO BOILER OR RETURN SYSTEM
5 PUMP
6 SIGHT GLASS
7 CITY WATER MAKEUP
8 FROM STEAM DRIPS
9 CONDENSATE RETURN
10 VENT TO OUTSIDE - TYPE "M"
   COPPER TUBE - SLOPE BACK
   TO RECEIVER
11 SOLENOID WATER MAKEUP
   VALVE
12 FLOAT SWITCH SET TO TAKE
   ON WATER BEFORE PUMP
   SUCTIONS ARE DRY
13 BACKFLOW PREVENTER -
   REDUCED PRESSURE TYPE

CONDENSATE RECEIVER
WITH DUPLEX PUMPS -
CAST-IRON TANKS -
LOW HEIGHT

D-15851

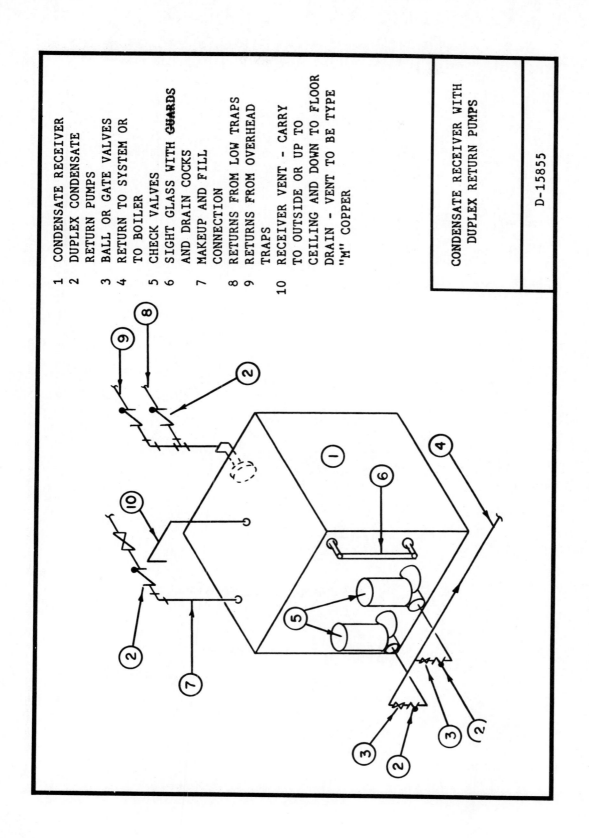

1 CONDENSATE RECEIVER
2 DUPLEX CONDENSATE
  RETURN PUMPS
3 BALL OR GATE VALVES
4 RETURN TO SYSTEM OR
  TO BOILER
5 CHECK VALVES
6 SIGHT GLASS WITH GUARDS
  AND DRAIN COCKS
7 MAKEUP AND FILL
  CONNECTION
8 RETURNS FROM LOW TRAPS
9 RETURNS FROM OVERHEAD
  TRAPS
10 RECEIVER VENT – CARRY
  TO OUTSIDE OR UP TO
  CEILING AND DOWN TO FLOOR
  DRAIN – VENT TO BE TYPE
  "M" COPPER

CONDENSATE RECEIVER WITH
DUPLEX RETURN PUMPS

D-15855

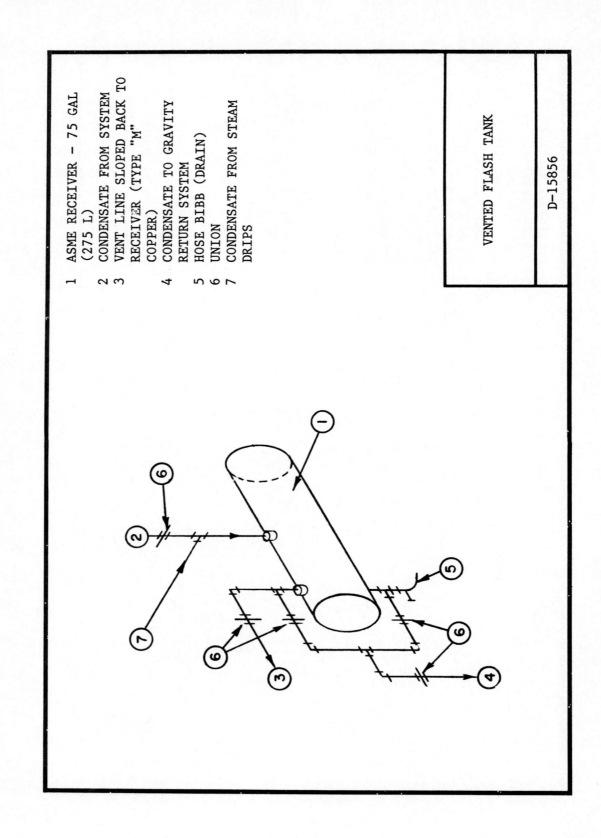

1 ASME RECEIVER – 75 GAL (275 L)
2 CONDENSATE FROM SYSTEM
3 VENT LINE SLOPED BACK TO RECEIVER (TYPE "M" COPPER)
4 CONDENSATE TO GRAVITY RETURN SYSTEM
5 HOSE BIBB (DRAIN)
6 UNION
7 CONDENSATE FROM STEAM DRIPS

VENTED FLASH TANK

D–15856

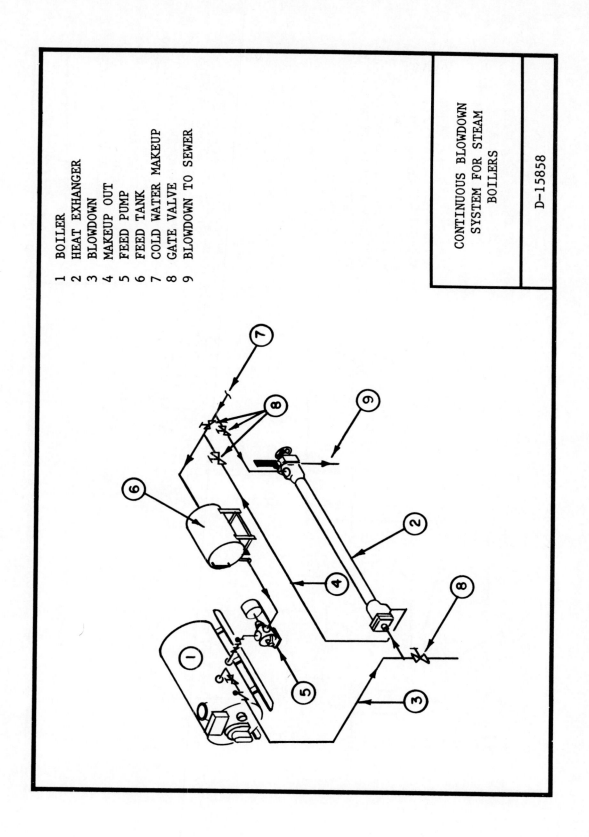

1 BOILER
2 HEAT EXHANGER
3 BLOWDOWN
4 MAKEUP OUT
5 FEED PUMP
6 FEED TANK
7 COLD WATER MAKEUP
8 GATE VALVE
9 BLOWDOWN TO SEWER

CONTINUOUS BLOWDOWN
SYSTEM FOR STEAM
BOILERS

D-15858

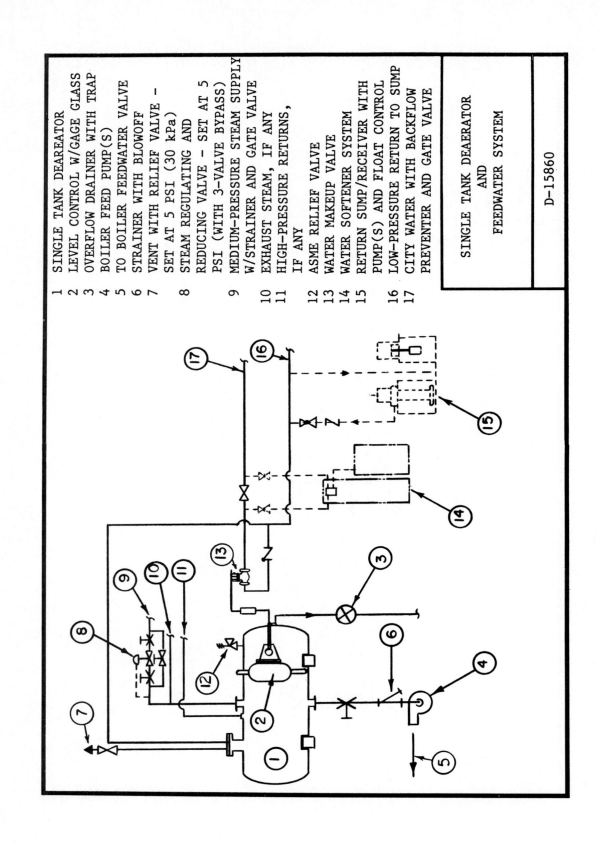

1   SINGLE TANK DEAERATOR
2   LEVEL CONTROL W/GAGE GLASS
3   OVERFLOW DRAINER WITH TRAP
4   BOILER FEED PUMP(S)
5   TO BOILER FEEDWATER VALVE
6   STRAINER WITH BLOWOFF
7   VENT WITH RELIEF VALVE –
    SET AT 5 PSI (30 kPa)
8   STEAM REGULATING AND
    REDUCING VALVE – SET AT 5
    PSI (WITH 3-VALVE BYPASS)
9   MEDIUM-PRESSURE STEAM SUPPLY
    W/STRAINER AND GATE VALVE
10 EXHAUST STEAM, IF ANY
11 HIGH-PRESSURE RETURNS,
    IF ANY
12 ASME RELIEF VALVE
13 WATER MAKEUP VALVE
14 WATER SOFTENER SYSTEM
15 RETURN SUMP/RECEIVER WITH
    PUMP(S) AND FLOAT CONTROL
16 LOW-PRESSURE RETURN TO SUMP
17 CITY WATER WITH BACKFLOW
    PREVENTER AND GATE VALVE

SINGLE TANK DEAERATOR
AND
FEEDWATER SYSTEM

D-15860

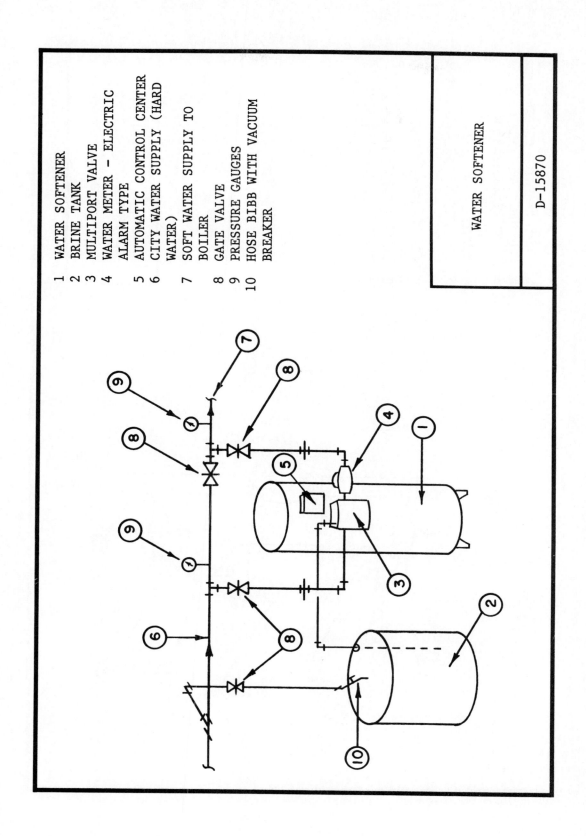

1 WATER SOFTENER
2 BRINE TANK
3 MULTIPORT VALVE
4 WATER METER – ELECTRIC
   ALARM TYPE
5 AUTOMATIC CONTROL CENTER
6 CITY WATER SUPPLY (HARD
   WATER)
7 SOFT WATER SUPPLY TO
   BOILER
8 GATE VALVE
9 PRESSURE GAUGES
10 HOSE BIBB WITH VACUUM
   BREAKER

WATER SOFTENER

D–15870

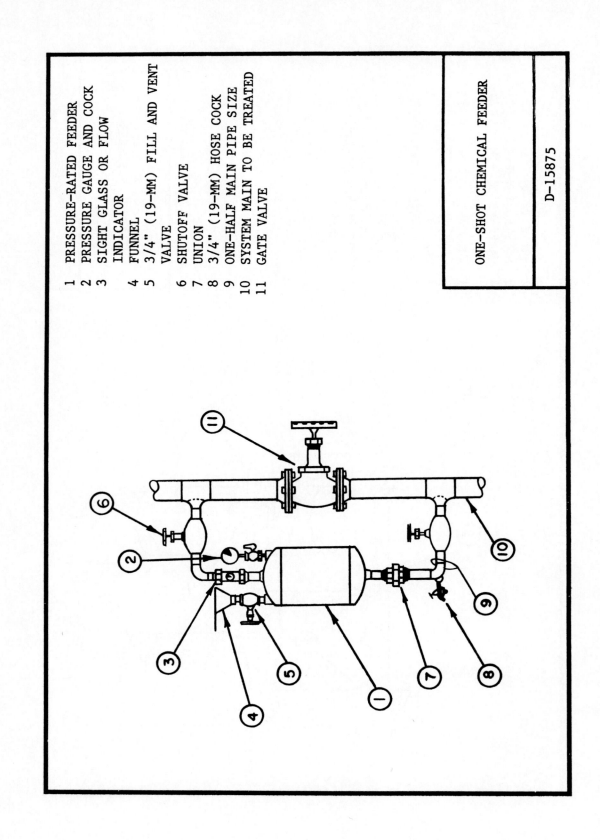

1 PRESSURE-RATED FEEDER
2 PRESSURE GAUGE AND COCK
3 SIGHT GLASS OR FLOW
   INDICATOR
4 FUNNEL
5 3/4" (19-MM) FILL AND VENT
   VALVE
6 SHUTOFF VALVE
7 UNION
8 3/4" (19-MM) HOSE COCK
9 ONE-HALF MAIN PIPE SIZE
10 SYSTEM MAIN TO BE TREATED
11 GATE VALVE

ONE-SHOT CHEMICAL FEEDER

D-15875

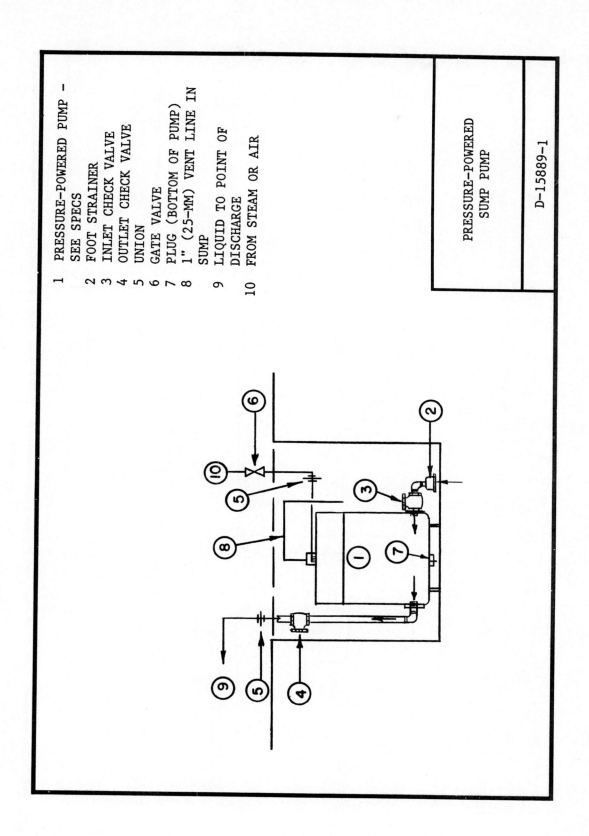

1 PRESSURE-POWERED PUMP – SEE SPECS
2 FOOT STRAINER
3 INLET CHECK VALVE
4 OUTLET CHECK VALVE
5 UNION
6 GATE VALVE
7 PLUG (BOTTOM OF PUMP)
8 1" (25-MM) VENT LINE IN SUMP
9 LIQUID TO POINT OF DISCHARGE
10 FROM STEAM OR AIR

PRESSURE-POWERED
SUMP PUMP

D-15889-1

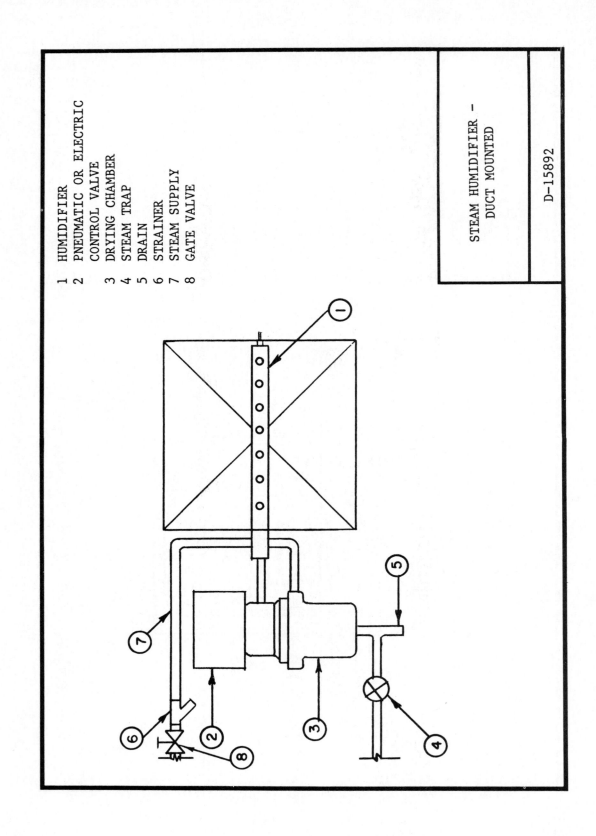

1 HUMIDIFIER
2 PNEUMATIC OR ELECTRIC
  CONTROL VALVE
3 DRYING CHAMBER
4 STEAM TRAP
5 DRAIN
6 STRAINER
7 STEAM SUPPLY
8 GATE VALVE

STEAM HUMIDIFIER –
DUCT MOUNTED

D–15892

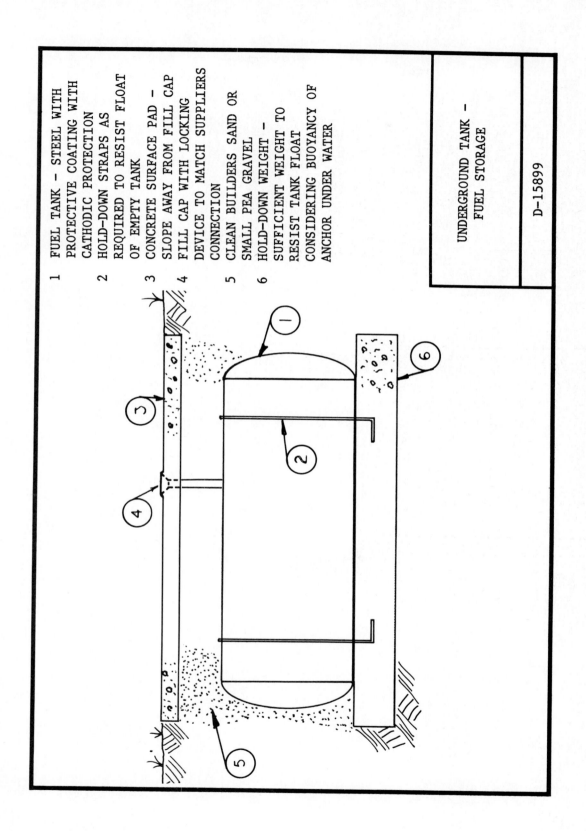

1 FUEL TANK – STEEL WITH
   PROTECTIVE COATING WITH
   CATHODIC PROTECTION
2 HOLD–DOWN STRAPS AS
   REQUIRED TO RESIST FLOAT
   OF EMPTY TANK
3 CONCRETE SURFACE PAD –
   SLOPE AWAY FROM FILL CAP
4 FILL CAP WITH LOCKING
   DEVICE TO MATCH SUPPLIERS
   CONNECTION
5 CLEAN BUILDERS SAND OR
   SMALL PEA GRAVEL
6 HOLD–DOWN WEIGHT –
   SUFFICIENT WEIGHT TO
   RESIST TANK FLOAT
   CONSIDERING BUOYANCY OF
   ANCHOR UNDER WATER

UNDERGROUND TANK –
FUEL STORAGE

D–15899

CHAPTER 10

Control Components

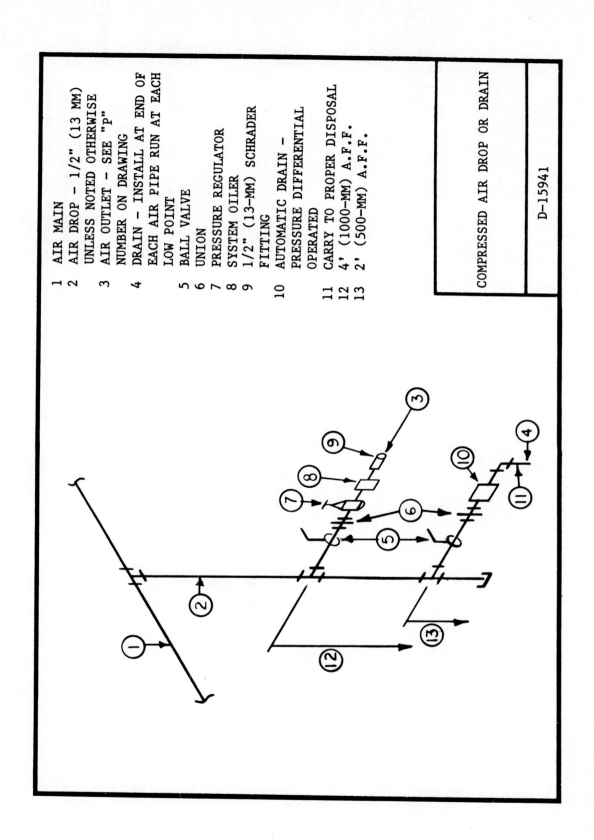

1 AIR MAIN
2 AIR DROP – 1/2" (13 MM)
  UNLESS NOTED OTHERWISE
3 AIR OUTLET – SEE "P"
  NUMBER ON DRAWING
4 DRAIN – INSTALL AT END OF
  EACH AIR PIPE RUN AT EACH
  LOW POINT
5 BALL VALVE
6 UNION
7 PRESSURE REGULATOR
8 SYSTEM OILER
9 1/2" (13–MM) SCHRADER
  FITTING
10 AUTOMATIC DRAIN –
   PRESSURE DIFFERENTIAL
   OPERATED
11 CARRY TO PROPER DISPOSAL
12 4' (1000–MM) A.F.F.
13 2' (500–MM) A.F.F.

COMPRESSED AIR DROP OR DRAIN

D–15941

1 REMOTE BULB THERMOSTAT
2 CAPILLARY BULB
3 SUPPORT FOR CAPILLARY –
1/2" (13–MM) EMT CONDUIT
4 SUPPORTS IN DUCTWORK FOR
CONDUIT

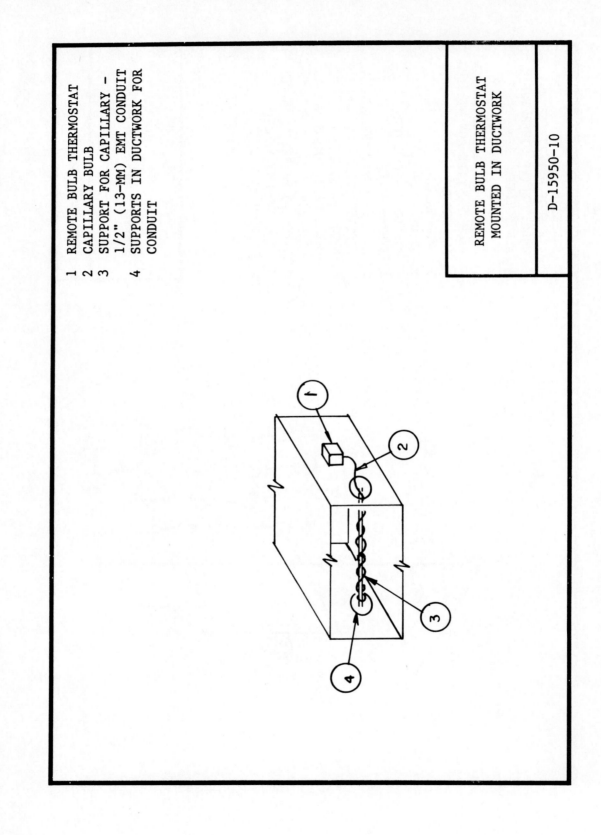

REMOTE BULB THERMOSTAT
MOUNTED IN DUCTWORK

D–15950–10

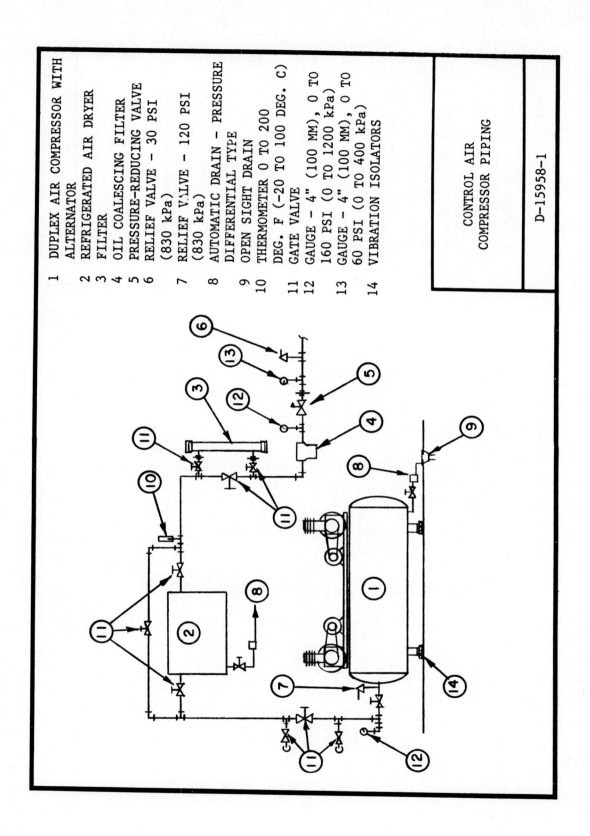

1 DUPLEX AIR COMPRESSOR WITH ALTERNATOR
2 REFRIGERATED AIR DRYER
3 FILTER
4 OIL COALESCING FILTER
5 PRESSURE-REDUCING VALVE
6 RELIEF VALVE – 30 PSI (830 kPa)
7 RELIEF VALVE – 120 PSI (830 kPa)
8 AUTOMATIC DRAIN – PRESSURE DIFFERENTIAL TYPE
9 OPEN SIGHT DRAIN
10 THERMOMETER 0 TO 200 DEG. F (-20 TO 100 DEG. C)
11 GATE VALVE
12 GAUGE – 4" (100 MM), 0 TO 160 PSI (0 TO 1200 kPa)
13 GAUGE – 4" (100 MM), 0 TO 60 PSI (0 TO 400 kPa)
14 VIBRATION ISOLATORS

CONTROL AIR
COMPRESSOR PIPING

D–15958–1

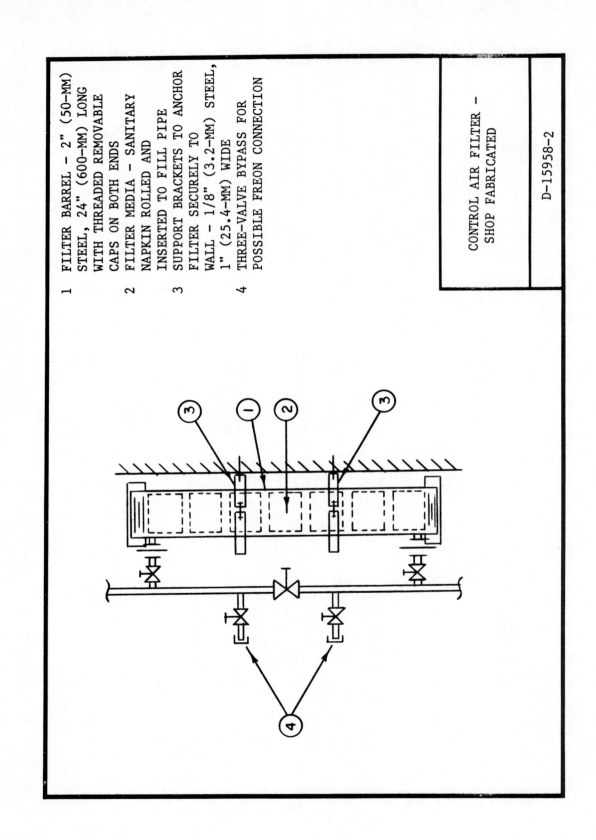

1 FILTER BARREL – 2" (50-MM) STEEL, 24" (600-MM) LONG WITH THREADED REMOVABLE CAPS ON BOTH ENDS

2 FILTER MEDIA – SANITARY NAPKIN ROLLED AND INSERTED TO FILL PIPE

3 SUPPORT BRACKETS TO ANCHOR FILTER SECURELY TO WALL – 1/8" (3.2-MM) STEEL, 1" (25.4-MM) WIDE

4 THREE-VALVE BYPASS FOR POSSIBLE FREON CONNECTION

CONTROL AIR FILTER – SHOP FABRICATED

D-15958-2

CHAPTER 11

Schedules

11-14	CEILING-MOUNTED CENTRIFUGAL FANS	AIR QUANTITY, STATIC, AND POWER REQUIRED
11-15	FAN, LIGHT, HEATER COMBINATION	AIR QUANTITY, STATIC, AND POWER REQUIRED
11-16	CABINET FANS	AIR QUANTITY, STATIC, AND POWER REQUIRED
11-17	IN-LINE CENTRIFUGAL FANS	AIR QUANTITY, STATIC, AND POWER REQUIRED
11-18	WALL-MOUNTED EXHAUST FANS	AIR QUANTITY, STATIC, AND POWER REQUIRED
11-19	ROOF-MOUNTED PROPELLER FANS	AIR QUANTITY, STATIC, AND POWER REQUIRED
11-20	ROOF-MOUNTED CENTRIFUGAL EXHAUST FANS	AIR QUANTITY, STATIC, AND POWER REQUIRED
11-21	ROOF VENTILATORS-PROPELLER TYPE-VERTICAL SHAFT	AIR QUANTITY, STATIC, AND POWER REQUIRED
11-22	HOOD EXHAUST FANS	AIR QUANTITY, STATIC, AND POWER REQUIRED
11-23	UTILITY VENT SETS	AIR QUANTITY, STATIC, AND POWER REQUIRED
11-24	UTILITY FANS CENTRAL AIR HANDLING SYSTEMS	AIR QUANTITY, STATIC, AND POWER REQUIRED
11-25	WALL-MOUNTED PROPELLER EXHAUST (SUPPLY) FANS	AIR QUANTITY, STATIC, AND POWER REQUIRED

CHILLER SCHUDULE

CHILLER NUMBER OR SYMBOL	NOMINAL CAPACITY TONS (WATTS)	EVAPORATOR						AUXILIARY EQUIPMENT	
		QUNATITY GPM (M³/S)	TEMP. ENTERING DEG F (C)	TEMP. LEAVING DEG F (C)	% GLYCOL MIXTURE	PRESSURE DROP FT WATER	NUMBER OF PASSES	FREE COOLING	VARIABLE SPEED DRIVE

CONDENSER					MOTOR				
QUANTITY GPM (M³/S)	TEMP. ENTERING DEG F (C)	TEMP. LEAVING DEG F (C)	PRESSURE DROP FT WATER	NUMBER OF PASSES	MAXIMUM POWER DRAW IN KW (DESIGN)	ALLOWABLE MAX. DRAW AT			VOLTAGE
						25%	50%	75%	100%

AIR HANDLING UNIT SCHEDULE

BLOWER SECTION (CONSTANT VOLUME)

UNIT NUMBER OR SYMBOL	SUPPLY AIR, CFM (M³/S)	EXTERNAL STATIC, IN WATER (PA)	OUTDOOR AIR, CFM (M³/S)			FAN		CASING		FILTERS			
			NORMAL (1)	MAX (2)	MIN (3)	TYPE (4)	MAX. HP	TYPE (5)	LOSS	PRE-FILTERS		FINAL	
										AREA	TYPE	AREA	TYPE

(1) OUTDOOR AIR OCCUPIED TIMES.
(2) OUTDOOR AIR FOR ECONOMIZER COOLING.
(3) OUTDOOR AIR DURING UNOCCUPIED TIMES.
(4) SUPPLY FAN TYPE AND CLASS.
(5) CASING TYPE (BU) BUILT-UP
          (MFG) MANUFACTURERED
          (BT) BLOW-THROUGH
          (DT) DRAW-THROUGH

AIR HANDLING UNIT SCHEDULE

BLOWER SECTION (VARIABLE AIR VOLUME)

UNIT NUMBER OR SYMBOL	SUPPLY AIR, CFM (M³/S)	EXTERNAL STATIC, IN WATER (PA)	OUTDOOR AIR, CFM (M³/S)			FAN (1)		CASING		FILTERS			
			NORMAL (2)	MAX (3)	MIN (4)	TYPE (5)	MAX. HP (WATTS)	TYPE (6)	LOSS	PRE-FILTERS		FINAL	
										AREA	TYPE	AREA	TYPE

(1) METHOD OF AIR QUANTITY VARIATION.
    (IV) INLET VANES
    (VS) VARIABLE SPEED FAN DRIVE

    TYPE OF DRIVE (VF) VARIABLE FREQUENCY
                 (VP) VARIABLE PITCH
                 (EC) EDDY CURRENT
                 (HC) HYDRAULIC CLUTCH

(2) OUTDOOR AIR OCCUPIED TIMES.
(3) OUTDOOR AIR FOR ECONOMIZER COOLING.
(4) OUTDOOR AIR DURING UNOCCUPIED TIMES.
(5) SUPPLY FAN TYPE AND CLASS.
(6) CASING TYPE (BU) BUILT-UP
               (MFG) MANUFACTURERED
               (BT) BLOW-THROUGH
               (DT) DRAW-THROUGH

AIR HANDLING UNIT SCHEDULE (CONTINUED)

COOLING COIL (WATER)

ENTERING DEG F (C)		LEAVING DEG F (C)		MAXIMUM FACE VELOCITY FT/MIN (M/S)	MAXIMUM STATIC PRESSURE DROP	CHILLED FLUID (WATER)					COIL CONSTRUCTION	
DB	WB	DB	WB			QUANTITY GPM (M³/S)	SUPPLY DEG F (C)	PRESSURE LOSS IN WATER	TEMP RISE DEG	GLYCOL %	ROWS	FINS PER FOOT

AIR HANDLING UNIT SCHEDULE (CONTINUED)

COOLING COIL (DX)

ENTERING DEG F (C)		LEAVING DEG F (C)		MAXIMUM FACE VELOCITY FT/MIN (M/S)	MAXIMUM STATIC PRESSURE DROP	REFRIGERANT		COIL CONSTRUCTION	
DB	WB	DB	WB			TYPE	SUCTION TEMP. DEG F (C)	ROWS	FINS PER FOOT

AIR HANDLING UNIT SCHEDULE (CONTINUED)

HEATING COIL (WATER)

ENTERING DEG F (C)	LEAVING DEG F (C)	MAXIMUM FACE VELOCITY FT/MIN (M/S)	MAXIMUM STATIC PRESSURE DROP	HEATING FLUID (WATER)						COIL CONSTRUCTION	
				QUANTITY GPM (M³/S)	SUPPLY DEG F (C)	FLUID PRESSURE DROP	PRESSURE LOSS IN WATER	TEMP. DROP DEG	GLYCOL %	ROWS	FINS PER FOOT

AIR HANDLING UNIT SCHEDULE (CONTINUED)

STEAM HEATING COIL

ENTERING DEG F (C)	LEAVING DEG F (C)	MAXIMUM FACE VELOCITY FT/MIN (M/S)	MAXIMUM STATIC PRESSURE DROP	STEAM SUPPLY		COIL CONSTRUCTION		TRAP		
				POUNDS/HR	SUPPLY PSIG (kPa)	ROWS	FINS PER FOOT	TYPE	ORIFICE SIZE	PRES. PSIG (kPa)

SCHEDULE OF ROOFTOP UNITS - ELECTRIC COOLING - GAS HEAT

UNIT NO. OR SYMBOL	AIR QUANTITY, CFM (M³/S)	EXTERNAL STATIC, IN WATER (MM WATER)	EVAP. FAN POWER, HP (WATTS)	NOMINAL TONS A.R.I.	HEATING OUTPUT REQD. (1)	SERVICE/ LOCATION	ECONOMIZER REQUIRED (2)	SUGGESTED MANUFACTURERS (SEE SPECIFICATIONS)	
								MAKE	MODEL

(1) NATURAL (LP GAS) FIRED, 80% NOMINAL EFFICIENCY, MBH (WATTS).
(2) ECONOMIZER FOR FRESH AIR COOLING TO BE FURNISHED WITH THE UNIT, COMPLETE WITH CONTROLS.

SCHEDULE OF ROOFTOP UNITS - ELECTRIC COOLING - ELECTRIC HEAT

UNIT NO. OR SYMBOL	AIR QUANTITY, CFM (M³/S)	EXTERNAL STATIC, IN WATER (MM WATER)	EVAP. FAN POWER, HP (WATTS)	NOMINAL TONS A.R.I.	HEATING OUTPUT REQD. (1)(2)	SERVICE/ LOCATION	ECONOMIZER REQUIRED (3)	SUGGESTED MANUFACTURERS (SEE SPECIFICATIONS)	
								MAKE	MODEL

(1) KW OF ELECTRIC RESISTANCE HEAT INCORPORATED IN THE UNIT AND SERVED FROM SAME POWER SOURCE AS THE UNIT.

(2) KW OF ELECTRIC RESISTANCE HEAT INCORPORATED IN THE UNIT OR IN ADJOINING DUCTWORK, AND SERVED FROM SEPARATE POWER SOURCE.

(3) ECONOMIZER FOR FRESH AIR COOLING TO BE FURNISHED WITH THE UNIT COMPLETE WITH CONTROLS.

SCHEDULE OF ROOFTOP UNITS - ELECTRIC COOLING ONLY

UNIT NO. OR SYMBOL	SUPPLY AIR QUANTITY, CFM (M³/S)	EXTERNAL STATIC, IN WATER (MM WATER)	EVAP. FAN POWER, HP (WATTS)	NOMINAL TONS A.R.I. (WATTS)	HEAT (1)	SERVICE/ LOCATION	ECONOMIZER REQUIRED (2)	SUGGESTED MANUFACTURER (SEE SPECIFICATIONS)	
								MAKE	MODEL

(1) SEE DRAWINGS FOR HEAT REQUIRED, IF ANY.
(2) ECONOMIZER FOR FRESH AIR COOLING SHALL BE FURNISHED WITH THE UNIT, COMPLETE WITH CONTROLS.

SCHEDULE OF ROOFTOP SINGLE-PACKAGED HEAT PUMPS - COMMON POWER SOURCE

UNIT NO. OR SYMBOL	SUPPLY AIR QUANTITY, CFM (M³/S)	EXTERNAL STATIC, IN WATER (MM WATER)	EVAP. FAN POWER, HP (WATTS)	NOMINAL TONS A.R.I. (WATTS)	HEAT OUTPUT (1)	SERVICE/ LOCATION	ECONOMIZER REQUIRED (2)	SUGGESTED MANUFACTURER (SEE SPECIFICATIONS)	
								MAKE	MODEL

(1) HEAT REQUIRED FROM THE UNIT AT STANDARD CONDITIONS OF 17 DEG DB/15 DEG WB WITH 70 DEG DB TO THE EVAPORATOR (-12 DEG DB/-13 DEG WB C.) AND AUXILIARY HEAT (KW) REQUIRED TO MEET THE HEATING DEMAND.

(2) ECONOMIZER FOR FRESH AIR COOLING TO BE FURNISHED WITH THE UNIT CMPLETE WITH CONTROLS.

SCHEDULE OF ROOFTOP SINGLE-PACKAGED HEAT PUMPS - SEPARATE POWER SOURCE

UNIT NO. OR SYMBOL	SUPPLY AIR QUANTITY, CFM (M³/S)	EXTERNAL STATIC, IN WATER (MM WATER)	EVAP. FAN POWER, HP (WATTS)	NOMINAL TONS A.R.I. (WATTS)	HEAT OUTPUT (1)	SERVICE/ LOCATION	ECONOMIZER REQUIRED (2)	SUGGESTED MANUFACTURER (SEE SPECIFICATIONS)	
								MAKE	MODEL

(1) HEAT REQUIRED FROM THE UNIT AT STANDARD CONDITIONS OF 17 DEG DB/15 DEG WB WITH 70 DEG DB TO THE EVAPORATOR (-12 DEG DB/-13 DEG WB C.) AND AUXILIARY HEAT (KW) REQUIRED TO MEET THE HEATING DEMAND.

(2) ECONOMIZER FOR FRESH AIR COOLING TO BE FURNISHED WITH THE UNIT CMPLETE WITH CONTROLS.

SCHEDULE OF THROUGH WALL HEATING AND COOLING UNITS - ELECTRIC COOLING - ELECTRIC HEAT

UNIT NO. OR SYMBOL	SUPPLY AIR QUATITY, CFM (N³/s)	COOLING CAPACITY, A.R.I.	HEATING CAPACITY, MBH	VOLTAGE/ PHASE	AUXILIARY EQUIP. (1)(2)(3) (4)	SERVICE LOCATION	SUGGESTED MANUFACTURERS (SEE SPECIFICATIONS)	

(1) ARCHITECTURAL CONDENSER COIL GRILLE.
(2) DECORATIVE CABINET FRONT.
(3) SUBBASE TO SUPPORT UNIT FOR CURTAIN WALL CONSTRUCTION.
(4) REMOTE CONTROLS FOR UNIT. SEE SPECIFICATIONS.

SCHEDULE OF CEILING-MOUNTED CENTRIFUGAL FANS

FAN NO. OR SYMBOL	AIR QUANTITY, CFM (M³/S)	EXTERNAL STATIC, IN WATER (MM WATER)	MOTOR POWER, HP (WATTS)	FAN RPM (TIP SPEED)		SERVICE/ LOCATION	CONTROLS (1)(2)(3) (4)(5)	SUGGESTED MANUFACTURERS (SEE SPECIFICATIONS)	
								MAKE	MODEL

(1) MANUAL VARIABLE SPEED CONTROL (ELECTRONIC).
(2) CONTROL WITH LIGHTS WITH OFF-TIME DELAY.
(3) PROVIDE "OFF-TIME" DELAY TIMER.
(4) MANUAL ON-OFF SWITCH (SEPARATE FROM LIGHTS).
(5) INTERLOCK WITH AIR SYSTEM SUPPLYING AREA.

SCHEDULE OF COMBINATION FAN, LIGHT, AND HEATER

FAN NO. OR SYMBOL	AIR QUANTITY, CFM (M³/S)	EXTERNAL STATIC, IN WATER (MM WATER)	MOTOR POWER, HP (WATTS)	LIGHT, WATTS	HEATER, WATTS	SERVICE/ LOCATION	CONTROLS (1)(2)(3)	SUGGESTED MANUFACTURERS (SEE SPECIFICATIONS)	
								MAKE	MODEL

(1) MANUAL SWITCHES FOR LIGHT, FAN, AND HEATER.
(2) CONTROL FAN WITH LIGHTS WITH "OFF-TIME" DELAY.
(3) PROVIDE "OFF-TIME" DELAY TIMER FOR FAN.

SCHEDULE OF CABINET FANS

FAN NO. OR SYMBOL	AIR QUANTITY, CFM (M³/S)	EXTERNAL STATIC, IN WATER (MM WATER)	MOTOR POWER, HP (WATTS)	FAN RPM (TIP SPEED)	NOISE LEVEL, SONES (dBA)	SERVICE/ LOCATION	CONTROLS (1)(2)(3) (4)	SUGGESTED MANUFACTURERS (SEE SPECIFICATIONS)	
								MAKE	MODEL

(1) MANUAL MOTOR STARTER - SEE DRAWING FOR LOCATION.
(2) MAGNETIC MOTOR STARTER WITH START/STOP STATION.
(3) INTERLOCK WITH SUPPLY AIR SYSTEM SERVING AREA.
(4) SEE SECTION ON CONTROLS FOR INTERLOCKING.

SCHEDULE OF IN·LINE CENTRIFUGAL FANS

FAN NO. OR SYMBOL	AIR QUANTITY, CFM (M³/S)	EXTERNAL STATIC, IN WATER (MM WATER)	MOTOR POWER, HP (WATTS)	FAN RPM (TIP SPEED)	NOISE LEVEL SONES dBA	SERVICE/ LOCATION	CONTROLS (1)(2)(3)(4)	SUGGESTED MANUFACTURERS (SEE SPECIFICATIONS)	
								MAKE	MODEL

(1) MANUAL MOTOR STARTER - SEE DRAWING FOR LOCATION.
(2) MAGNETIC MOTOR STARTER WITH START/STOP STATION.
(3) INTERLOCK WITH SUPPLY AIR SYSTEM SERVING AREA.
(4) SEE SECTION ON CONTROLS FOR INTERLOCKING.

SCHEDULE OF WALL-MOUNTED PROPELLER TYPE EXHAUST FANS

FAN NO. OR SYMBOL	AIR QUANTITY, CFM (M³/S)	EXTERNAL STATIC, IN WATER (MM WATER)	MOTOR POWER, HP (WATTS)	FAN RPM (TIP SPEED)	NOISE LEVEL, SONES dBA	SERVICE/ LOCATION	CONTROLS (1)(2)(3) (4)	SUGGESTED MANUFACTURERS (SEE SPECIFICATIONS)	
								MAKE	MODEL

(1) MANUAL MOTOR STARTER - SEE DRAWING FOR LOCATION.
(2) MAGNETIC MOTOR STARTER WITH START/STOP STATION.
(3) INTERLOCK WITH SUPPLY AIR SYSTEM SERVING AREA.
(4) SEE SECTION ON CONTROLS FOR INTERLOCKING CONTROLS.

SCHEDULE OF ROOF-MOUNTED PROPELLER TYPE EXHAUST FANS

FAN NO. OR SYMBOL	AIR QUANTITY, CFM (M³/S)	EXTERNAL STATIC, IN WATER (MM WATER)	MOTOR POWER, HP (WATTS)	FAN RPM (TIP SPEED)	NOISE LEVEL, SONES (dBA)	SERVICE/ LOCATION	CONTROLS (1)(2)(3)(4)	SUGGESTED MANUFACTURERS (SEE SPECIFICATIONS)	
								MAKE	MODEL

(1) MANUAL MOTOR STARTER - SEE DRAWING FOR LOCATION.
(2) MAGNETIC MOTOR STARTER WITH START/STOP STATION.
(3) INTERLOCK WITH SUPPLY AIR SYSTEM SERVING AREA.
(4) SEE SECTION ON CONTROLS FOR INTERLOCKING CONTROLS.

11-19

SCHEDULE OF EXHAUST FANS - ROOF MOUNTED - CENTRIFUGAL

FAN NO. OR SYMBOL	AIR QUANTITY, CFM (M³/S)	EXTERNAL STATIC, IN WATER (MM WATER)	MOTOR POWER, HP (WATTS)	FAN RPM (TIP SPEED)	DRIVE (B) BELT (D) DIRECT	SERVICE/ LOCATION	CONTROLS (1)(2)(3) (4)	SUGGESTED MANUFACTURERS (SEE SPECIFICATIONS)	
								MAKE	MODEL

(1) MANUAL MOTOR STARTER - SEE DRAWING FOR LOCATION.
(2) MAGNETIC MOTOR STARTER WITH START/STOP STATION.
(3) INTERLOCK WITH SUPPLY AIR SYSTEM SERVING AREA.
(4) SEE SECTION ON CONTROLS FOR INTERLOCKING CONTROLS.

SCHEDULE OF ROOF VENTILATORS - PROPELLER TYPE - VERTICAL SHAFT

FAN NO. OR SYMBOL	AIR QUANTITY, CFM (M³/S)	EXTERNAL STATIC, IN WATER (MM WATER)	MOTOR POWER, HP (WATTS)	FAN RPM (TIP SPEED)	DRIVE (B) BELT (D) DIRECT	SERVICE/ LOCATION	CONTROLS (1)(2)(3) (4)	SUGGESTED MANUFACTURERS (SEE SPECIFICATIONS)	
								MAKE	MODEL

(1) MANUAL MOTOR STARTER - SEE DRAWING FOR LOCATION.
(2) MAGNETIC MOTOR STARTER WITH START/STOP STATION.
(3) INTERLOCK WITH SUPPLY AIR SYSTEM SERVING AREA.
(4) SEE SECTION ON CONTROLS FOR INTERLOCKING CONTROLS.

SCHEDULE OF HOOD EXHAUST FANS

FAN NO. OR SYMBOL	AIR QUANTITY, CFM (M³/S)	EXTERNAL STATIC, IN WATER (MM WATER)	MOTOR POWER, HP (WATTS)	FAN RPM (TIP SPEED)	NOISE LEVEL, SONES (dBA)	SERVICE/ LOCATION	CONTROLS (1)(2)(3)(4)	SUGGESTED MANUFACTURERS (SEE SPECIFICATIONS)	
								MAKE	MODEL

(1) MANUAL MOTOR STARTER - SEE DRAWING FOR LOCATION.
(2) MAGNETIC MOTOR STARTER WITH START/STOP STATION.
(3) INTERLOCK WITH SUPPLY AIR SYSTEM SERVING AREA.
(4) SEE SECTION ON CONTROLS FOR INTERLOCKING CONTROLS.

SCHEDULE OF UTILITY VENT SETS

FAN NO. OR SYMBOL	AIR QUANTITY, CFM (M³/S)	EXTERNAL STATIC, IN WATER (MM WATER)	MOTOR POWER, HP (WATTS)	FAN RPM (TIP SPEED)	DRIVE (B) BELT (D) DIRECT	SERVICE/ LOCATION	CONTROLS (1)(2)(3) (4)	SUGGESTED MANUFACTURERS (SEE SPECIFICATIONS)	
								MAKE	MODEL

(1) MANUAL MOTOR STARTER - SEE DRAWING FOR LOCATION.
(2) MAGNETIC MOTOR STARTER WITH START/STOP STATION.
(3) INTERLOCK WITH SUPPLY AIR SYSTEM SERVING AREA.
(4) SEE SECTION ON CONTROLS FOR INTERLOCKING CONTROLS.

11-23

SCHEDULE OF UTILITY FANS - CENTRAL AIR HANDLING SYSTEMS

FAN NO. OR SYMBOL	AIR QUANTITY, CFM (M³/S)	EXTERNAL STATIC, IN WATER (MM WATER)	MOTOR POWER, HP (WATTS)	FAN RPM (TIP SPEED)	NOISE- SOUND POWER	SERVICE/ LOCATION	CONTROLS (1)(2)(3) (4)	SUGGESTED MANUFACTURERS (SEE SPECIFICATIONS)	
								MAKE	MODEL

(1) MANUAL MOTOR STARTER - SEE DRAWING FOR LOCATION.
(2) MAGNETIC MOTOR STARTER WITH START/STOP STATION.
(3) INTERLOCK WITH SUPPLY AIR SYSTEM SERVING AREA.
(4) SEE SECTION ON CONTROLS FOR INTERLOCKING CONTROLS.

SCHEDULE OF WALL-MOUNTED PROPELLER EXHAUST (SUPPLY) FANS

FAN NO. OR SYMBOL	AIR QUANTITY, CFM (M³/S)	EXTERNAL STATIC, IN WATER (MM WATER)	MOTOR POWER, HP (WATTS)	FAN RPM (TIP SPEED)	NOISE LEVEL, SONES (dBA)	SERVICE/ LOCATION	CONTROLS (1)(2)(3) (4)	SUGGESTED MANUFACTURERS (SEE SPECIFICATIONS)	
								MAKE	MODEL

(1) MANUAL MOTOR STARTER - SEE DRAWING FOR LOCATION.
(2) MAGNETIC MOTOR STARTER WITH START/STOP STATION.
(3) INTERLOCK WITH SUPPLY AIR SYSTEM SERVING AREA.
(4) SEE SECTION ON CONTROLS FOR INTERLOCKING CONTROLS.

Cross References to Sourcebook of HVAC Specifications

The user of these details and schedules may find this list of specifications, as published in a companion volumne, SOURCEBOOK OF HVAC SPECIFICATIONS, to be of interest and help in the preparation of drawings and schedules associated with these system components.

DETAIL	DESCRIPTION OF DETAIL	SPECIFICATION REFERENCE
D-15150-1	RECIPROCATING COMPRESSOR REFRIGERANT PIPING	15150
D-15150-2	RECIPROCATING CHILLER - PIPED WITH EVAPORATOR ABOVE COMPRESSOR	15150
D-15150-3	RECIPROCATING CHILLER - PIPED WITH EVAPORATOR BELOW COMPRESSOR	15150
D-15151-1	WATER-COOLED CONDENSER PIPE CONNECTIONS	15151, 15152, 15153, 15160, 15162, 15163, 15164, 15165
D-15152-1	CHILLER-EVAPORATOR PIPE CONNECTIONS	15151, 15152, 15153, 15160, 15162, 15163, 15164, 15165, 15169
D-15152-2	MULTIPLE CHILLER PIPING DIAGRAM	15150, 15160, 15162, 15163, 15165
D-15153	MULTIPLE CHILLER/BOILER PIPING DIAGRAM	15150, 15152, 15153, 15160, 15163, 15165, 15800, 15806, 15810, 15820
D-15155-1	STEAM-POWERED ABSORPTION CHILLER PIPING HOOKUP	NONE
D-15155-2	HOT WATER-POWERED ABSORPTION CHILLER HOT WATER PIPING	NONE
D-15155-3	TYPICAL CONDENSER WATER PIPING FOR ABSORPTION CHILLER	NONE
D-15155-4	STEAM PIPING FOR ABSORPTION CHILLER	NONE
D-15160	WATER-COOLED CENTRIFUGAL CHILLER PIPING	15160, 15162, 15163, 15164, 15165
D-15175-9	CONCRETE PAD FOR GROUND-MOUNTED EQUIPMENT	15175, 15176, 15180, 15182, 15185, 15186, 15250, 15801
D-15180	COOLING TOWER PIPING - PROPELLER FAN TYPE	15180, 15182

DETAIL	DESCRIPTION OF DETAIL	SPECIFICATION REFERENCE
D-15180-1	EQUIPMENT SUPPORT - GROUND-SUPPORTED PIERS	15175, 15176, 15180, 15182, 15185, 15186, 15187
D-15182-2	COOLING TOWER PIPING - PACKAGED TOWER	15182
D-15183-1	COOLING TOWER WITH THREE-WAY CONDENSER WATER CONTROL VALVE	15958
D-15183-2	COOLING TOWER WITH TWO-WAY CONDENSER WATER CONTROL VALVE	15958
D-15185	COOLING TOWER PIPING - CENTRIFUGAL TYPE FAN	15185
D-15188	EVAPORATIVE COOLER FOR COMMERCIAL/INDUSTRIAL USE ("SWAMP COOLER")	15188
D-15218	SPLIT SYSTEM HEAT PUMP	NONE
D-15219	WATER SOURCE HEAT PUMP - PIPING HOOKUP	NONE
D-15225-1	THRU-WALL UNIT - BRICK WALL INSTALLATION	NONE
D-15225-2	THRU-WALL UNIT - PANELWALL INSTALLATION	NONE
D-15225-3	WINDOW TYPE UNIT MOUNTED IN WALL	NONE
D-15225-4	WINDOW TYPE UNIT MOUNTING	NONE
D-15225-5	THRU-WALL PACKAGED UNIT	15225
D-15225-6	THRU-WALL UNIT DUCT EXTENSION	NONE
D-15225-7	SMALL THRU-WALL UNIT - BRICK WALL INSTALLATION	15225
D-15225-8	SMALL WINDOW TYPE UNIT MOUNTED THRU THE WALL	15225
D-15230-1	EQUIPMENT SUPPORTS	15325, 15327, 15329, 15331
D-15230-2	EQUIPMENT SUPPORT - ROOF MOUNTING	15175, 15176, 15180, 15182, 15185, 15186, 15187, 15188, 15250, 15801
D-15240-1	SLAB-MOUNTED MULTIZONE UNIT	15300
D-15248-1	ROOF CURB FOR EXISTING ROOF	15200, 15205, 15210, 15215, 15216, 15217
D-15248-2	CURB FOR ROOFTOP UNIT MOUNTING	15200, 15205, 15210, 15215, 15216, 15217
D-15249-1	ROOF MOUNTING CURB FOR CRITICAL AREA	15200, 15205, 15210, 15215, 15216, 15217, 15249

DETAIL	DESCRIPTION OF DETAIL	SPECIFICATION REFERENCE
D-15249-2	ROOF MOUNTING CURB FOR ROOFTOP UNIT - WOODEN ROOF DECK	15200, 15205, 15210, 15215, 15216, 15217
D-15249-3	ROOFTOP UNIT WITH OFFSET UNDER CURB	15200, 15205, 15210, 15215, 15216, 15217
D-15176-1	AIR-COOLED CONDENSER REFRIGERANT PIPING	15176
D-15250-1	AIR-COOLED CONDENSING UNIT - SLAB MOUNTED	15250
D-15250-2	AIR-COOLED CONDENSING UNIT - MOUNTED ON TIMBERS ON LOW-SLOPE ROOF	15250
D-15250-3	AIR-COOLED CONDENSING UNIT - CIRCULAR UNIT MOUNTED ON TIMBERS ON ROOF	15250
D-15251	REFRIGERANT LINES BELOW GRADE IN PVC CONDUIT	15250
D-15300-1	CHILLED AND/OR HOT WATER COIL PIPING IN AIR HANDLING UNIT	15300
D-15300-2	DX (DIRECT EXPANSION) COIL PIPING IN AIR HANDLING UNIT	15300
D-15300-3	STEAM AND DX COIL PIPING IN AIR HANDLING UNIT	15300
D-15300-4	STEAM COIL PIPING IN AIR HANDLING UNIT	15300
D-15300-5	HEATING AND COOLING COIL PIPING HOOKUP	15300
D-15300-6	CHILLED WATER COOLING COIL PIPING HOOKUP	15300
D-15300-7	HOT WATER COIL PIPING HOOKUP	15300
D-15325-1	UPFLOW GAS FURNACE WITH DX COOLING COIL	15325, 15327
D-15325-2	DOWNFLOW GAS FURNACE WITH DX COOLING COIL	15325, 15327
D-15325-3	HORIZONTAL GAS FURNACE WITH DX COOLING COIL	15325, 15327
D-15335-1	ELECTROSTATIC AIR CLEANER - UPLFOW FURNACE - SIDE INSTALLATION	15325, 15327
D-15335-2	ELECTROSTATIC AIR CLEANER IN DOWNFLOW FURNACE	15325, 15327
D-15340	GUARD POST FOR GROUND-MOUNTED UNIT	15175, 15176, 15180, 15182, 15185, 15186, 15187, 15250
D-15345-1	GAS VENT THRU ROOF WITH VENT CAP	15325, 15327, 15329
D-15345-2	GAS VENT THRU WALL	15325, 15327, 15329

DETAIL	DESCRIPTION OF DETAIL	SPECIFICATION REFERENCE
D-15350-1	UNIT VENTILATOR DETAIL - SINGLE COIL - VALVE CONTROL	NONE
D-15350-2	UNIT VENTILATOR DETAIL - SINGLE COIL - FACE AND BYPASS CONTROL	NONE
D-15350-3	UNIT VENTILATOR DETAIL - TWO COILS - FOUR PIPE CONTROL	NONE
D-15355	UNIT VENTILATOR PIPING HOOKUP - SINGLE COIL UNIT	NONE
D-15402	EXHAUST FAN AND LIGHT COMBINATION	15402
D-15403	EXHAUST FAN, HEATER, AND LIGHT COMBINATION	NONE
D-15407	AIR CURTAIN/FLY FAN - CEILING EXHAUST FAN WITH SUPPLY OUTLET	15407
D-15410	IN-LINE FAN WITH DAMPER	15410
D-15414	CENTRIFUGAL WALL EXHAUST FAN WITH BACKDRAFT DAMPER - INLET GRILLE	15414
D-15414-1	CENTRIFUGAL WALL EXHAUST FAN WITH BACKDRAFT DAMPER IN DUCT	15414
D-15416-1	DIRECT-DRIVE PROPELLER TYPE DOME EXHAUST FAN	15416
D-15416-2	DIRECT-DRIVE CENTRIFUGAL DOME EXHAUST FAN WITH SOUND CONTROL CURB	15416
D-15420	ROOF-MOUNTED EXHAUST FAN - DOME TYPE - REFER TO SCHEDULE FOR TYPE OF FAN	15420, 15421
D-15421-1	DOME TYPE BELT-DRIVEN CENTRIFUGAL ROOF EXHAUSTER	15421
D-15421-2	DOME TYPE BELT-DRIVEN CENTRIFUGAL ROOF EXHAUSTER WITH SOUND CURB	15421
D-15423	KITCHEN EXHAUST HOOD WITH MAKEUP AIR - NO HEAT IN MAKEUP AIR - NO DETAIL ON HOOD	15423
D-15427-1	PROPELLER WALL EXHAUST FAN - DIRECT DRIVE - LIGHT DUTY	15427
D-15427-2	PROPELLER WALL FAN - DIRECT DRIVE - HEAVY DUTY - INTAKE WITH FIXED LOUVER - DUCT CONNECTION	15427, 15460, 15461, 15462, 15463
D-15428	PROPELLER TYPE WALL FAN - BELT DRIVE - EXHAUST SHUTTER	15428, 15455

DETAIL	DESCRIPTION OF DETAIL	SPECIFICATION REFERENCE
D-15428-1	PROPELLER TYPE WALL FAN - NO LOUVER OR SHUTTER SHOWN	15428
D-15428-2	PROPELLER TYPE WALL FAN WITH INSULATED MOVABLE LOUVERS	15428, 15460, 15461, 15462, 15463
D-15450-1	RIDGE-MOUNTED VENTILATOR - GRAVITY TYPE	15450
D-15450-2	VENTILATOR ON FLAT ROOF - GRAVITY TYPE - MANUAL DAMPER - CEILING RING GRILLE	15450
D-15450-3	VENTILATOR ON PITCHED ROOF - GRAVITY TYPE - MANUAL DAMPER	15450
D-15450-4	HORIZONTAL RELIEF CAP - ROOF MOUNTED	15450
D-15455-1	SHUTTER TYPE RELIEF DAMPER - WALL DISCHARGE	15455
D-15455-2	WALL RELIEF SHUTTERS WITH BIRD SCREEN	15455
D-15460-1	WALL LOUVER INTAKE - FIXED LOUVER - BIRD SCREEN - MANUAL DAMPER	15460
D-15461	INSULATED MOVABLE DAMPERS MOUNTED BEHIND WEATHERPROOF WALL LOUVERS WITH GYM GUARD - INTAKE SERVICE FOR VENTILATION SYSTEM	NONE
D-15465-1	LOUVERED PENTHOUSE - INTAKE OR EXHAUST - MOTORIZED DAMPERS	15465
D-15465-2	LOUVERED PENTHOUSE - RAISED DUCT FOR STORM PROTECTION OF FRESH AIR INTAKE	15465
D-15468-1	INTAKE HOOD WITH PREFABRICATED ROOF CURB	NONE
D-15469	GOOSENECK TYPE OUTSIDE AIR INTAKE	15469
D-15479	DISHWASHER HOOD WITH CENTRIFUGAL EXHAUST FAN	15479
D-15500	SHEET-METAL DUCT HANGERS	15500
D-15500-1	REINFORCED ANGLE "S" SLIP CONNECTOR	15500
D-15500-2	SUPPORT FOR DUCTWORK AT FLOOR PENETRATION	15500
D-15501	RETURN AIR PLENUM FOR UPFLOW FURNACE	15325, 15327, 15329
D-15502	UNDERFLOOR DUCT	15502
D-15504	WEATHERPROOF ROOF CURB FOR DUCT CONNECTION THROUGH ROOF	15504
D-15505-1	ROOF CURB FOR GAS LINE PENETRATION	15505

DETAIL	DESCRIPTION OF DETAIL	SPECIFICATION REFERENCE
D-15505-2	DUCT-SUPPORT ROOF CURB FOR DUCT MOUNTED ON ROOF	15504
D-15505-3	ROOF CURB AT ROOF PENETRATIONS FOR REFRIGERANT LINES, GAS LINES, CONDUIT, ETC.	15505
D-15506	ROOF CURB AT STRUCTURAL SUPPORTS	15505
D-15515	FLEXIBLE DUCT CONNECTION TO DUCTWORK OR EQUIPMENT	15515
D-15525	AIR SUPPLY DIFFUSER DUCT TAKEOFF	15525
D-15525-1	AIR SUPPLY DIFFUSER TAKEOFF WITH ADJUSTABLE VOLUME DAMPER AND AIR SCOOP	15525
D-15530	TOE SPACE RETURN AIR GRILLE	NONE
D-15531	STAIRWAY SUPPLY/RETURN GRILLES	NONE
D-15583	BELOW WINDOW (LOW SIDEWALL) SUPPLY AND RETURN FOR SLAB-MOUNTED UNIT	NONE
D-15586	CONSTANT CFM RETURN GRILLE	NONE
D-15595-1	TYPE "A" FIRE DAMPER WITH WALL GRILLE OR REGISTER	15595
D-15595-2	TYPE "A" FIRE DAMPER WITH CEILING GRILLE OR REGISTER	15595
D-15595-3	TYPE "B" FIRE DAMPER IN WALL WITH GRILLE OR REGISTER	15595
D-15595-4	TYPE "B" FIRE DAMPER IN LAY IN TYPE CEILING	15595
D-15595-5	TYPE "C" FIRE DAMPER FOR SIDEWALL AIR REGISTER OR GRILLE	15595
D-15595-6	TYPE "C" FIRE DAMPER FOR CEILING GRILLE OR REGISTER	15595
D-15595-7	FIRE DAMPER IN FLOOR SYSTEM	15595
D-15595-10	1-1/2-HOUR FIRE DAMPER IN WALL	15595
D-15595-11	FIRE DAMPERS FOR 3-HOUR RATED WALL	15595
D-15601-1	GAS-FIRED UNIT HEATER - HIGH EXPOSED MOUNTING - PROPELLER TYPE - POWER VENTED	15601
D-15601-2	GAS-FIRED UNIT HEATER - HIGH EXPOSED MOUNTING - CENTRIFUGAL TYPE - POWER VENTED	15601

DETAIL	DESCRIPTION OF DETAIL	SPECIFICATION REFERENCE
D-15601-3	HORIZONTAL HOT WATER UNIT HEATER	NONE
D-15612	GAS REGULATOR - POUNDS TO INCHES	NONE
D-15612-1	GAS PIPE SUPPORT ON ROOF	NONE
D-15616	RADIANT HEATER - CEILING MOUNTED	15616
D-15626	ELECTRIC WALL HEATER - FAN TYPE WITH BUILT-IN THERMOSTAT	15626
D-15640	HOT WATER CONVECTOR PIPING - WALL TO WALL	NONE
D-15640-1	HOT WATER CONVECTOR PIPING - INDIVIDUAL WALL-MOUNTED TYPE	NONE
D-15640-2	HOT WATER CONVECTOR - RECESSED	NONE
D-15641-1	WALL FIN RADIATION - HOT WATER OR STEAM - ONE TIER	NONE
D-15641-2	WALL FIN RADIATION - HOT WATER OR STEAM - TWO TIERS	NONE
D-15661	STEAM UNIT HEATER PIPING	15700
D-15670	NONFREEZE STEAM COIL PIPING	15700
D-15700-3	CLEVIS TYPE PIPE HANGER	15700
D-15700-5	CLAMP TYPE PIPE HANGER	15700
D-15700-6	PIPE ANCHOR/GUIDE FOR BARE PIPE	15700
D-15700-10	CLEVIS TYPE PIPE HANGER FOR NONMETALLIC PIPE	15700
D-15700-11	STRAP GUIDE/SUPPORT FOR INSULATED PIPE	15700
D-15700-12	TRAPEZE HANGER WITH ROLLER AND SPRINGS	15700
D-15700-13	TRAPEZE HANGER FOR INSULATED PIPE	15700
D-15700-14	TRAPEZE HANGER FOR BARE PIPE OR INSULATED FOR HEAT LOSS ONLY (NO VAPOR BARRIER)	15700
D-15700-15	CLAMP HANGER FOR BEAM PIPE OR EQUIPMENT SUPPORT	15700
D-15700-17	FLOOR FLANGE FOR USE AS PIPE OR EQUIPMENT SUPPORT	15700

DETAIL	DESCRIPTION OF DETAIL	SPECIFICATION REFERENCE
D-15700-19	PIPE CRADLE FOR FLOOR SUPPORT	15700
D-15700-21	SPRING TYPE HANGER FOR PIPE OR EQUIPMENT	15700
D-15700-23	FIBERGLASS HANGER FOR NONMETALLIC PIPE	15700
D-15700-24	HANGER FOR NONMETALLIC PIPE - CLEVIS TYPE	15700
D-15700-25	PIPE HANGER (OVERHEAD SUPPORT) - SPLIT RING TYPE	15700
D-15700-27	STRAP ANCHOR FOR NONMETALLIC PIPE	15700
D-15700-30	PIPE SADDLE FOR INSULATED HOT PIPE (NO VAPOR BARRIER)	15700
D-15700-32	CONCRETE INSERT ANCHOR SUPPORT FOR PIPE OR EQUIPMENT	15700
D-15700-34	EYE ROD HANGER - WELDED OR OPEN EYE	15700
D-15700-36	SIDE BEAM CLAMPS FOR EQUIPMENT OR PIPE SUPPORT	15700
D-15700-38	SIDE BEAM CLAMPS FOR EQUIPMENT OR PIPE SUPPORT	15700
D-15700-40	BEAM CLAMPS FOR PIPE OR EQUIPMENT SUPPORT	15700
D-15700-42	WELDED STEEL HANGER BRACKET	15700
D-15700-44	SPRING ISOLATED HANGER FOR PIPE OR EQUIPMENT	15700
D-15700-46	SPRING/ELASTOMERIC HANGER FOR PIPE OR EQUIPMENT	15700
D-15731	PIPE INSULATION UNDERGROUND - FOAMGLASS AND MASTIC WITH GLASS FABRIC AND MASTIC COVERING	NONE
D-15735	PRESSURE GAUGE WITH TEST GAUGE CONNECTION	15700, 15704, 15706
D-15735-1	THERMOMETER INSTALLATION IN INSULATED PIPE	15700, 15704, 15706
D-15736	EXPANSION TANK CONNECTIONS	15704, 15706
D-15739	STEAM SEPARATOR - LOW- AND MEDIUM-PRESSURE STEAM (REMOVES MOISTURE AND TRASH) - SHOP FABRICATED	15700
D-15748	CONDENSATE METER FOR HOT WATER RETURN	NONE

DETAIL	DESCRIPTION OF DETAIL	SPECIFICATION REFERENCE
D-15756	SUBMERSIBLE SUMP PUMP - FLOAT CONTROL	NONE
D-15764	IN-LINE PUMP CONNECTIONS	15764
D-15770-1	BASE-MOUNTED CENTRIFUGAL PUMP	15770
D-15770-2	TYPICAL PUMP INSTALLATION	15770
D-15780	RUBBER TYPE EXPANSION JOINT - TYPICAL APPLICATION FOR EXPANSION AND NOISE CONTROL	15776, 15780
D-15780-5	EXPANSION TANK WITH AIR ELIMINATOR FOR BOILER - DIAPHRAM TYPE	15780
D-15805-1	VENTED GAS TRAIN - SAFETY VENT BETWEEN MOTORIZED GAS VALVES	15806, 15810, 15812, 15813, 15820, 15821, 15822
D-15805-2	MEDIUM- TO LOW-PRESSURE GAS REGULATOR	15806, 15810, 15812, 15813, 15820, 15821, 15822
D-15805-3	VENTED GAS TRAIN WITH OVER-PRESSURE SAFETY TRIP	15806, 15810, 15812, 15813, 15820, 15821, 15822
D-15807	MULTIPLE STEAM BOILER PIPING HOOKUP	15807, 15808, 15810, 15811
D-15807-1	BOILER TRIM FOR LOW-PRESSURE STEAM	15807, 15808, 15810, 15811
D-15810	STEAM PIPING AND TRIM FOR LOW-PRESSURE STEAM BOILER	15807, 15808, 15810, 15811
D-15812-1	PIPING FOR VERTICAL STEAM BOILER WITH SOFTENER - HIGH MAKEUP REQUIREMENTS	15812
D-15812-2	DUPLEX BOILER FEED SYSTEM - SERVING SINGLE BOILER	15808, 15810, 15811
D-15822	SAFETY VALVE DISCHARGE PIPING - HIGH-PRESSURE STEAM	15812, 15822
D-15830-1	TWO-STAGE PRESSURE REDUCING STATION	NONE
D-15830-2	PRESSURE-REDUCING VALVE STATION FOR STEAM - HIGH CAPACITY - SINGLE STEP OF REDUCTION	NONE
D-15830-3	PRESSURE-REDUCING VALVE STATION FOR STEAM - SMALL CAPACITY - SINGLE STEP OF REDUCTION	NONE
D-15832	STEAM MAIN DRIP LEG	NONE

DETAIL	DESCRIPTION OF DETAIL	SPECIFICATION REFERENCE
D-15833	STEAM HEADER CONNECTION	15700
D-15850	CAST-IRON CONDENSATE RETURN UNIT - LOW HEIGHT	15850
D-15851	CONDENSATE RECEIVER WITH DUPLEX PUMPS - CAST-IRON TANK - LOW HEIGHT	15851
D-15855	CONDENSATE RECEIVER WITH DUPLEX RETURN PUMPS	15855
D-15856	VENTED FLASH TANK	NONE
D-15858	CONTINUOUS BLOWDOWN SYSTEM FOR STEAM BOILERS	NONE
D-15860	SINGLE TANK DEAERATOR AND FEEDWATER SYSTEM	15860
D-15870	WATER SOFTENER	15870
D-15875	ONE-SHOT CHEMICAL FEEDER	15875
D-15889-1	PRESSURE-POWERED SUMP PUMP	15880
D-15892	STEAM HUMIDIFIER - DUCT MOUNTED	NONE
D-15899	UNDERGROUND TANK - FUEL STORAGE	NONE
D-15941	COMPRESSED AIR DROP OR DRAIN	NONE
D-15950-10	REMOTE BULB THERMOSTAT MOUNTED IN DUCTWORK	15958
D-15958-1	CONTROL AIR COMPRESSOR PIPING	15958
D-15958-2	CONTROL AIR FILTER - SHOP FABRICATED	15958

Index

About the Author

Frank E. Beaty, Jr. graduated from Clemson University with a B.S. in Mechanical Engineering and served as a sales engineer with Westinghouse Electric Corporation and a design engineer with James A. Evans Consulting Engineers before establishing his own firm, specializing in heating, ventilation, and air conditioning; plumbing; and fire protection. His consulting and design experience has included projects ranging from design of facilities for construction of nuclear reactors, water and sewage treatment plants, and large industrial plants to schools, churches, libraries, dormitories, and office buildings. Beaty is presently a staff engineer with the Energy Management Department of the University of Alabama at Birmingham.